WINNING IS NEVER ENOUGH

Winning
is never
Enough

SUFFERING, SPORTS & HOPE

(How to Deal with the Friday Night Loss on Monday Morning)

BRADLEY D. BAILEY

the publishing CIRCLE.

the **publishing** CIRCLE.

Send permission requests to the publisher at:
admin@thepublishingcircle.com.
Attention: Permissions Coordinator
Regarding Bradley D. Bailey

I would like to thank all the authors cited in this work. "Fair use" quotes have been cited using proper attribution. Extra gratitude and thanks are given to those authors who have allowed and granted permission for larger expression of their ideas than normally occur in proper attribution. They are listed below:

Alistair Begg, *Made for His Pleasure*, Moody Press, 1996.

Chad Bladow, *Seven Years Seven Ways*, Starrider Books, 2007.

Some content taken from *The Blessing of Humility*, Jerry Bridges, 2016. Used by permission of NavPress, represented by Tyndale House, a division of Tyndale House Ministries, 2016. All rights reserved.

"8 Major Worldviews," parts 1 & 2, Dr. Brian Chilton, CrossExamined.org., 2017.
https://crossexamined.org/8-major-worldviews-part-1/
https://crossexamined.org/8-major-worldviews-part-2/

Dr. Cunningham, P.C., "Letter from the President." *Taylor University Alumni Magazine* (Upland, IN), volume 121, Spring 2021.

Reggie Marra, *The Quality of Effort: Integrity in Sport and Life for Student-Athletes, Parents and Coaches* (From the Heart Press, 2013). Used with permission of the author.

Dr. Curt Thompson, *The Soul of Shame,* InterVarsity Press, 2015.

Dr. Christopher Watkins, *Biblical Critical Theory,* HarperCollins Christian Publishing, 2022. www.harpercollinschristian.com

Published by The Publishing Circle
www.thepublishingcircle.com

WINNING IS NEVER ENOUGH: SUFFERING, SPORTS & HOPE
FIRST EDITION

ISBN 978-1-955018-60-9 (PAPERBACK)
ISBN 978-1-955018-61-6 (HARDCOVER)
ISBN 978-1-955018-62-3 (LARGE-PRINT PAPERBACK)
ISBN 978-1-955018-63-0 (E-BOOK)

Cover and book design by Michele Uplinger

DEDICATION

As I wrote this book, the faces of my grandchildren filled my mind. This book is for them, whether or not they played a sport, I could see them as I wrote many of the ideas in this book. My desire is to share lessons, information, and thoughts, which I would like to pass on to them, both in sport and life.

I would also like to honor the athletes whom I have had the privilege to coach, their faces fill my memories with gratitude.

Dedication is shared with the hundreds of athletes and competitors who have struggled with the sorrow and disappointment associated with failing in pursuing their dreams. I pray they will find hope in these words.

To my wife, Karen, who loves me, win or lose, and who knows the heartbreak that the losses have cost firsthand.

To my son, Peter Bailey, who endured his dad's coaching in both the highs and the lows.

And to the rest of our children, Dr. Michael Salazar, Kristen Villas, Allison Vogann, Dr. Rachel Bailey Anaya, and Abigail Khavari, and their spouses and children, who God allows me to share life.

To my parents Vincent and Marilyn Bailey who loved and cared for me and my sisters and their spouses, Vickie and Dr. Carson Reed, and Melodie and Ron Bissonnette.

In conclusion, I dedicate this work to these ideals:

"I want to know Christ and the power of his resurrection and the fellowship of sharing in his sufferings, becoming like him in his death, and so, somehow, to attain to the resurrection from the dead" (PHILIPPIANS 3:10–11).

And this certainty, "a faith and knowledge resting on the hope of eternal life, which God, who does not lie, promised before the beginning of time" (TITUS 1:2).

ACKNOWLEDGMENTS

I want to honor several individuals for their impactful work in my life. Some of them are no longer with us, however they deserve credit just the same. I would like to thank Dr. John J. Davis, my advisor at Grace Theological Seminary, who many years ago took on this graduate student proposing a thesis looking into the relationship between *The Bible* and sports. The thesis topic at the scholarly institution was unconventional. He graciously embraced the challenge and led me to successful completion. This book was in my heart.

I would like to thank and express my indebtedness to the many outstanding administrators and leaders in my life and coaching journey, my college coach at Taylor University, Don Odle, Dr. Randy Crist, Bud Schindler, Jim Kessler, Dr. Larry Crabb, Lynn Nutall, Jim Crinan, Steve Sonmor, Arnold Doerksen, Tim Grant, D.J. Saucedo, Dane Kennon, Leo Garcia, Loren Cushman, Brandon Siqueiros, Bill Sanderlin, Joy Walkey, Ron Hendrix, Marvin Wiseman, Dr. W. C. Stephens, John Pickett, and Patrick Tebbano, all people who led and or encouraged me for which I am grateful.

My high school coach at Tecumseh High School, Doug Chaffins, who instructed and trained me in the art of basketball, for which I will forever be in his debt.

Last, I would like to extend deep appreciation to Linda Stirling who took on this project and believed there is value to pass on to those who choose to read this book. She was supportive and patient to the point of extraordinary. Linda brought Candace Sinclair alongside as editor, and Candace has poured untold hours into this effort and made great contributions to this finished product. I wish to sincerely thank them both.

CONTENTS

Winning
is never
Enough

SUFFERING, SPORTS & HOPE

(How to Deal
with the Friday Night Loss
on Monday Morning)

BRADLEY D. BAILEY

Part One

Introduction
&
Chapters 1–9

**Ideas about Sports and Life
We Commonly Think about
Without Much Consideration**

INTRODUCTION:

FIVE VIGNETTES

WINNERS HAVE A VOICE. HANDSOME PEOPLE have a voice. Rich people have a voice. Successful people have a voice. This book presents a case for the others: those who have lost, those who are invisible, those who are hurt, and those who remain silent.

While watching *The Last Dance* during COVID, thinking back on my enthusiastic interest in sports, having NBA hoop dreams, being mesmerized by the nanoseconds between winning and losing in the 2021 Olympics, and bantering with athletes on my basketball team after a Super Bowl game, started the wheels of thought turning.

Do we think about our life's path, or do we just float downstream with the popular populace? What shapes our values and beliefs about the world in which we live? Is there a reason to think differently from the narrative of our culture?

Here are five vignettes or short story sketches that each capture ideas that were food for thought as this writing unfolded. These stories unveil nine sports-themed chapters clarifying things we think about without delving too deeply. The marketplace presents us with sports ideas in chapters 10–18, examining the thoughts of our day and considering both typical pathways and challenging ideas. Chapters 19–25 inspire us to find higher ground, revealing the truth that empowers ourselves and others. Chapters 26–31 cover sports applications and ideas to consider.

And the last three chapters, 32–34, contain inspiring true stories of triumph mixed with closing thoughts.

#1

Michael Jordan speaks, and people listen. Michael Jordan declares, "Go out and win at any cost," and "win at all costs." People hear these types of exhortations and believe him. During the COVID broadcast of the docudrama "The Last Dance," a ten-part series highlighting the accomplishments of Michael Jordan from his perspective, Michael Jordan proclaimed in various phraseologies, I am a winner, and winning is all that matters.[1] The basis for Michael Jordan's philosophical bravado was based on his ability to lead his team to three straight NBA titles, take off almost two years, and upon returning for full seasons, win three more NBA championships, for six championships. This remarkable accomplishment gives him credibility and is the stuff of adult legends and little boy dreams. Winning is all that matters, written in the skies, immortalized in phrases, and quipped in motivational speeches. This idea ignites motivation from the playground to the rec gym to the high school, college, and finally to the NBA hardwood.

#2

The win is all that matters, and people express its philosophical position in almost an infinite variety of ways. Charles Barkley said on a TNT broadcast, "Kobe [Bryant] and Michael [Jordan] would kill you for the win."[2] Kobe, while filming "Kobe Bryant's Muse," played a Chinese youngster and was determined to win. Writer Chris Ballard said, "Sometimes you gotta challenge some punk teenager to a double-or-nothing game. And then you have to elbow him in the post, cheat on the out-of-bounds play, and impose your will on the poor sap because when it comes down to it, sometimes that's what it takes to win, son."[3] Years ago, in the spellbinding movie "Draft Day," there's a poignant scene where the general manager of the Cleveland Browns, played by Kevin Costner, asks the potential number one draft pick, Bo Callahan, how important winning is. And with pure Hollywood flare and pomp, Bo Callahan says, "Well, winning is everything, Mr. Weaver; nothing else matters."[4] Hollywood bought it. We agree that gorging on all manner of slogans uttered by sports heroes places them on exquisitely carved pedestals. And heroes have an audience, and audiences follow the pied piper of our day. We, the audience, listen, hear, believe, and emulate this declaration, patterning our lives after the mantra "Winning is all that matters!"

#3

Shooting baskets in the driveway started a quest for basketball excellence. The pursuit of basketball greatness commenced with shooting hoops in the driveway, followed by intense training and workouts at the nearby concrete court, where skills are sharpened and aspirations are born. From playing the babysitter one-on-one at four years old to games against friends at recess to playing three men at once and winning, I carved a path toward basketball obsession. Thousands of hours of development created the skills and passion needed to excel in basketball artistry. This skinny, uncoordinated kid, who longed to make the first team, went from being cut abruptly and not being selected to play against the skilled older hoopers because I was not good enough, to finally, competing against all comers and sought to stretch for the "pot of gold at the end of the rainbow." This pathway created the formation, care, and feeding of an athlete. Like millions of other youngsters, the NBA dream took root, and vivid daydreams of hitting the last-second jumper as the clock expired flowed from a hopeful and passionate imagination. High school hoop dreams, college ball, and eventually NBA stardom were all daily thoughts of one so young.

When the end arrives, and the end always arrives, hoop dreams all end. Hoop dreams crash! Dreamers turn to other ventures and pursuits, whether the athlete retires decorated with championship rings on each finger or falls short of the NBA bid. The athlete cannot earn a college scholarship or high school joys are the height of accomplishment, or the hoopster is just not good enough for a variety of reasons. The budding star withers before he blossoms and cannot play at any level. No matter where the end occurs, all have this in common: the end comes, and they must explore other pursuits. For some, coaching basketball extends playing basketball, and coaching careers spawn. Coaching becomes the new dream, carrying its unique challenges, burdens, and celebrations.

#4

Watching the Olympics in 2021 brought forth some stunning oxygen deprivation, taking one's breath away moments. One such moment was the Women's 4 X 200-meter freestyle swimming finals. Three teams broke the previous world record. Let's consider this: three teams broke the previous world record, but only one emerged as the winner, two teams set world records and lost! Likewise, in track, five of the eight runners ran personal bests in the Men's 400-meter hurdles, two broke the previous world record, and three of the finishers ran the fastest times ever run in one race simultaneously and yet only one winner emerged! Despite personal bests and world-record times, all but one loses! In this same Olympics, in the Women's 400-meter hurdles, two women set world records, five of the seven finishers ran personal bests, and yet only one winner! World-class athletes perform multiple world record times and walk away without the gold! No words. Can't breathe!

#5

Walking into practice in 2020, making small talk with the athletes at a local high school, all were discussing yesterday's Super Bowl clash between the San Francisco 49ers and the Kansas City Chiefs. As the talking and banter grew louder and more intense, the guys recounted the exciting play and action of this phenomenal game. Then someone said the only thing that mattered was that the Chiefs won and the 49ers were bums because they were losers. In shocking disbelief, someone challenged this idea. "You're saying the 49ers are bums?" And to no one's amazement, except the coach, the athlete laughed and said, "Yeah, winning is all that matters." Using this line of reasoning, the semifinal conference game between the Buffalo Bills and the Kansas City Chiefs on January 23, 2022, would signify that the Buffalo Bills are Bums, even though this was one of the most exciting all-time heavyweight football matchups in recent history. During these same playoffs, a quarterback brilliantly masterminded a barely short comeback to fall victim to loss, making this quarterback a bum! Yes, Tom Brady of the Tampa Bay Buccaneers is a chump/bum; they lost!

These vignettes contain deep passion and emotion that a quick reading could overlook. They contain the kerygma of sport and life with exceptional force and power. These five vignettes, all in one fashion or another, introduce us to the world of sports philosophical epistemology, or more simply put, what we believe and think about life and sports. This journey through sports philosophy will look from the theoretical to the practical. Often, the context will involve basketball, as this is the background which I am most familiar.

These vignettes more subtly point out a not-so-obvious struggle, the struggle with failure, disappointment, missed goals, broken dreams, and suffering. The struggle found in sports has more to do with suffering than people first recognize. To excel in anything requires a multiple intricate set of skills, but at the core of the venture is discipline. Discipline provides a foundation without which accomplishment of the end goal will result in failure. Failure produces a mixture of outcomes: pain, shame, despair, depression, and, most importantly, suffering. The effort to build skill sets that allow for success and a heart-breaking loss, though on opposite ends of the spectrum, requires suffering. The discipline needed for development walks hand in hand with suffering. Who has not felt the pain in a wind sprint, the burn of muscles in an effort, the heartbreak of a missed opportunity, the outcome below expectations? Suffering wraps its arms around each of these aspects and puts a painful ribbon on them. However, suffering has a side of glory often missed in the frantic pursuit of the victor's prize, trophy, gold medal, and victory lap.

These vignettes all beg for a framework, a point of reference. There is a need for a takeoff point or a perspective on the outcome. No human pursuit exists in isolation. How we pursue, what we pursue, why we pursue, all outcomes find themselves in a philosophical milieu. We live, move, and have our being in a context. Different factors shape all our contexts. And most people would agree that in pursuit of all endgames, character is important. Whether we are congruent with our beliefs is another crucial point.

ENDNOTES: INTRODUCTION

1. Hehir, Jason, director. Jason Hehir, Michael Tollin, and Peter Gruber, producers. *The Last Dance,* a ten-part documentary. ESPN Films & Netflix, 2020.

2. Tim Kiely, producer. *Inside the NBA,* TNT Network, September 9, 2020.

3. Chris Ballard, *"Twilight The Saga,"* VAULT Archives, *Sports Illustrated,* August 25, 2014.

4. Ivan Reitman, director. Ivan Reitman, Ali Bell, & Joe Medjuck, producers. *Draft Day.* USA: Lion's Gate Entertainment, 2014.

CHAPTER 1

WIN BABY WIN

JUST LIKE MICHAEL JORDAN DECLARING THE philosophy—play to win! Do whatever it takes to grab victory—winning requires tremendous sacrifice at a high price. Our culture and world daily shout this mantra in an endless variety of ways. Just win baby! A sign on the interstate by a law firm states, "Winning matters," and some form of this message found on most of their billboards declares, "We will win!" Our society parrots these words and this attitude in every facet of life, like the sweatshirt logo seen at an airport, boldly announcing, "Winners don't take days off." Likewise, sports figures, comedians, and Hollywood pokes fun at anyone who wins a silver medal or comes in second. "Congratulations, you almost won." "Second place is the first loser." "Of all the losers you were first." Audiences roar with laughter and nod their heads in approval.

Vince Lombardi did not say it first, but it's attributed to him that "Winning is not everything, it is the only thing!" ESPN talking heads utter frequently at the start of NFL playoffs, that only the Super Bowl winner is a winner, and the other thirty-one teams have all failed; basically, they are losers. When sports broadcasts, talk shows, and evaluations by so-called experts express these sentiments dozens, if not hundreds of times a day, a cacophony of noise emphasizes that winning is all that matters. Literally, millions of fans, athletes, and coaches from all walks of life mouth the same rhetoric and the same sentiments.

Years ago, a two-time NFL coach of the year, George Allen, said, "The winner is the only individual who is truly alive . . . every time you win, you're reborn; when you lose, you die a little."[1]

Hall of Fame basketball guard Pete Maravich said, "Personal things like leading the league in scoring don't get you a cup of coffee. My obsession is to be on a championship team. As soon as I am, I'll retire. Definitely. Right then. Because then I will have been successful. I'm really only happy when I'm winning."[2]

ESPN's Bill Parcells has said, "You are what your record says you are." This phrase, as if truth, has been repeated by high school coaches across our country.

An announcer broadcasting the Baltimore Ravens and Tennessee Titans football game said of Lamar Jackson, "He didn't win it in high school. He didn't win it in college. Now winning a championship, that's all he cares about and that's all he should care about."

ESPN analyst Bart Scott preached fervently, "I don't care who you are as a person, you're a nice guy. Congratulations . . . you got to win some damn games."[3]

A popular commercial finds Josh Allen parroting, the "just win" mantra, with an emphasis on getting the job done no matter what it takes.

Coach Raheem Morris, in 2020, when he took over as the head football coach of the Atlanta Falcons, stated, "Nothing else matters. Just win."

Win at any cost produces sentiments represented by Dwight Howard's comments after the Los Angeles Lakers won the 2020 NBA championship "Winning the championship was everything . . . What really matters is just holding up that trophy. That would be my message to everybody on the team: what are you willing to give up to get that trophy? Sometimes you got to give up everything."[4]

Jerry Jones, in evaluating a dismal season in 2020, says, "Do y'all have any idea how much I'd write a check for if I knew I could get that Lombardi trophy? And so, my whole point to you is it is a big, big thing. It is the foremost thing, not money. There's never been but one thing, and that is to win."[5]

Texas A & M University wrote the check. They decided their coach, Jimbo Fisher, could not get the job done, so they sent him packing. Fisher received the outlandish buyout price of $77.6 million on November 12, 2023. Texas A & M University believed the problem was with the coaching staff. But is something wrong with a university willing to throw that kind of money away? The problem might be within their own walls. It appears no price is too high for wins.

"Winning is all that matters" because it appears to fill voids in our hearts and soul. The void that we all have . . . who am I? What is my purpose? Why am I here? Winning tells us it has filled our empty void; the hole in our hearts has been satisfied. We are a winner. That's why we're here. That's our purpose. Winning makes us important.

The virtues of winning have been celebrated for decades. Leaders today and leaders of yesteryear, actors, political figures, broadcasters, sports legends, CEOs, business leaders, bankers, and lawyers all fuel the philosophy that winning is the ultimate grand prize. Our value is determined by whether we win or lose. We can only fulfill our validation, existence, and reason for being by winning. This truth has persisted throughout human existence, dating back to ancient history, where winners during the Isthmian games, the ancient Olympic Games, and the Athenian games received glory, honor, power, and influence as a result of winning! Validation, wealth, and "the spoils" are brought by winning. Winners build castles and edifices declaring their success, notoriety, and omnipotence! Money and achievement are what winners use to build their kingdoms! Winners receive endorsements, prime-time coverage, and even game-day coverage. This is clearest in the modern Olympic Games, where contestants only receive coverage if they are first, second, or third. The audience will not see a contestant who is back in the pack. A non-front-runner participant is not worthy of coverage.

If Olympic participants do not participate in a "sexy sport," they may not receive any attention or be given a token spot. Broadcasts rarely feature Olympic javelin throwers, shot putters, discus throwers, fencers, or non-marquee boxers because they are not considered significant, sadly the winners may receive only minimal attention. Broadcasts often overlook the event because it is not considered popular or will not draw enough viewers. Winning isn't just being the best, but being the best in the right events or sports. Real winning are the champions who everyone else thinks elite: "A showman worthy, creme de la crème."

ENDNOTES: CHAPTER 1

1. Thomas Tutko and William Burns, *Winning Is Everything and Other American Myths*, Macmillan, 1976, 5–6.

2. Thomas Tutko and William Burns, *Winning Is Everything and Other American Myths*, Macmillan, 1976, 5–6.

3. Mike Greenberg, producer. *Get Up!* ESPN Studio, February 28, 2023.

4. Ryan Young, "Dwight Howard Said Doc Rivers, 76ers Were the Only Team to Reach Out to Him During Free Agency", Yahoo!sports, November 25, 2020.

5. Nicole Poell, "Cowboys Owner Criticizes Himself", *USA Today*, December 13, 2020.

CHAPTER 2

PLATITUDES
OF SWISS CHEESE

"WINNING ISN'T EVERYTHING. IT'S THE only thing," one of sports' most popular platitudes neatly sums up how so many view life and sports. Platitudes have the unenviable literary acumen combining profound truths with a hint of reality, spun with large doses of insanity. Platitudes possess the attractiveness of being believed no matter how absurd and uttered with the popular appeal of money given away during game shows. Wow! Our world is full of platitudes, which make great slogans, wonderful posters, and motivational trinkets but carry very little substance. Throughout history, people have used platitudes to call us to victory, despite their lack of substance.

- "Our greatest weakness lies in giving up. The most certain way to succeed is always to try it just one more time" Thomas Edison.

- "If you believe it, you can achieve it."

- "Work hard, and you can accomplish anything."

- "Give 110 percent." (This is a mathematical impossibility.)

- "No pain, no gain."

- "You only get out what you put in."

- "God helps those who help themselves."

- "You must pull yourself up by your own bootstraps."

- "Sports is a microcosm of life."

- "Sport is war."

- "Sports build character."

Platitudes usually have an element of truth, which is why they persist. However, they cannot stand alone, require context, and have one thing in common: they are incomplete and may miss the truth. I'll address each of these last three platitudes separately.

Unfortunately, the tired idiom "sports is a microcosm of life," though true in a handful of lessons, misses many life reality points, the most obvious being that life is not all about recreation, leisure, entertainment, and competition. Work is a very real aspect of life that does not stop when the buzzer sounds. Adults continue to labor day in and day out, and it does not result in headlines, post a "win," or finish when events are drawn to a close. The daily tasks of a job are seldom confused with play. Sports do not produce goods or resources. Sports only contribute 1% to The Gross National Product. Sport is a consumer entertainment business without any long-range value. People forget winners as quickly as the wind blows. Life has few heroes; broadcasters do not broadcast about someone's work performance. Life always ends in death, does not always have winners and losers, has no offseason, and doesn't get an instant replay review. Life is pregnant with many shades of gray. These facts and many other concerns highlight the problems in the "microcosm of life" mantra.

"Sport is war," oft overused quote misses that sport is not life and death. Players should play with passion, enthusiasm, focus, and strive for their best effort, but in the end, it is a game. The sport's purpose is not to bring about the death of the participants. In fact, if death were to occur, it would be a gross failure by the participants or organizations. Sport is not war, no matter how many inane sports enthusiasts parrot the expression. By definition, we should never compare sport to war. These are gross misrepresentations of each. War contains the seeds of the worst humanity offers, whereas sport has the potential of arousing benefit. When people use the sport to war comparison, it suggests they are taking themselves too seriously.

That sports build character, sports build better people, sports correct "all wrongs" may be the worst of all platitudes. Dick's Sporting Goods ran a major ad campaign in 2023, emphasizing "Sports Changes Lives."[1] Dick's promotes the idea that sports change lives. They go into great detail, stating that teams, fields, athletic seasons, and coaches all create positive changes. The changing lives idea is the primary message. It would appear some emotional stories, catchy music, and we have a truth. This ad campaign has been their biggest ad campaign over the last seventy-five years, and last year they spent $412 million on advertising. They are betting millions upon millions of dollars on the benefit of sport. Sports change lives all right, but for the better, how, or for the worse? Think and decide.

Researchers have studied the benefits of sports for over a hundred years and have arrived at very similar conclusions. Sports do not inherently make us better people, even though this cliche sells sports participation and sporting goods and dupes communities into paying billions of dollars to build stadiums for billionaires. It is simply not true. The idea that sports foster attributes that could build character has some truth to it, but as early as the 1920s, people started challenging the belief that sports build character. John R. Tunis, a sportswriter, wrote: "The Great Sports Myth . . . is a fiction sustained and built up by . . . the news gatherers . . . who tell us a competitive sport is health-giving, character-building, brain-making, and so forth . . . Let us cease the elevation of [sport] to the level of religion."[2]

In another study written about sports' intrinsic worth, Dr. Bruce

Ogilvie and Dr. Thomas Tutko wrote in *Psychology Today* in 1971, "For the past eight years, we have been studying the effects of competition on personality . . . we found no empirical support for the tradition that sports builds character. Indeed, there is evidence that athletic competition limits growth in some areas."[3]

Wells Twombly, a San Francisco columnist, wrote in 1972: "Not only is it obvious that sports do not build character, it is even questionable if they have any socially redeeming aspects."[4]

James A. Michener, in his classic and exhaustive work on sports says, "Haywood Hale Broun, who has written much in this field, has said, 'Sports do not build character. They reveal it.' Darrell Royal, of Texas, phrased it this way: 'Football doesn't build character. It eliminates the weak ones.'"[5]

A twenty-year study examined 80,000 college, professional, and high school athletes regarding character. The author, Sharon Stull, found that: "Athletes score worse on tests of moral reasoning. In fact, from the moment athletes enter big-time sports, their moral reasoning never improves and usually declines. Athletes tested as high school freshmen rarely score higher when tested at the end of college." She found that girls and women who historically scored higher than men in moral reasoning have shown regression to where by 2012, they will be like their male counterparts. Too often, today's young athletes don't care if it is morally wrong; they will do whatever it takes to be successful.[6]

Fast forward to today, and professional athletes expect to enjoy load management, thereby taking games off, "recovering from injuries," getting ready for the playoffs, all of which create questionable stints where they simply do not play. This is frequent behavior by numerous athletes regularly for a variety of reasons. Management is often held hostage by athletes who demand a better team and refuse to play or have a semi-legitimate grievance that justifies their refusal to work. Some athletes demand more money for the simple reason, "I am better than that guy," and should earn more than him. Pro's regularly challenge officials, displaying a lack of honesty and sportsmanship and taunt opponents when they make an outstanding play, flaunting one-upmanship.

These attitudes are now part of the college scene, where changing schools for more NIL money, playing time, chance to win, and to develop their professional stock rises above a college education or loyalty to a university for developing and believing in them. Top players sit out bowl games to "prepare" for the NFL or avoid risk of injury. The confusion that this creates for universities, coaches, teammates, and fans is one that may take years to sort out. However, it is clear far too many college athletes are now paid professionals changing college sport landscapes forever.

Colleges are semi-pro sports factories, and high schools are getting into "the act." High school players pay thousands of dollars for personal trainers, AAU travel and fees, area-wide leagues, and equipment. High school athletes change schools if they don't "like" the coach, don't play enough, or get what "I want." While listening to a football coach on the radio speaking of the importance of football and sports to the development of young people, he equated the practices of sports to the classroom. He stated that plenty of learning occurs on that field, and numerous values are learned on the path toward the state championship. True enough, players learn values on any team, but what if a team is not on a path toward a state championship? Would there be values, then? And research demonstrates there may not be as many rewards "out there on that field" as he thinks.

It's obvious with just a short list of examples that an endless sea of platitudes will not produce the bedrock resolve or opportunities to form a lifestyle of substance or even the proverbial "win." Platitudes and cliches provide fodder for the perpetuation of lies and are simply too shallow to hold up under the weight of truth. The fallout of this is that people accept these ideas, creating a poor ideology. Platitudes and cliches will not provide the baseline bedrock for the mental and physical resolve necessary to become a winner or produce a mature character. The "win-at-all-costs philosophy" loses its luster as it is meticulously examined and reveals the underbelly of just another shaky platitude, a saying much like Swiss cheese, full of holes.

ENDNOTES: CHAPTER 2

1. Dick's Sporting Goods, television commercial. *Sports Change Lives*. USA: Multiple Media Outlets, 2023.

2. Thomas Tutko and William Burns, *Winning Is Everything and Other American Myths*, Macmillan Publishing Co., Inc., 1976, 38–39.

3. Thomas Tutko and William Burns, *Winning Is Everything and Other American Myths*, Macmillan Publishing Co., Inc., 1976, 39

4. Thomas Tutko and William Burns, *Winning Is Everything and Other American Myths*, Macmillan Publishing Co., Inc., 1976, 49.

5. James A Michener, *Michener On Sport*, UK: Secker & Warburg, 1976, 16.

6. Sharon Stull, "Do College Athletics Corrupt?," *Sports Illustrated* (March 5, 2007), 67.

CHAPTER 3

CAN YOU KEEP A SECRET?

WHAT IS REQUIRED TO WIN? TALENT, giftedness, genius, cunning, size, strength, toughness, and the list goes on and on. If winning is all that matters, then we would all have an equal shot at it. In this fair, everyone is a winner, pass out ribbons to all participants, and level the playing field world, where everyone has equal rights and opportunities. It seems like the formula for winning is just a research assistant project away. We could pass down the research knowledge to the masses and make most if not all, winners.

"Self-esteem education demands everyone get a trophy ... It insists that every child is exceptional, [don't criticize,] which sends a very wrong message ... Many college students today do not know how to fail; they have no idea what to do when the trophy isn't handed to them."[1]

Born out of this discussion is a hideous, unattractive, and secret problem raising its grotesque head. A problem we do not talk about because it's akin to profanity and sacrilege or blasphemy at worst. Life Is Not Fair!

Life is supposed to be fair. Shouldn't life be fair? Two things are clear: one, we have an innate sense that fairness is a quality that should exist. We boldly assert that fairness is absolute. That something should be a certain way speaks to our sense of self-importance and arrogance.

Irrationally, we demand that things fit into "my" paradigm. I determine the grid of how outcomes are judged.

Life's unfairness is a truth that is overwhelmingly simple and gives us all a hair-standing-on-end, vinegar-on-teeth kind of experience. Life is fair puts a demand on all of us in some form or another because life is supposed to be fair, isn't it? Yes, fairness would be great, but life is not fair. This bears repeating because most of us have adopted a full-on-life-is-fair heartbeat. However, if we must establish one starting point, life is not fair. It's not always just, and people's circumstances are not equal. This is a deal-breaking, rain-on-your-parade statement, but we must have an honest discussion concerning winning and the mantra that "winning is all that matters."

The belief in moral absolutes, including fairness, suggests there are external standards and values that we inherently recognize. We do not have the capability or intelligence to accurately figure out how things should work, so how things should work must come from outside ourselves. This "outside ourselves" information is a quality referred to as God. But bringing God into this discussion is just another "four-letter" word or, in this case, a grotesque three-letter word. Nevertheless, it's our only basis for determining any absolutes or fairness. Something "other than ourselves" determines the moral absolutes. God determines the rules of life, and he has placed in our hearts a sense that things should be fair and just. For evidence of this, one needs only to watch Fox News or CNN to observe that people of all political spectrums seek fairness and justice. A brief observation reveals that people have different points of view on matters of fairness and justice, which proves we could not, through our own efforts, reach agreements on standards of fairness or rights. This reinforces the idea there must be outside directives in defining a term such as fairness. C.S. Lewis said, "My argument against God was that the universe seemed so cruel and unjust. But how had I got the idea of just and *unjust*? A man does not call a line crooked unless he has some idea of a straight line. What was I comparing this universe with when I called it unjust?"[2]

Humanity's sense of fairness and justice is so entrenched in our thinking all people think something should be a certain way or must be a particular way. Roughly, the idea of "should" or "must" are ideas incorporated by Albert Ellis's work in the fifties as part of his Rational Emotive Behavior Therapy. He coined a term that reflects that people think results should or must fit outcomes according to their preferences or standards. Many thinkers have discussed this treatise and have made numerous observations regarding the efficacy of the thought. At the end of the discussion, people believe things should or must be a certain way and other people should cooperate in like-minded pursuit of these ideals. Ellis argues thinking things must or should be a certain way is faulty thinking. We cannot always escape life's difficulties. Life's "musts" fuel personal problems. Life does not work out the way we think it must or should. Therefore, it's obvious the idea that "life is fair" is a 100 percent lie. The fact that we think it should be tells us we long for it to be so, but the reality we live in overwhelmingly demonstrates otherwise. We are not born equally attractive, equally intelligent, equally tall, equally charismatic, equally coordinated, equally athletic, equally strong, equally quick, equally intuitive, equally gifted in music or art, and the list is endless.

Inequality was shouted loud and clear when Michael Finebaum observed how an Alabama basketball player was treated related to involvement with men who murdered an innocent. Michael Finebaum said, "If this had been a bench warmer, would we be having the same conversation? We have all been in athletics long enough to know there is a double standard."[3] We are not here to debate the "hypocrisy of athletes in general." His comments point past the philosophical discussion and demonstrate the societal lack of fairness, which is loud and clear. None of us are equal; none are born the same; on the contrary, we are all born equally different. In fact, no two fingerprints are alike, no two retinal scans are the same, no two voice intonations are identical, no two DNA matches, and the list is endless. Since we are not identical and comparisons are subjective, fairness as a construct is hopeless. Put simply, life is not fair and cannot be fair!

Phillip Yancey explains, "Life is patently unfair and that people are unequal in their abilities." . . . "No two human beings have the same set of abilities, intelligence, appearance, and family backgrounds."[4]

Years ago, in what looked like an unfair accident, I was saddened to read of a coach who had been celebrating track and field accomplishments by doing standing backflips. He had performed them dozens of times, if not hundreds. One day, he lost his balance, fell, and broke his spine in a critical place, causing paralysis. Tragic unfairness abounds. One does not have to look far to see a child who is missing a limb or limbs, one who has deformities, accidents that forever change a person, adults who are injured in war, or who have been damaged by being a bystander at a tragic event. Tragically, the "life is fair" equation suddenly becomes a rational, feasible, and mathematical impossibility! Yes, there are standards of right and wrong, and we should want, desire, and seek fairness. However, because life is not fair, it does not remove our responsibility to treat people justly. Laws and morals are required for civilizations to exist, but we must understand reality. All too often, people scream to be heard in a search for fairness, demanding justice, when on planet Earth, it will never happen. Life is not fair.

ENDNOTES: CHAPTER 3

1. Kathleen M. Comerford, "A Hard Lesson," *Reader's Digest*, November 11, 2011, 36.

2. C.S. Lewis, *Mere Christianity*, Macmillan, 1943, 45–46.

3. James Dunn (producer). *First Take*, New York: ESPN, February 23, 2023.

4. Phillip Yancey, "Parkinson's—The Gift I Didn't Want", *Christianity Today*, February 20, 2023, www.christianitytoday.com/ct/2023/february-web-only/philip-yancey-ct-parkinson's-diagnosis-gift-i-didn't-want.

CHAPTER 4

BRIDGING THE GAP
THROUGH HARD WORK

IF WE MUST WIN, IF "WINNING IS ALL THAT MATTERS," and since life is not fair, how do we bridge the gap? How do we reach past the inequalities and succeed in a world where success is demanded? How do we succeed, define ourselves, and earn our significance and security?

Look at hard work. The theme of the early 1900s was virtue, hard work, breaks, luck, someone reaching down to help, and maximizing opportunities. This pattern or formula may cause the achievement of the American dream, i.e., respectability, middle-class living, and comfort. This theme was the undertow of Americana fleshed out in the stories popularized by Horatio Alger. His books and their influence reached far and wide, from modern-day presidents, business leaders, and pop culture to the how-to-get-ahead parade of speakers so prominent in the last half of the twentieth century. He promoted the idea of the self-made man and the famous rags-to-riches motif. His ideas epitomized we can all pull ourselves up by our own bootstraps and that we are self-sufficient for reaching success. This thinking produced countless converts, and frequently, they can be heard to say, "You can accomplish anything you want if you try hard enough and don't give up." Sports heroes, celebrities, leaders of the day, and local achievers are glittering examples of accomplishment. Carl Trueman declares, "The idea that we can be who or whatever we want to be is commonplace today."[1] Trueman points out that the popular thought of today is caught up in our self-creation. "Success in life is now seen as the individual's responsibility alone, and if someone is not supremely successful, they are at fault because the only thing stopping us following our dreams is our lack of desire."[2] The Alger motif laid a foundation that is still popular. These philosophical ideas have locked into our minds a foundation that hard work can make our imaginations into reality. Anyone can become president in the United States. Anyone can be a star. Anyone can play in the NBA.

"We are heirs to the Judeo-Christian ethic, which states in principle that man should work hard to succeed, that if a person does his best, works unceasingly, and makes the right sacrifices, he will win . . . Winners and losers are actually seen as good and bad people."[3]

We see this same mentality in the book of Job, where Job's three friends accuse him of all kinds of improprieties and sins, which is why Job incurred so much suffering. The friends stated if Job did things God's way, he would prosper, and all these bad things would not be happening. Three friends argue with Job for the better part of thirty-seven chapters, arguing success always follows doing or being right with God, "bad things just cannot happen to good people." Unfortunately, most people accept this idea, not realizing that the pinnacle of teaching truth in the book of Job is that bad things can happen to anyone and that God is not bound to a quid pro quo system. Blessings do not always follow good, and tragedy and suffering do not always grow out of evil. (Evil always has deleterious effects on the lives of everyone engaged in evil.) Just because bad things happen to a person does not mean that evil caused it. "It should be that hard work would always lead to prosperity, but now sometimes you can work hard and injustice or disaster wipes it away."[4]

In the world of sports, a friend and colleague of mine, Greg Berry, who was a career college coach, said: "A team does not win (on the court or in theory) merely by 'trying harder.' Amazingly, one occasionally encounters a coach, athlete, fan, or critic who thinks anyone can do anything if he or she only tries hard enough. Emotion, dedication, and motivation are essential to winning teams, particularly in a day when virtually every team is blessed with talent. But to succeed in the challenge of modern-day college basketball, motivation must be channeled through sound fundamentals, solid conditioning, an unselfish team spirit, and astute strategies. The team that tries hard but lacks these and other essentials as part of its foundation will seldom win."

When I was a young coach, the industry standard for a summer high school basketball program was holding an open gym a couple nights a week during the summer and a one-week tournament or league. This would place a team above the curve. Years later, the standard for summer high school basketball became traveling tournaments where a team played twenty to thirty games, and during the summer, there would be an open gym mixed throughout. Over time, top players began participating in an AAU summer schedule, where they were on the road for a month and played at least thirty local team games, which created a new industry standard. Today, rule changes in many states allow an AAU schedule that covers up to eight or nine months of participation. Local teams play fifty or more games, and many players employ private coach tutors and use daily open gyms. This schedule makes it very difficult to play multiple sports, and practice is usually in a structured environment, making it rare to find an athlete working out on his own at the local park.

Both athletes and coaches can buy into the work harder mantra, but at some point, adding more effort and work has diminishing returns. People will inevitably succumb to exhaustion or the reality of limited time in a day, and the need for sleep. During graduate school, I was exhorted to learn to get by on three to four hours of sleep and to spend more time studying. This eventually results in a continually increasing effort and intensity, which results in a grossly distorted and out-of-balance life, not to mention its detrimental impact on health. Everyone wants to find the silver bullet of success; hard work is not the only criterion for winning. An increasing workload is short-sided. There is more to success than just hard work. A team or athlete may lose because "the reason may simply be that your team is not as talented as the opponents on your schedule. Yet the faith persists that you'll never be a winner unless you work harder and harder and harder, that 'hard work has its just rewards.'"[5]

Hard work does not guarantee success. And if one strives to outwork all others, then at some point, working harder becomes both an impossibility and an illogical incongruity. More is better is a misnomer. Harder work by itself will not always produce the fruits of success.

ENDNOTES: CHAPTER 4

1. Carl Trueman, *The Rise and Triumph of the Modern Self*, Crossway, 2020, 164.

2. Christopher Watkins, *Biblical Critical Theory*, Zondervan Academic, 2022, 212.

3. Thomas A. Tutko and Bill Bruns, *Winning is Everything and Other American Myths*, MacMillan, 1976, 7.

4. Timothy Keller, *Walking With God Through Pain and Suffering*, New York: Dutton, 2013, 114.

5. Thomas A. Tutko and Bill Bruns, *Winning is Everything and Other American Myths*, MacMillan, 1976, 23–24.

CHAPTER 5

BRIDGING THE GAP, NEVER GIVE UP

F WE MUST WIN, IF NOTHING ELSE MATTERS, IF LIFE IS not fair, and if hard work alone is not the answer, then the magic formula must be a headlong pursuit of the goal until it is realized. A dogged platitude-fueled determination, "If you believe it, you can achieve it," and "Never stop until you reach the top." The if-you-believe-it-you-can-achieve-it mindset not only works in sports metaphors but is espoused across many walks of life. Even million-dollar TV evangelists use this mantra, declaring this message is found in God's message to man.

Movies like *Rudy* parrot this theme. *Rudy* was a movie about a young man who was laser focused on playing football for the Fighting Irish of Notre Dame. Rudy tirelessly pursued this dream, refusing to allow setbacks to stop him. However, if it were not for the mercy and kindness of his teammates, he would have never played one second of one game regardless of his overzealous, never-give-up life.[1] Do you believe his determination and dedication were admirable? Certainly! But movies showcasing countless athletes who possessed equal drive, passion, and focus yet lacked the luxury of a cinematic conclusion would not be box office hits. Their endings would feature shipwrecked hopes and dreams, not the fairy-tale ending of happily ever after. Who wants to watch that?

On October 29, 1941, Winston Churchill delivering a twenty-minute speech during World War Two declaring resolve to look at the future, wrestle with the issues at hand, and challenge his audience among other things to never give up. He exhorted his country, England, and the world with the following:

"This is the lesson: never give in, never give in, never, never, never, never—in nothing, great or small, large or petty—never give in except to convictions of honor and good sense. Never yield to force; never yield to the apparently overwhelming might of the enemy."

This is only an excerpt of his speech, which lasted for twenty minutes, but it achieved legendary fame as if Churchill had said, "Never give in, never give in, never, never, never," and sat down. But this is not true. He spoke for twenty minutes, and he stated one should never give up except for honor or good sense. The point people like to make quoting Churchill is to never give up under any circumstances, no matter the pain, cost, self-sacrifice, and suffering. But when one fact checks, we find that this is not how it played out. Modern day exhortations often grab a piece of an idea or speech and repeat it. They use motivational material in everyday parlance, attack a problem armed with the quip, and provide a position to move forward. When we repeatedly hear a historical quote from someone famous, we eventually accept it as accurate, especially if the quote aligns with mantras for success. We want to believe it.

Churchill's idea was part of a larger context and was not a one-size-fits-all formula for success. At some point, an athlete must know when to quit or accept the end. Never giving up is difficult in the clothing of humanity and aging. Churchill, in his famous speech, even provided an out. He said if an endeavor violates "convictions of honor" and when walking away makes "good sense."

How is it then, that his speech is incorrectly remembered? People pant for a recipe for success, a formula, and a panacea for reaching the elusive peak of the mountain. It is so important, "winning is everything," that we will believe lies, inaccuracies, or overgeneralizations. I once bought a book entitled *Winners Never Quit* by Phil Pepe, forward by Vince Lombardi. Poetic license sells books, platitudes excite, mantras motivate, and so we latch onto ideas, even when incorrect, and bow down to their propaganda.

Desire, determination, and a relentless will to excel are all necessary to reach the heights of athletic success, achievement, and winning. But never giving up, taken to its literal end, does not stand up to sensible reason. Perseverance, passion, determination, and desire all figure into a formula for success. But "never giving up" cannot stand alone; often, it is bad advice. We find wisdom in both a relentless pursuit of achievement and in the ability to stop or quit. I cannot see quitting as the rejection or destruction of human value. On the contrary, ceasing to do something may be the pinnacle of wisdom and valor. When I was in college, I spent many afternoons running long distances. Pain, exhaustion, and fatigue were never a reason to quit; the motto was just "fight through it." As aging and maturity blossomed, I learned that pain can be the body's way of signaling that something is wrong and that further continuation could cause serious damage. Pain was a friend, an ally, and information, not something to fight through, no matter the cost. This example, on a small scale, declares there is a time to give up. There is a time to start and a time to stop. Death, a profoundly sad reality on a larger scale, forces all of us to eventually give up.

ENDNOTES: CHAPTER 5

1. David Anspaugh, director. Robert N. Fried and Cary Woods, producers. *Rudy*. USA: TriStar Pictures, 1993.

CHAPTER 6

BRIDGING THE GAP, CHEAT

" ITS WATCHWORD IS PRAGMATIC EFFICIENCY: whatever means gets you to your desired end, those are the means to employ . . . It is the default human setting . . . achievement brings reward, and you do what you must to get what you want . . . it is how we do everything we do in the world."[1]

Moral relativism rules! Outcomes are defined by the culture. If winning is the goal, then whatever it takes to win is allowed. Since life is unfair, if hard work does not guarantee success, and refusing to give up does not gain the desired goal, then cheat!

How else are we going to achieve the results we seek? How do we earn the significance we crave? How do we showcase abilities validating personhood and earn scholarships and truckloads of money? If winning is all that matters, then the means of achieving it are not important to us . . . the ends justify the means. Cheat.

Intimidate, step on or over people, enhance performance, lie, steal, destroy, just win, baby! Learn to channel your inner strength, build your self-confidence, and find your peak performance. Read one of dozens of books detailing self-power, achievement, positive self-talk, and self-actualization. Double down on the motivational poster power, try harder, never give up, and accept the unfairness of life, and if your dreams are still not realized, just . . . cheat!

Cheating . . . everybody does it. Life taught us decades ago that the ends justified the means. Tour de France record-holder champion Lance Armstrong used this as his defense after years of lying to the press, his peers, and himself. Cheating was so obvious that he finally admitted it true with the caveat everybody was cheating. He cheated to compete. Ben Johnson, the Canadian sprinter, used performance-enhancing drugs in the 1988 Olympics, and they stripped him of his gold medal. Mark McGuire admitted steroid use after setting the single-season home run record but suffered a ban from the Baseball Hall of Fame as a result. Steroid and drug use encapsulated a time when it appeared everyone was using drugs to improve their performance. "The meltdown of drugs in sports has been pretty astounding," said David Callahan. "Never in US history have so many prominent athletes found themselves dealing with doping rumors . . . [contributing] to the general feeling that nobody is playing by the rules," said ethicist Jack Marshall.[2]

In the early 80s, two men wrote a how-to book chronicling steroid use. Duchaine and Zumpano authored *We're Going to Tell You How: Underground Steroid Handbook for Men and Women*. This book, aimed at the athlete willing to do anything to get ahead, outlined the underground steroid/drug use for those who wanted an edge. Duchaine and Zumpano instructed, "There is a large number of what we call the 'businessman doctor.' These guys are out to hustle a buck . . . Look for the young ones just out of medical school. Young doctors have a different morality than the older ones."[3] This attitude began changing the stigma surrounding drug enhancements to the point that the 1996 Olympics were mockingly called the HGH games.

An article was written about four minor-league baseball pitchers who were vying for a spot in the major leagues. The article describes in detail their similarities in size, age, throwing abilities, and desire. However, one used steroids, made the big leagues, and eventually regretted it to the point of considering taking his own life. Tom Verducci states, "This is a story about the hundreds, even thousands, of anonymous ballplayers whose careers and lives were changed by a temptation that defined an era. It is also a story about the secrets we keep and the casualties we create . . . This is a story about the real cost of steroids in baseball."[4]

The cost of cheating carries consequences impacting one's physical health, mental health, and ethical health. It appears Moral Relativism rules the day. Gaining an edge has become the norm, and cheating, top-down, from the professional ranks to middle school, is a reality. Culturally, we are driving a stake into the heart of the idea that "Life is fair," "Cheaters never win," "Hard work," and "Never giving up" will always foster success and victory.

Phil Taylor, in his 2011 article, "How Low Can You Go?" mocks cheating and scandals by setting up an imaginary game show. The article starts like this: "Welcome to the premier of America's newest game show . . . in which coaches, parents and sports executives compete to see who tried to slip the most blatant violations and ethical misdeeds passed the NCAA, the public or both—all for fabulous cash and prizes!"[5]

He then lists improprieties by Ohio State football coach Jim Tressel, Tennessee basketball coach Bruce Pearl, parent Cecil Newton, and CEO of the Fiesta Bowl, John Junker. It is a hilarious article with the powerful, sad point that cheating and rule violations are rampant.

Over the past decade, hoping against hope, wishing, wanting, and believing that drugs have gone away, hoping performance-enhancing drug use are remnants of a bygone era, we are left to wonder if illegal substances are more a part of the mainstream than ever before. We wonder as we watch specimens on the football field, basketball court, baseball field, track, MMA arenas, and other venues. Then, as if confirming our worst nightmares, it was discovered that even a horse was drugged! We scratch our heads and ask, does anyone play by the rules? Bob Baffert is implicated in the headline, "Exposed," which poses questions of horse race cheating and a clear willingness to give drugs to a horse in an attempt to win the Kentucky Derby.[6] In a New York Post article, Baffert blames the positive test results on anti-fungal cream. Likewise, blame was also placed on the "horse [ate] hay in a stall that had been urinated on by a groom who had ingested cough medication."[7] If this were the first positive drug finding of a Baffert horse, it would not have made the news, but this happened so often and with so many excuses that it appears he cannot escape guilt. Soon, the headlines were quick to read, "Medina Spirit drug test confirmed." "Churchill Downs on Wednesday suspended the Hall of Fame trainer for two years after an additional drug test of Medina Spirit confirmed the presence of the steroid betamethasone in the Kentucky Derby winner's system."[8] "But no matter how many breakdowns, how many get injured or how many drug violations he has on his record, losing is the only thing that would stop owners from sending Baffert their horses. Saturday's Preakness showed why that isn't going to happen anytime soon."[9]

In this foray into drug use, many would argue drugs are good for you. No, if our bodies were as healthy and free of illness as we should like them to be, we would unequivocally not need any drug. We would not need or use caffeine, alcohol, medicine, or mind-altering chemicals, nothing! Legal drugs can be helpful, but even legal drugs have side effects. ALL drugs do! People may use a drug for healing and physical improvements. Some would contend if there are health benefits, all drugs should be made legal because all drugs have health benefits. However, some drugs whose health benefits are so far outweighed by their negative side effects are deemed illegal. In a perfect world, human beings would not need any type of drug. However, we do not have perfect bodies, and we do not live in a perfect world. Should athletes use drugs to enhance their performance? The rules say no—Olympic rules, professional rules, NCAA rules, and NFHSAA rules. Do athletes use drugs? Yes. In what quantities and frequency only guesses can be made. However, through the years, this question has risen repeatedly and with an ethic that states the ends justify the means. Therefore, some athletes will pursue any course, legal or illegal. Some athletes are determined to do anything necessary to reach the pinnacle of their sport, and they view recreational drugs, anabolic steroids, growth hormones, and other substances as the path to success.

Sadly, articles and books challenging important questions about fair play are not prominent in our culture. Years ago, *Sports Illustrated* writer, Alexander Wolff, stirred us to ponder the direction of sports. He challenged the status quo as he blasted and critiqued the Miami football team, mentioning that many universities shared in rules malpractice in the 80s.[10] Many things were wrong, but a popular national magazine was challenging and even exposing them.

Today, sideline-and on-field antics are normal. Camera operators zoom in on the athlete to observe their gestures and grandstanding. Athletes in college can now get paid and earn endorsement monies, sex is marketed and consumed in a variety of venues, and student-athlete is an oxymoron where players change schools as fast as changing clothes. They can play one year in college with no intention of graduating and move on to a multimillion-dollar payday with fanfare and the blessing of the NCAA and universities. Professionals, like football great Tom Brady, deflated footballs to win. His coach, Bill Belichick, has illegally filmed, scrambled headsets, and used other antics, causing an NBC podcaster to cry foul, stating, "Dude's a cheater. A relentless, incorrigible, clinical cheater." The Houston Astros, in 2017, were caught cheating while winning a World Series. Baseball pitchers have cheated so often that the league instituted rule changes to stop baseball doctoring on June 15, 2021. On November 25, 2023, the University of Michigan received disciplinary action not once, but twice, for rule violations during the same season, yet they continue to march brazenly into the national spotlight without hindrance, ultimately winning the college football national championship.

Articles questioning the blights of sport are difficult to find, and popular books rarely question sport ethics. One should read three outstanding books that were written during a time when virtue mattered. One can only grieve that these kinds of authors are uncommon today. *Competition* by Gary Warner, 1979, *The Quality of Effort* by Reggie Marra, (first copyrighted in 1991) 2013, and *Winning is Everything and Other American Myths* by Tutko and Bruns, 1976. These books point to thoughts and philosophical precepts aimed toward healing sports maladies. Typically, today, we choose to focus on the results, exploits, and, by the way, truckloads of money, "just win, baby."

ENDNOTES: CHAPTER 6

1. Christopher Watkins, *Biblical Critical Theory*, Zondervan Academic, 2022, 186–187.

2. Knight Ridder, "Dark Clouds of Allegations Hang Over Top U.S. Athletes," subtitled, "Is Anybody Playing By the Rules?" *Springfield News-Sun*, July 3, 2004, 7C.

3. Shaun Assael, *Steroid Nation*, ESPN Books, 2007, 7.

4. Tom Verducci, "Special Report: To Cheat or Not to Cheat," *Sports Illustrated* (June 12, 2012), 38–51.

5. Phil Taylor, The Point After [column], "How Low Can You Go?" *Sports Illustrated*, April 11, 2011, 84.

6. Dan Wolken, "Exposed," *USA Today* printed in *Las Cruces Sun-News*, May 12, 2021, 1B, 3B.

7. Peter Botte, "Bob Baffert Comes Clean in Medina Spirit Scandal," *The New York Post* online (May 11, 2021).

8. Associated Press. Gary B. Graves and Stephen Whyno, "Medina Spirit Drug Test Confirmed," *Las Cruces Sun-News*, June 3, 2021, p.4B.

9. USA Today. Dan Wolken, "Winning Keeps Baffert in Horse Racing," *Las Cruces Sun-News*, May 22, 2023, 1B, 2B.

10. Alexander Wolff, "Broken Beyond Repair: Why the University of Miami Should Drop Football," *Sports Illustrated*, June 12, 1995, 22.

CHAPTER 7

YOU CAN'T BE ANYTHING YOU WANT TO BE!

DON CLIFTON BELIEVED HE COULD BE ANYTHING he aspired to be. He spent hundreds of hours practicing basketball, going to basketball camps, looking for the formula to become the next Michael Jordan. No matter how hard he tried, he was not destined for the bright lights of NBA stardom. In fact, he failed to even make the high school junior varsity team. Desire did not cut it, maximum effort did not work, and daily practice was not the key to success. Don Clifton just wasn't created to become a basketball star. Early in life, he learned that no matter how hard he tried, you can't be anything you want to be. He laments that people all too often pursue dreams and careers that do not fit their strengths and weaknesses. He, along with a Gallup study, sought to direct people toward their areas of strength and build on those talents and gifts. He says in his book *Strengthsfinder 2.0* from Gallup and Tom Rath, *Discover Your CliftonStrengths,* that if we invest ourselves in our strengths, we will experience greater rewards and satisfaction. One needs to identify their strengths and interests and build upon qualities of giftedness. "In every culture we have studied, the overwhelming majority of parents think that a student's *lowest* grades deserve the *most* time and attention. Parents and teachers reward excellence with apathy instead of investing more time in the areas where a child has the most potential."[1]

Parents need to carefully study their children and lovingly encourage them toward pathways where they are best suited. Realizing we cannot achieve everything we desire is a harsh reality. This message needs to be shouted from every roof and mountain top unless a person still believes in Santa Claus and the Easter Bunny. The sooner we accept this, the better.

Instead, adults lie to young people millions of times: in schools, commencement speeches, motivational messages, movies, TV, music, and virtually everywhere, and it is not true! Wake up! People are different, and those differences make us unique and created in the image of God, but it does not mean we are all going to grow up to be rock stars, bigger-than-life celebrities, G.O.A.T.S., "generational" athletes, Hall of Famers, Pope, President of the United States, Noble Peace Prize winners, Nobel Laureates, or fill-in-the-blank hero. It Just Ain't Going To Happen!

Reality check, but it happens. How do we explain this? Extraordinary giftedness is obvious most of the time. Everyone will know who the outstanding individuals are in certain fields or venues. A person will have "IT"—that blessing, miracle, talent, or ability that is so clear that everyone recognizes it. These people can excel at the highest levels of accomplishment. They have a prodigious talent.

For example, I had a third-grade schoolteacher who had such an incredible voice that everyone who heard her sing would say something like, "You need to go to Nashville and pursue singing. You would be a surefire, can't-miss country headliner." Virtually, every time she sang, people would flock to congratulate her with generous encouragement, thank her, and tell her she had "it," go use it. (By the way, she did, and she did.)

A boy, a contemporary of mine, had "it." As a little leaguer at six or seven years old, he was told he would be great. He was amazing, won most games he participated in, and played any sport he chose with equal skill, dexterity, and aplomb. Athletically, he was a gifted prodigy, and everyone in our small, sleepy little town knew it. Everyone talked about him, and his peers measured themselves against his athletic prowess. This young man could go far! However, the personal decisions that he made kept him from reaching his potential.

Lebron James had so much of "it" that *Sports Illustrated* featured him on a cover as the "Chosen One" his junior year in high school![2]

Julio Jones had "it." His middle school coaches would ask their team the question, "Who are the younger players who are going to be the outstanding talents next year?" And every time, those boys would say the same name: "Quintorris, Quintorris, Quintorris. O.K., *great. Is he in the sixth grade? Fifth grade?* 'Third,' Hinson remembers them replying,"[3] . . . Quintorris Jones became known as Julio Jones, one of the great NFL receivers.

Certain individuals are destined for exceptional achievements in a specific field, and success flourishes. They blossom early many times, but even the late bloomers are seen in their resplendent colors. They might make it, win, become successful, earn riches, and notoriety. I say might because even with prodigious talent, other factors come into play that sort out a destiny. But one thing is for sure: remarkable abilities infrequently go unnoticed.

We clearly are not that special. In all walks of life, we desire to be extraordinary, but life is a bell-shaped curve, and most of humanity is in the middle of the bell. We see the incongruent nature of humanity in today's classroom. "In the new economy we're calling mediocre work good and good work excellent." The endgame for students in our schools is about "protecting delicate sensibilities seems a major part of the impetus—the old self-esteem thing again."[4]

Naturally, we all resist being average, and we want to be extraordinary, and especially, we yearn for our children to be wonderful. We see it in sports, parents investing in their little darlings with "love, money, time . . . their own unrealized childhood dreams . . . All the while they refuse to accept the simple truth that athletes are born not made, no matter how much zeal, talk and cash you throw at the project." The kid isn't a star . . . " the coach is negligent, incompetent, ought to be fired."[5] Ideas are expressed like my kid is going to shine because he is super special, and we have spent $10,000 training our boy this year. This alone is reason enough that he should play all the time. We are so invested and enthusiastic. This makes him special. A few years ago, an article in the newspaper chronicled the life of a young man whose parents had spent around $200,000 over his lifetime to guarantee that their son's skills would be ready for a college scholarship.

But did these athletes have "it?" Were they going to be "big-time" Division One star athletes? How do we know? Honestly, no one can know for sure because even prodigious talent requires discipline, hard work, opportunity, and breaks. Many athletes have been featured on the cover of magazines, only to be forgotten. Stardom or failure can be seen in the number of first-round draft picks that never contribute significantly to the organizations that selected them. Some are a bust, and with great sadness, some are even cut from the team. But without "it," they are not even on the draft board. So, how does the parent and child negotiate the world of sports and the reality that we are not that special?

Exploring the limits of our potential is a noble endeavor. Competing for playing time and pushing the limits of one's abilities can bring great satisfaction. It's good to test ourselves and determine our strengths and weaknesses. Taking a chance or a risk to find out where one stands in the scheme of things is a strength. Theodore Roosevelt is often quoted in a speech titled "Citizenship in a Republic" spoken at Sorbonne, France on April 23, 1910. Words uttered during the speech are as follows: "who at the best knows in the end the triumph of high achievement, and who at the worst, if he fails, at least fails while daring greatly, so that his place shall never be with those cold and timid souls who neither know victory nor defeat." Risk or daring greatly deepens us and failure may strengthen us. Roosevelt states that even in failure one can "nobly venture." It is difficult to succeed without risk. But how do we know how hard to strive, what level to reach, and when to quit and try something else? Should I invest myself in one activity over another? For those of faith, was I created by God to do this endeavor? The following are suggested markers for determining what level a young person is best suited.

#1–3 Recreational league:

1. Does the child have an interest in a particular activity?

2. Are they willing to dedicate time toward this pursuit?

3. Do they have the opportunity to engage in their area of interest? For example, if a person does not own a piano or has access to one, they will not be a concert pianist. If a school does not offer football as a sport, it is not likely one will become a football player. If a town does not have materials for art, or if you cannot afford materials, then the youngster will not develop into an artist.

#4–6 Competitive league:

4. Is this activity something the child loves to do?

5. Are they willing to develop the tools, and do they have the discipline required to excel in this venture?

6. Do they have a passion for this, and does it energize dreams?

#7–11 Top high school or college performer:

7. Could one see oneself going "all in" to accomplish one's specific dreams?

8. Is there good instruction or coaching available?

9. Does someone believe in and have an interest in helping the young person reach their goals?

10. Does the youngster have the mental abilities needed to take part?

11. Physically, do they have the attributes that increase chances

of success?

#12–14 Elite and professional:

12. Is it possible to be placed in a situation where breaks and opportunities are a strong reality?

13. Has development included multisport and tapping other interests?

14. Is there an intense passion, so much so that the person will do the activity for free and invest large quantities of time?

15. Does one ultimately possess the genetics for the activity?

This last category, **#15 Genetic,** is a watershed criterion and is worthy of some detailed consideration. It's perhaps the one criterion that holds the greatest sway over future high-caliber elite success. Genetics must face steel-cold objectivism, honestly, and without bias. We must recognize that our minds and bodies are influenced by numerous variables: the contribution of our genetic material births our physical and mental capabilities. Our genetics are God-given components that play an incredible role in our lives. Before the cries of discrimination bellow up in a cacophony of naysayers, we need to look at the present-day research in genetics. All geneticists would agree that key and important vital genetic information influences the traits of human beings. Athletes have long recognized the role of genetics in influencing choices available to them in the world of sports. Athletes with fast-twitch muscle are quick and excellent jumpers, and athletes with slow-twitch muscle have muscles that can maintain long exertion in a steady state. Slow twitch is an asset for excellent distance runners. These fibers are part of the genetic makeup of an individual, and the combination of these fibers is given to us at birth. We increase the number of fast or slow-twitch muscles through exercise and diligent work outs, specific training, advanced techniques, and diet. These training methods have demonstrated that we can enhance the muscle tissue that we possess. However, at birth, the percentage quantities of these fibers create a ceiling that we cannot surpass. Intense training may create some fiber changes, but there are genetic limitations.[6]

These fibers are part of the genetic makeup of an individual. When I was in high school, a dear friend was blessed with a majority of slow-twitch muscle fibers. He liked to run and became an outstanding distance runner. Why did he choose to be a distance runner? He loved running; that is simple enough, but why didn't he pick being a sprinter? After all, sprinting has always been a glamour event when it comes to the sport of track and field. The answer is genetics. My friend became a distance runner because his muscle fiber was primarily slow twitch. Slow-twitch fiber allows for prolonged use and results in strong, steady states. This means he could run for an incredibly long period of time at an amazing pace, but in a sprint to the finish line, he was in trouble.

To be a sprinter, a person needs fast-twitch muscle fiber, and preferably, the more of it, the better. Unfortunately, my friend did not have large quantities of fast-twitch muscle fiber, so he became a distance runner. Our bodies and our minds develop based upon our genetic signals, thereby influencing our bents. The body size of an individual or the fiber makeup of our muscles is a very definitive factor in the selection of activities that a young person may choose to take part in. This is undeniably a fact. Genetics profoundly impacts what we can and cannot do, and we are not all created equal physically or mentally. Genetics in sports is accepted; in the arena of athletics, it isn't even a question. The question is, to what degree does the environment influence the development of an individual?

Science has been asking, "What is the role of environment, or nature versus nurture controversy?" for decades, and there's no definitive answer. We know that environment plays a key role in the expressive element of a gene. The difficulty is the percentage and how great an influence the environment plays in our genetic and physical attributes. What is the environmental effect, and how much does genetics predetermine the path in which we choose to excel? There will be people who are very uncomfortable with this discussion, and rightly so. It is obvious it could be a short jump to imply that genetics predetermines the opportunities of an individual and, therefore, creates a class system. Genetics does determine opportunities; it does not predispose opportunities solely on its own merit.

A more dangerous conclusion is that certain genetic characteristics make one person more valuable than another. The "right" genetics entitles one person to life and another to the snuffing out of their life. The "right" genetics increases the person's value, and the "wrong" genetics allows no such benefits. This line of reasoning would be reprehensible! But to state genetic factors do not affect who we are and what kinds of endeavors we find ourselves pursuing will be blatantly naive. The point is we must recognize the factors that impact our lives. The genes we are born with do affect the way we learn, how we develop, and even our temperaments. Genetic factors determine strengths and weaknesses during the development of the body and brain. The DNA of Shaquille O'Neal, who's over seven feet tall, would have created a terrible horse jockey, but his size helped fashion a superior NBA Hall of Fame Champion basketball player. Likewise, William Shoemaker, a Hall of Fame horse jockey who stood four feet ten inches tall and weighed ninety-one pounds, would have been a terrible football lineman.

While it is true genetics carry incredible weight when shaping our ability, the environment has a profound impact. Externals, in plain terms, affect everything. The environment has infinite variations, producing outcomes affecting all human growth and development. Air pollution, health hazards, limited resources, parental or lack of parental impact, socioeconomic status, and the list goes on. These outside influences affect the expression and usage of our genetic makeup, as seen in our physical maturation. Environmental influences can even begin at conception.

Parents may compromise their unborn child even before birth, using alcohol, drugs, tobacco, or poor nutrition. People typically ignore that their choices and decisions can negatively impact the genetic potential of their unborn child. This is a subject deemed too sensitive and controversial to openly talk about. However, we would be wise to recognize the treasure of our infinite genetic variety and protect children from genetic damage.

It needs to be clear when discussing the origin and factors that influence our minds and bodies; we are not arguing the value of human life. Human life is immeasurably precious. However, genetics play a huge part in the physical and mental development of a human being. Therefore, in the classical sense of fairness, a child may not be anything they dream up because of physical attributes, mental attributes, or environmental factors, even as early as in the womb; a person can't be anything they aspire to be!

ENDNOTES: CHAPTER 7

1 Don Clifton and Tom Rath, *StrengthsFinder 2.0: Discover Your CliftonStrengths,* Gallup Press, 2017, 5–7.

2 LeBrecht, M. J., photographer. LeBron James, subject. *Sports Illustrated,* February 2, 2002, cover.

3 Ben Baskin, "The Legend of Julio Jones: How the Falcons WR Became One of the NFL's Best," *Sports Illustrated,* November 15, 2017, 48–55.

4 David McCullough, *You Are Not Special and Other Encouragements,* HarperCollins, 2014, 101.

5 David McCullough, *You Are Not Special and Other Encouragements,* HarperCollins, 2014, 185.

6 Danile L. Plotkin, Michael D. Roberts, Cody T. Haun, and Brad J. Schoenfeld, authors. Anthony J. Blazevich, academic editor, "Muscle Fiber Type Transitions with Exercise Training: Shifting Perspectives," National Library of Medicine, National Center for Biotechnology Information, September 10, 2021 online.

CHAPTER 8

BUILDING
THE FOUNDATION
(LIFE PHILOSOPHY 101)

WHERE DOES SOMEONE START TO GET ON THE right path? How should we think since life is not fair and hard work combined with never giving up are both balloons with holes in them? Once a person determines the level they want to pursue, and they believe it's reasonable to pursue an endeavor or athletic adventure, and they feel strongly about their hopes and goals, they have found the "good fit," what is the lift-off process? The start point or the launchpad are foundations. Foundations of thought are the bedrock upon which the athlete's dream begins and where it must start. What is the seminal building block for life and sport? Is it planned in a do-whatever-it-takes-to-win attitude, and the end justifies the means? If so, then the previous chapter on cheating, instead of being found wanting, is the formula for success. "Winning is all that matters" is a foundational position and ultimately will end in moral relativism and situational ethics. Moral relativism states there is no absolute rule to determine right and wrong. And ethical relativism argues action is right or wrong depending on the norms of the society in which they're practiced. Therefore, societal mores determine how we live in a context where there are no absolutes. Winning as the standard for life is acceptable. "Americans are making up their own rules and laws . . . We choose which laws of God we believe. There is absolutely no moral consensus, as there was in the 1950's and 1960's,"[1] and this was written in 1991.

"A single-lens anthropology sees all reality through one optic: the present. It considers the present human condition to be normative: how things are at the moment is the only available measure for what is normal . . . the would-be cultural critic [would have] no leverage point."[2]

With no moral law, nothing other than the present, and myself as the determiner of knowledge or truth, produces someone like Nietzsche who could emphatically rail, "I am no mess; I am dynamite."[3] He defines his own existence by his declaration that is wholly found within himself. He declares his omnipotence and his power. However, this foundation is cracked and ready to crumble. Without a basis for fairness, justice, and life, the meaning of life is vacuous. Nietzsche's idea that I am the starting and finishing point to all values, existence, and outcomes is absurd.

How do we get to the place where we accept that winning is the only thing, and it doesn't matter how we win, just win? What choices did we make philosophically to arrive at this epistemology? Do we believe what the sports giants tell us accepting that winning is all that matters, buying into the platitudes and the shallow philosophies. Does it occur to us to think deeply about our foundations. It is rare to formulate a personal epistemology. Yet, oddly enough, we all have a worldview from which we operate, whether it is realized or not. All of us surmise and deduce how the world works and the premises by which it operates. We determine our foundations for life, fairness, justice, and mercy. These ideas and positions form our constructs concerning life, our values, and how we live. Our worldview is the lens or the glasses by which we evaluate; it is our foundation. Our worldview is handed down to us by our parents and the generations that have gone on before, as well as society. "A person's worldview consists of the values, ideas, or the fundamental belief system that determines his attitudes, beliefs and ultimately, actions. Typically, this includes his view of issues such as the nature of God, man, the meaning of life, nature, death, and right and wrong."[4]

A discussion of worldviews may seem like an odd place to look, but the tools we use to define our world in general, sports specifically, and winning in particular, will lead us very clearly down a path. This path we choose will impact the assimilation of our careers, money, love, values, recreation, success, and failure. It is important to know what we believe and why. It is easy to be told what and how to believe, the media moguls and the political entities will be happy to do this for us. Mike Greenberg of ESPN once said before going to commercial break, "We are going to tell you what to think, we'll tell you if Charles [Barkley] is right . . . regarding what he said about load management."[5] This is the true underbelly of media. They may not state openly, "We are going to tell you what to think," but they do.

One of my favorite poems is by Robert Frost, "The Road Not Taken." Robert Frost exhorted us to think for ourselves and to recognize the significance of our pathway.

> "Two roads diverged in a yellow wood,
> And sorry I could not travel both,
> And be one traveler, looking I stood
> I looked down one as far as I could
> To where it bent in the undergrowth;
>
> Then, took the other, as just as fair,
> And having perhaps the better claim,
> Because it was grassy and I wanted to wear it;
> Though as for the passing, there
> Had worn them really about the same,
>
> And both that morning equally lay
> In leaves, no step had trodden black.
> Oh, I kept the first for another day!

Yet knowing how way leads to way.
I doubted if I should ever come back.

I shall be telling this with a sigh
Somewhere ages and ages hence:
Two roads diverged in a wood, and I—
I took the one less traveled by,
And that has made all the difference."

The path we choose and travel by makes all the difference. It's imperative to examine our foundations and our worldview. Worldviews are many, but they fall basically into three to eight categories. It is this writer's intention to explain, in broad brushstrokes, eight groupings or perspectives on the world. If one desires more in-depth study, plenty of books, articles, and lectures can explain the intricacies of all these worldviews in far greater detail.

Atheism/Naturalism purports that there is no god. Only the natural world exists. Why does anything exist? It just does.

Agnosticism focuses on the idea that it's impossible to know if God exists. No religion is correct. Atheistic Agnostics would state there is no god.

Pantheism offers there is an impersonal force, aka *Star Wars*, including the idea that god is everywhere. Being enlightened, one seeks to remove desire, thus eliminating good and bad and accepting that human life includes suffering, but the less we desire, the less we will suffer. Life operates in a circle, much like the popular movie *Lion King*. Buddhism is the greatest example of this worldview, and the goal is to end up as nothing; nothing is Nirvana.

Panentheism states everyone is god and we find that god is in everything, with no distinction between god and physical creation. God's existence in everything creates a problem for the existence of evil. Hinduism is an example of this worldview.

Polytheism asserts the existence of multiple gods. This is best seen in the Greek and Roman system of beliefs and Mormonism. Hindus believe in one universal god manifested in hundreds of gods or avatars on Earth.

Dualism holds the idea that the physical and spiritual realm is irreconcilably separated. The spiritual dimension is good, and the physical realm is bad. God and Satan are equals. That a god could rise bodily is not possible. This belief is best seen in Platonism, Greek thought, and New Age.

Deism believes that god exists and is worthy of praise. However, god created everything and then stepped away. God is no longer involved in our world or affairs. There are no miracles, and there is no reason for god to be involved or concerned with his creation. Thomas Jefferson, John Locke, and Benjamin Franklin were famous Deists.

Monotheism teaches there is one god who is separated from creation but works in creation. God is in the universe and outside of the universe. He reveals himself to humanity by revelation. All Christians are theists, but not all theists are Christian. Judaism, Christianity, and Islam are all monotheistic.[6]

Many see the digesting of the philosophical underpinnings of our thought processes as irrelevant, too much ado about nothing, or just too exhausting. What difference does it make, anyway?

But it truly matters! The beliefs we hold impact our lives and birth our deepest core values. It matters in this life if we believe "now" is all there is, if there is a "tomorrow," or whether there is an afterlife. We will think differently, make decisions differently, and hold to values based on which side of the philosophical fence we choose to stand. If a person believes there is a higher moral order and success is found in living out the principles, then that person will make choices limiting their personal freedoms. We form our existence through a structure. But if a person believes there's nothing higher than oneself, then they will pursue those interests and activities that bring them the greatest satisfaction and happiness. Since my happiness is the benchmark, then what happens to "you" is not important. Therefore, "go out and win at any cost" produces an individual or a team where if they win, they are validated, and the methodology is validated. The championship is the sum total criterion for success, and how we go about it is irrelevant. Right is equated with results, not any type of concrete objective criterion. Endgame win, methods justified!

One can observe this same win-at-all-costs attitude in the everyday workings of commerce. Recently, a Wall Street tycoon stated, "Yeah, if there's a market for it, they should do it." If people have an appetite for something, someone will sell it. This is money as king. It doesn't matter if the appetite is good or bad, fair or unfair. Make money. Money means winning and winning is all that matters. If money is the endgame, then sell it; the "it" is irrelevant. If "it" is illegal drug consumption and the eventual outcome is drug addiction, then creating a steady stream of sales makes money. How many drug dealers wreck millions of lives, breathing this mantra? This attitude occurs in the day-to-day marketplace; it doesn't have to be an illegal activity. Making money drives multiple capital enterprises with the ends justifying the means. Make money, baby. Win baby. What does this thinking reflect? What is the foundational worldview? It clearly is not a higher standard than oneself. Nietzsche anyone?

We behave based on what we believe to be true, and the goals we set are based on our system of beliefs. It matters what a person believes. Wrestling with the ideas behind our behaviors is healthy. This is not easy work but deeply worthwhile. If I play for myself and only myself, I am a different athlete than if I play for the benefit of those around me, and I am different if I pursue delighting the one who created me.

All three positions reveal an enormously important worldview, and consequently, behaviors that spring out of the viewpoint are embraced. If there is no god, or if there isn't a god who actively influences the world and my life directly, then I pursue my own pleasure through play, work, and life. However, if God pays attention to my comings and goings and what happens to me and all others on this planet, then I may play to achieve something more than a "win" or a success. So, in the end, what I believe matters. In this wrestling with the philosophical underpinnings of our humanity, we recognize our choices are important. Which road do we take? What does it mean to choose? Many people don't wrestle with their foundational positions. They accept outcomes as fate, or "that's life," or do the best they can, and everything will work out. But the choice is important! One of the foundational aspects of human life is choice. The ability to look at a problem and find a solution is distinctly human. Human beings have the talent, skills, and intellect to solve incredible problems. We do not operate solely by instinct. That's what animals possess—instinct. They feel pain, experience emotions, and reproduce. An animal's reasoning and power of choice are very limited, and they have no self-consciousness or God-consciousness. Choice, self-consciousness, and abstract thought are integral to what it means to be human. Our humanity can set us on an incredible journey, a path where life blossoms and flourishes.

ENDNOTES: CHAPTER 8

1. James Patterson and Peter Kim, *The Day America Told the Truth: What People Really Believe About Everything That Really Matters*, Prentice Hall Direct, 1991 235.

2. Christopher Watkins, *Biblical Critical Theory*, Zondervan Academic, 2022, 160.

3. Carl Trueman, *The Rise and Triumph of the Modern Self: Cultural Amnesia, Expressive Individualism, and the Road to Sexual Revolution*, Crossway 2020, 192.

4. Tracy F. Munsil, "What's Your Worldview?" Focus on the Family, October 22, 2014, https://www.focusonthefamily.com/faith/whats-your-worldview/.

5. Mike Greenberg, producer. *Get Up!* ESPN Studio, February 28, 2023.

6. Brian Chilton. "*8 Major Worldviews*" Podcast. CrossExamined.org.,
Part 1 January 18, 2017, https://crossexamined.org/8-major-worldviews-part-1/
Part 2 January 25, 2017, https://crossexamined.org/8-major-worldviews-part-2/

CHAPTER 9

WHAT IF I LIVE TO WIN?

I DON'T NEED YOUR STINKING PHILOSOPHIES. I JUST LIVE life. People make comments like, "I'll sleep when I'm dead," or "I just want to have a good time," or "I can do it myself. I don't need anyone's help," or like a small child, "Look, Mommy, look, Daddy, look at what I can do." These attitudes sometimes reflect today's philosophical points of view. To expose today's philosophy, scrutinize the messages of popular music; music declares ideologies and pinpoints perspectives. One needs only peruse popular song titles to zero in on a cross-section of modern life philosophy. Songs are statements of life philosophies put into music.

The life philosophy of "winning at all costs" is a foundational position born out of an "in the moment" self-gratification, culminating in an egocentric happiness ethos. Culture swims in an ocean filled by bankruptcy of standards. Throughout history, sport has never held up under the weight of character and morality. Sports have always been littered with misplaced priorities and disturbing scenarios. "In 1869, the very year that Princeton and Rutgers inaugurated intercollegiate football, a game between the two schools was canceled because the faculties feared over-emphasis."[1] Can one imagine how those institutions would view the college sports scene today? Leaders from yesteryear would undoubtedly be aghast and sickened by the loss of educational importance and the rise in a money-grabbing mentality using a "just win" ethic. How much deeper down the rabbit hole have we ventured during those intervening years? And at what cost?

Sport has long strangled our lives and left us in confusion. A popular book, *Friday Night Lights*, puts the struggles of values into focus, "I'm only 18. I spent six years working for it and all the time before thinkin' about it. When I got to the 8th grade, I found out I wasn't going to be able to play college ball . . . high school ball was the best thing for me. And now it's history."[2]

Randy Gregory, when playing for the Dallas Cowboys, said, "I was like, if football isn't here, then what am I? What am I going to do? What do I have to offer? Will my friends and my family still see me the same way? Am I a failure? There's a lot of things I had to figure out."[3]

In 2003, *Sports Illustrated* dedicated an article to mental health issues, "Prisoners of Depression." The article chronicles several different athletes and their very real struggles with the pain of winning and losing. "The biggest risk factor for depression is stress. Performing in front of thousands of fans, having your work scrutinized and judged regularly, laboring in a field where success and failure are so clear-cut—all that can exact a huge psychic toll."[4]

Failure can show itself in many forms, and the pain of failure is real. It can cause damage to our hearts and soul to the point where we just fall on our sword. A prominent baseball player, after winning the World Series, decided his life was a failure, a life of hypocrisy, and he asked his driver to pull the limousine over so he could jump off the bridge. He had won the World Series, but so what? He was a cheater living a lie; death was better than living. Shame can rear its ugly head even in winning the ultimate prize.[5]

Our philosophy drives us, and if we cannot win, then emptiness can condemn us by yet another loss; the world sees us as failures. We are told winning is real life, and we drink deeply of success and power with winning quantifying our humanity. So, when it comes to movies, books, stories, and tales of wonder, we drink deeply from the well of fantasy. Could you tell me why we gravitate toward these stories, movies, and fairy tales? Because we are told to believe them. We enshrine them in legend and folklore. They are branded into our consciousness. The pinnacle of all humanity is the hero, the overachieving, odds-defying, never-say-die "Americana" mantra, the best of man and mankind. Of course, could the sports fetish and idolatry be from another source? Could we bow to and ingest the idol of the importance and God-like nature of sports and sports accomplishment? Why would this happen? Thirty-five billion to forty billion dollars a year can create the magic of sport. This much money provides egregious amounts of mantra, PR feeding, hero-worshipping, and blatant idolatry to keep the professional sports franchises earning and pumping money into their coffers. In short, someone brainwashes us, making us believe we are choosing our values, ideas, philosophies, and life meaning, when actually we are consuming the beliefs that the steady diet of billion-dollar enterprises feeds us.

S.L. Price writes, of course, young people, specifically Black youth, believe their best chance for getting out of poverty and pursuing lucrative careers comes from sports prowess and success. Price says, "That blacks have overcome—or are overcoming—barriers to success in all sports is welcome news, but some African Americans view it as a mixed blessing ... [leaders] worry that too many of today's Black youths unrealistically focus on becoming professional athletes." Price mentioned that Dr. Joseph Carroll of Colby Sawyer College said years ago that when large groups of people form a belief that they can rise above their class by outstanding performance or involvement in an activity, it is called a "false consciousness." False consciousness or expecting too much from oneself and the outcome of a particular activity can create fantasy and disappointment.[6]

College athletes in every college in America traffic in "false consciousness." The athlete often makes plans to go all-in on his basketball, football, baseball, or a sports career, hoping to become a professional. The statistical reality and the sheer difficulty make the dream next to impossible. Yet, many college athletes, and too often athletes of color, even with a college degree, believe their best way to earn a living is to pursue professional sports. This is tragic because millions of young Black men's illusionary dreams die every year and way too often, they do not develop other gifts which could produce extraordinary opportunities.

Athletes are not unlike most Americans from every walk of life. We are told what to believe, what values to have, and that winning is the pathway to the pot of gold at the end of the rainbow. Sadness and despair intensify as example after example find winning is often shallow and cannot have substance without a strong foundational philosophy. Instead, deep ravines of hopelessness can surface with terrifying consequences.

Years ago, a nationally accomplished runner, during the Championship of the NCAA 10,000-meter race in Indianapolis, fell off the pace and then struggled back to fourth place. She apparently decided she had failed to accomplish her objective, yet while still in the throes of this college race, she ran out of the stadium and jumped off the nearby White River bridge.

In 1982, a tragic example of suicide in an athlete caught the public's attention. Soccer hero John Lyons spoke about his disappointment in his performance to teammates, and after a particularly bad game where fans booed him, he went home and hung himself.

Simone Biles, in the 2021 Olympics, openly broke down and failed to compete during the Olympic Games, citing extreme mental health instability, which would create tremendous risks if she were to compete.

Basketball players of the NBA, Kevin Love and DeMar DeRozan, have both admitted to depression and its impact on their mental health and lives. Jerry West, an NBA Hall of Famer, wrote a book that included his battle with mental health issues during his career.

Michael Phelps, winner of the most gold medals in swimming in Olympic history, has openly admitted to struggling with suicide during the height of his accomplishments. He declares that depression and suicide among Olympic athletes is epidemic. Research shows that at least 187 Olympic and former Olympic athletes have committed suicide in the past one hundred years. This devastatingly backs up his point. One only has to do an internet search of athletes who have committed suicide to be scandalized and saddened by this phenomenon.

Tragic events and mental health consequences surround sports and life, which forces us to challenge the "winning-is-all-that-matters" philosophy. It is very clear that winning can prove to be a very low bar. It can leave us with a tornado of dysfunctional priorities and a life of meaninglessness and despair. Therefore, it is imperative that athletes and all of us build a healthy and valid foundation to guide our lives. Our philosophies and beliefs ignite our performances and can truly be life and death.

ENDNOTES: CHAPTER 9

1. Frank Deford, "No Longer a Cozy Corner" *Sports Illustrated*, December 23, 1985, 4–61.

2. H.G. Bissinger, *Friday Night Lights*, Boston: Addison-Wesley, 1990.

3. Jori Epstein, "'It's not something I can really X out of my life': Cowboys D E Randy Gregory opens up on tackling anxiety." USA Today, November 5, 2020, usatoday.com/story/sport/nfl/cowboys/2020/11/05/cowboys-randy-gregory-nfl-mike-mccarthy-jerry-jones/6170276002.

4. Jon Wertheim, "Prisoners of Depression," *Sports Illustrated*, September 8, 2003, 73.

5. Tom Verducci, "Special Report: To Cheat or Not to Cheat," *Sports Illustrated*, June 12, 2012, 38–51.

6. S. L. Price, "Whatever Happened to the White Athlete?" *Sports Illustrated*, September 8, 1997, 42.

Part Two

Chapters 10–18

**Sports Marketplace
Thoughts,
Reality Checks,
&
Drilling Down
on Ideas of Our Day**

CHAPTER 10

A POUND OF BALONEY, PLEASE

THERE ARE THIRTY-SIX NATIONAL SPORTS NETWORKS and thirteen Regional Sports Networks in the United States (plus or minus). These networks estimated annual revenue is generously above $22 billion, which is slightly under 50 percent of the worldwide market revenue, even though there are hundreds of sports networks worldwide. The networks broadcast everything from sporting events to sporting news programs to "talking about sports." Sports broadcasting in all forms is big business, really big business. And this business provides lots of information and opinions. Unfortunately, all this noise results in brainwashing. The endless commentary and analysis of all things "sport" creates "follow-the-leader thinking." Sports are broadcasted mindlessly 24/7, in living color on the big screen, and shown at every bar, restaurant, airport, and bedroom.

For the uninitiated or causal viewer, one may think sports networks are all about sporting events. They are not. Many sports news outlets exist primarily as infomercials for the NFL, and secondarily for the NBA, MLB, MLS, and NHL. Sports networks have moved from reporting news and finding out facts to creating news with lots of opinions and brainwashing sprinkled alongside. Selling opinions and predicting outcomes sometimes in conjunction with gambling odds, are regular and standard fare on most sports networks. When they predict upcoming games and expected results, one could even call it prophecy. Prophecy is telling, predicting, or speaking about the future. Sports networks spend hours telling us about the future. Telling us nothing. They tell us what is going to happen, what might happen, what they predict will happen, or in some cases, by their destruction of a player, team, management, or coach making something happen. They do this by predicting and questioning all news pertaining to sports. Sometimes, incredibly little real news is reported, but excessive numbers of hours are dedicated to prognosticating and predicting the future of a team or individual and dissecting a performance that has just occurred. Mistakes a team or player committed are endlessly analyzed. How could that player be so stupid or inept? Is this player playing up to his potential? Is this athlete worth his salary?

And regarding the future, who will be the picks in the NFL draft? Who will be the picks in the NBA draft? Who will go to the playoffs, who will get home-court advantage, who will win the playoffs, and when a playoff is over, will they repeat? Will this playoff winner be the start of a dynasty? What are the Las Vegas odds for a team winning the conference, a playoff game, or a championship? What are the odds?

Pause and think. When we let Las Vegas tell the future regularly, we have sunk to a new low. Sports networks, Las Vegas, or expert analysts *have no idea what will happen!* They do not have the ability to see into the future. Therefore, they are telling the viewers absolutely *nothing!* They are prophesying stupidity and, worse yet, by their mean-spirited reporting, they have destroyed countless careers. Their banter becomes the creator of MVPs, G.O.A.T.s, Super Bowl heroes, and makers of team market branding. Sports networks report little and proclaim loudly, employing vast quantities of empty hot air sprinkled with a large dose of bravado, creating and building elaborate yarns. Let's just call these entities what they truly are: entertainment with infomercials.

We are on a trajectory of destruction when we allow sports outlets to shape our belief systems and tell us how to think. When they set the cultural norms and moral compass with their "reporting," and when we allow them to form our attitudes about life and sports, we have problems. Sports and truth, whether in politics, culture, social issues, or religion, are rarely compatible or even logical. Athletes rarely receive a thorough education in the arts, literature, the world's socioeconomic geopolitical landscape, philosophy, politics, or other societal needs and ills. Why do sports heroes and sports networks seek a platform to speak about anything outside their areas of expertise? They are attempting to shape public opinion. Athletes want a voice in all societal matters, whether or not they are knowledgeable. They attempt to speak because the sports networks give them a platform. And why wouldn't sports networks give them this platform? They're protecting their own interests. Building viewership and influence creates wealth and power.

Sports magnets display their power by creating the "lemming effect," demanding that a "draft" be moved to the "right" city with the "right" attitude and social policy from the place that embodies the "wrong" social ideologies. All-Star games are juggled from one place to another generated by a room full of suits who maneuver to create public policy using the venue of sports networks. Networks that do not create goods, networks that do not produce resources, networks that consistently speak inanities, and networks whose sole purpose is to make money and entertain. They tell us how to think, and we let them. Sad. "Winning is all that matters."

Sports provide small talk banter. Sports give us a team to root for, something to talk about so we don't have to talk about anything, a neutral epistemology promulgated not to offend. Cotton candy for our brains. We believe we are rooting for a team, when all we are cheering for is a group of mercenaries willing to sell their skills and talents to the highest bidder. Players in professional sports hop from team to team as fast as lightning strikes a tall tree. Their loyalty and management/ ownership loyalty are a usury combination that is ghastly to behold and based on, let us guess, winning! Or maybe, money. Oh, money and winning, winning and money, bedfellows unified in their sloppy imaginations. There is no loyalty.

The professional attitude has invaded the once "innocent" lower levels of sports. College players jump to the best NIL deal, team, coach, and playing stardom opportunity with equal mercenary passions as their professional counterparts. A college coach must build a new team every year, and an opportunity to earn a college education as an incentive is now laughable. Why value a college education? "I am going to strike it rich and make tons of money." Today the Power Five conferences are realistically minor league sport teams attached to a university.

Sadly, because our youth emulate their heroes, jumping from team to team is a normative high school experience. High school coaches placate players and parents who threaten to pack up their toys and go somewhere else. High school athletes learn in the process to use, manipulate, and control their team and those around them. The team's job is to showcase their talents, as they seek herodom, stardom, and riches. It sounds like a game show. And so, the "game" begins—outsmarting your high school administration, coach, teammates, community, and fans. Sadly, we seldom have a basis for the decisions we make, how we choose to live, and whether we are pursuing the moral high ground.

People worship at the altar of sport to gain a lottery-isque salary, so astronomical that high schools will spend millions of dollars building training grounds for naive athletic neophytes with the agenda that one may get a NIL or scholarship promoting their school and program to the community, with the ultimate prize or pipe dream of a professional career. High schools and taxpayers pay to have their children educated, and they are being educated. "Winning is all that matters," loyalty has no value, and schools too often promote extracurriculars at the expense of education. Schools appear to be about education, but the gymnasiums, sports complexes, the number of games, travel time, sports classes, rule-bending, pep rallies, homecoming week, dances after the game, fundraising, community donations for big and flashy (you name it), forces us to consider that maybe the tail is wagging the dog.

Years ago, Dr. Tom Tutko saw this problem. He said, "You can believe that sport is building character, and you can believe it's making a contribution educationally, but if you actually look at the facts, those things are not occurring." High school sports are a mirror of a pro model. "The pro model basically is win."[1]

The value and character development of athletes are shaky and illusionary. The sport ends up being overhyped, oversold, and overmarketed. Sport is placed on a pedestal made of smoke and mirrors. Satirically, we are left just rooting for the teams' jerseys. At the end of the day, with loyalty evaporated, players from all levels of athletic teams jump from organization to organization and school to school. The professional team changes every year and even within a season. College athletes move to new schools with dizzying frequency through the "transfer portal." Even high school athletes seek greener grasses. The trajectory that we are on looks like a downward spiral and where sports are taking us may not be where we really want to go. Is winning enough?

---

1. Bob Slough, "An Ethics Wake-Up Call: Interview with Dr. Tom Tutko," *Athletic Directory*, vol. 10, issue 2, Winter-Spring, 1990.

CHAPTER 11

IF ONLY
I COULD MAKE
A LOT OF MONEY

WINNING IS HYPED AS THE ULTIMATE HUMAN achievement. It is hyped by docudramas; is hyped by players and coaches; is hyped by sports networks; it is hyped by John Q. Public, and riches that can barely be counted hype it. Riches may be the most powerful hype of all.

We never ask the question if an athlete is worth the riches they are being paid. Is a franchise worth six billion dollars? Is an endorsement worth millions, or in Stephen Curry's case, a billion dollars over his lifetime, as paid by Under Armour? Is the latest quarterback payout of $275 million fair, reasonable, or right? Is Shohei Ohtani worth almost three quarters of a billion dollars? Are people who play a game worth millions of dollars to the consumer, to anyone? It is no wonder values are skewed, and tails in every school in America wag the dog. Is it any wonder we are a society and culture who are confused, disillusioned, and disenchanted? We do not know what is important. There is nowhere to "hang our hat." True North is lost. Questions must be asked about ourselves, our community, our culture, and our country. Would riches solve all our problems? Is money a quick fix? Does winning the lottery that millions upon millions of people play every day provide security?

Winning, money, and laurels may appear to be all that matters since they provide rewards most of us would want. Ease and comfort, significance and security, affluence and accoutrements, are the riches we desire as our blanket. People in the United States want more money to purchase more items to augment their lifestyle. Our ease, comfort, and recreation appear vital. People will invest in sketchy schemes to get rich quickly. Businesspeople will work night and day to claw the success ladder. And parents will spend thousands of dollars to train their child, hoping their son or daughter will be the "goose that lays the golden egg." They believe happiness, honor, and glory will be theirs and their child's by signing a lucrative sports contract. We will work hard, chase the golden trophies of success, and sign up for the youth sports bonanza, even though the consequences are often tragic. The obvious tragedy is many potential young scientists, engineers, builders, businesspeople, artists, musicians, and other very talented individuals waste years or decades and do not pursue or ever use their gifts because the sports star sweepstakes has consumed them.

Why not pursue the sports star sweepstakes? The newspaper headlines and the sports outlets trumpet every contract negotiation and celebratory detail. Headlines of the past celebrate Bobby Hull, a National Hockey League player, who signed for $1.75 million for ten years in 1972. (That was a large sum of money in 1972.) Dave Parker, a Major League Baseball player, signed a deal for $5 million for five years, making him the first professional athlete to sign for $1 million a year in 1978. At about that same time, Nolan Ryan was actually paid $1 million a year. Moses Malone, an NBA basketball player, also signed for $1 million in 1978.

Estimated earnings in 2004 for Tiger Woods were $77 million, Shaquille O'Neal made $40 million, and LeBron James made $39 million. It's no wonder a comment in 2004 by the NBA's, Letrell Sprewell, who was making millions, made news when he said, "Why would I want to help them win a title? [Minnesota Timberwolves] They're not doing anything for me. I'm at risk here. I got my family to feed. Anything could happen."

On the heels of the Great Recession of 2008, sports salaries continued to increase, with Tiger Woods earning $99.7 million, Phil Mickelson $53 million, and LeBron James $42.4 million.

Today the beat goes on; earnings dwarf payouts from just a few years ago. One example is a good tight end for the Dallas Cowboys, Dalton Schultz, signed for $11 million for one year. He is a good player, but this salary is pedestrian by the new standards. New contracts for stars continue to rise at an astronomical rate. In 2022, total earnings for Lionel Messi were $130 million, LeBron James $121.2 million, and Stephen Curry $92.8 million. And Shohei Ohtani signed an out-of-this-world contract in December, 2023, for $700 million over ten years with the Los Angeles Dodgers, a number that staggers the imagination.

Do these numbers influence how we think, both positively and negatively? What would the average person do to reach the sports platform of mega success? What would a person do to make hundreds of millions of dollars? Is it any wonder people will cheat, lie, manipulate, and take any manner of performance enhancer to grasp the ring of success?

Perspective cries out: will money solve all our problems? Will it provide us with what we truly want or need? We're forced to ask the question, is it worth it? Who has not heard of the sports figure making a seven-figure salary who files bankruptcy after ceasing to play their sport? The money has wings and is as fleeting as a bird darting through the backyard on a balmy, breezy summer's day. Poof! It has disappeared. "The closest analog to a pro athlete isn't a white-collar executive. It's a lottery winner—often in his early twenties."[1]

The Hall of Fame in all major sports should list the number of heroes who have squandered great sums of money at the end of their yellow brick road of gold. At first, doing this research was interesting, studying the stories of athletes who squandered untold millions. But it became depressing; sad story after sad story pointed out how superstar athletes had squandered vast riches only to see their lives crash with great pain, disappointment, and sorrow. Money has wings; just like winning, riches are illusionary. It appears all the edifices to human achievement, in essence, are a "house of cards."

Superstars go broke so often that getting accurate statistics is difficult. Many articles parrot the statistics found in the *Sports Illustrated* article, "How (and Why) Athletes Go Broke." In the article "How (and Why) Athletes Go Broke," Pablo S. Torre states, "By the time they [NFL players] have been retired for two years, 78% of former NFL players have gone bankrupt or are under financial stress because of joblessness or divorce." He states that 60 percent of former NBA players go broke within five years, and MLB follows similar patterns.[2]

Athletes filed for bankruptcy or came dangerously close by squandering millions and millions of dollars in reckless spending and common-sense defying decisions. Athletes have been known to gamble away millions of dollars and by "living in the fast lane" burn through hundreds of millions more. Besides the fast-lane lifestyle, professional athletes fail financially because of divorce, child support, addictions, gambling, and unscrupulous advisors or friends. Hero after hero stumbles fueled by a giant ego and pursuing shallow goals like, keeping up with the Joneses, involvement with women, and spending money for no real reason or purpose. These monumental failings and the wasting of enormous amounts of funds basically go unreported by the sport-talk machines. The sport machines want to paint stories of success, excitement, and thrills. Bankruptcy, personal tragedies, and heartache are not the fairy tale happily-ever-after-endings that fuel the ranks of high school sports, colleges, and minor league feeder systems. Bankruptcy does not create imaginary and illusionary dreams birthed in childhood; one does not see themselves hitting the game-winning shot, riding in the ticker-tape parade, and then filing bankruptcy. The tragic waste of millions of dollars is common, and once retired, the athlete too often is bankrupt and penniless.

A who's who of past NBA stars have squandered their incomes and have ended up working at places like McDonald's and Starbucks. Some end up homeless. Hundreds have lost their fortunes. These fortunes were not NBA minimum salaries; they were multimillion-dollar jackpots. These players made All-Star teams and hundreds of millions of dollars in career earnings.[3]

Unfortunately, there are plenty of big-name legends from all sports who have failed financially. Athletes from the NHL, MLB, MLS, PGA, Olympic gold medalists, and world boxing champions have all shared the sad story of lost fortunes. Athlete after athlete who reached their dreams only to find that riches are fleeting, ultimately resulting in stories ending in the heartbreak of riches to rags.

Hundreds of our heroes have revealed that having success in the arena or on the field does not guarantee the right values, disciplines, perspectives, foundations, or attitudes in finances or life. Failures clearly point out once again the need for a solid personal foundation. Finances and life fail in a vacuum. Athletes, along with the rest of us, need direction and purpose. Fame, success, and wealth are fleeting; being a rich sports celebrity does not guarantee a stress-free, happy-ever-after life.

Sometimes, it takes a life-changing event for people to reevaluate their lives and philosophy. Past baseball players Dave Dravecky and Jim McGlothlin experienced wake-up calls. Dave Dravecky's arm shattered during a pitch, revealing life-threatening cancer, which resulted in the loss of his left arm. This event caused him to question everything and form new life-changing directions. Jim McGlothlin realized the temporary nature of material glory. Jim McGlothlin, a major league baseball player for the Cincinnati Reds, California Angels, and Chicago White Sox, died at the age of thirty-two. He died two years after pitching his last game. Prior to his death, he lost forty-five pounds and said, "It all came at a bad time". . . But I had a lot of time to think. I've found out there's more to life than baseball." Many athletes, like these two men, have hit hard times over the years and realized life holds deep challenges.

What is success? Who are the real heroes? What are our goals? What is important? These and many other questions should be part of our conversation with our children and a dialogue discussed among the professionals. What do we live for? What matters to us? Do we pursue money? Do we have to win? Will success give us a sense of significance or provide security? Are we caught up in becoming a hero?

ENDNOTES: CHAPTER 11

1. "Pablo S. Torre, "How (and Why) Athletes Go Broke," *Sports Illustrated*, March 23, 2009, 96.

2. "Pablo S. Torre, "How (and Why) Athletes Go Broke," *Sports Illustrated*, March 23, 2009, 92.

3. Ross Kelly, "NBA Stars Who Blew Their Millions." Stadium Talk, December 5, 2018, www.stadiumtalk.com/s/nba/-stars-who-lost-millions-of-dollars-542c2eb2266441f3.

CHAPTER 12

WHO IS THE BEST OR THE G.O.A.T.?

T HE HERO OF THE CLASSIC FICTIONAL 1980s movie *The Natural* centers on a young man gifted with prodigious talent in baseball. His name is "Roy Hobbs." He takes a wrong turn, and this decision changes his youthful life. He makes a comeback as an aging rookie and leads his team, the "Knights", to the playoffs. During the movie, Hobbs mentions he wants his name to mean something, he wanted to be remembered as "There's Roy Hobbs, the best there ever was." The first time he says it, he speaks to the villainess who is unimpressed as she fires a quick "And then what?" He reiterates that when he walks down the street, people will say, "There's Roy Hobbs, the best there ever was."[1] Roy Hobbs wants significance.

This is a breathtaking moment in the movie. It is all of us and none of us. Who among us does not aspire to be the best at something? And yet, who among us even gets close to being the best at something? We all seek immortality. We all aspire to accumulate immense wealth and leave a lasting legacy. We all want to be remembered and know our lives matter. However, we cannot define the terms that stamp our lives as worthwhile. "The best" and "the G.O.A.T." (or GOAT) are terms of undefinable definition. For those unfamiliar with the anachronism, "GOAT" is shorthand for Greatest Of All Time. I will detail these quandaries in the following discussion.

Recent chatter about the football GOAT is Tom Brady. After just winning a Super Bowl and defeating Dallas in the home opener in 2021, Tom Brady is the proclaimed GOAT of football. Talking heads love to toss the idea around of who the GOAT of this or that is, filling the airwaves with shallow glory. Many professional athletes seek fulfillment in pursuing greatness in a field of endeavor. We often think Michael Jordan is basketball's GOAT. Recently, lobbying for that moniker, LeBron James threw his hat into the ring. Wouldn't that be an accomplishment to be considered the GOAT in a particular field or activity? We all desire to make a difference and receive affirmation. The only problem is that it is difficult to garner. And even if we could be immortal, the designation leaves everybody on planet Earth out except one. Only one GOAT exists. Clothing manufacturers are clamoring to market GOAT shirts for young people because young people are naïve enough, vain enough, and self-centered enough to buy one and wear it in public. But there exists only one greatest of all time, only one in every field of endeavor, there exists only ONE!

Since there is only one, this would amount to fulfillment for a couple thousand people throughout the history of the world. If Aristotle was the GOAT of philosophers, then he is it. One! And moving on to the next category and so forth.

Being "the best" or GOAT is shallow. Why is it shallow? It is shallow to believe in the existence of a singular "par excellence." The best is only relevant at a moment in time on a particular day, in a particular game, for a particular strike of the clock. The word is fluid and shadowy. We cannot even define "the best;" the definition is fluid. And "GOATNESS" is impossible. Many people say, "Here is the best player on this team," "This is the best player in this league," "This is the best player in this division," and "This is the best player in this state," or "This is the best player in the country," and so forth. These conversations are philosophical conundrums. Number one, the best, along with the GOAT discussion, struggles to define terms of valuation. If the best player is part of a team, one must also refer to teammates; there is no best player by himself. One player cannot defeat a team. Key teammates often enable another teammate to have outstanding performances.

During the Super Bowl between Tampa Bay and the Kansas City Chiefs in 2021, Patrick Mahomes, who is supposed to be personified greatness, failed with the help of his key teammates. His offensive line had several injuries, and critical players did not get to play. Patrick Mahomes was well below his normal performance level, hampered by a foot injury. He was not the best that day; on that day there were no GOATs, the Kansas City Chief's team could not perform their usual heroics.

It becomes excruciatingly obvious when we talk about the best individual in a team game, we have another intellectual incongruency. We find the terms GOAT and "the best" full of intellectual incongruences. These struggles are reflected in an article where the author concisely details the qualities of basketball greats LeBron James, Kareem Abdul-Jabbar, and Michel Jordan. Their talents, global recognition, and legacies make a GOAT debate impossible. Reynolds concludes his article by stating, "The answer to the GOAT debate is there isn't one. There are many. Personal preference prevails."[2]

If one wished to speak in terms of "the best" in an individual sport, one would be well served to look at their body of work. Even the best can fail on any day, which then calls into question whether they are the best. The best in golf or the best in tennis can have an off day. So, how are we defining "the best" from an event point of view? Is someone the best if they defeated the best of all time on a given day? On that day, the "not the best" defeated "the best." So, who in that space of time is "the best?" Is the winner "the best" by defeating "the best?" Or is "the best" the best even though today they lost? The questions are endless. It is obvious the term "the best" is a nebulous fluid term or designation. The terms "the best" and "GOAT" are fraught with hyperbole and impossibilities. So, if the term "the best" is an elusive impossibility from a practical standpoint, then how much more preposterous is it to throw the term Greatest Of All Time around?

The Super Bowl in 2021 pitted the Tampa Bay Buccaneers against the Kansas City Chiefs. The discussion on many networks fell to who's the greatest football player of all time. It was Tom Brady. The problem with the idea of "Greatest Of All Time" is greatest compared to what? Greatest in skill, ability, a particular aspect of the game, mental preparation, physical preparation, ability to mesh with the other players, attitude, humility, compared to the generation's best in that time period, or in an algorithm proportional computation covering all time? What is the criterion, or can there be a criterion? And the term "Greatest Of All Time" is an intellectual incongruity because it cannot consider the future. The term "all time" would imply there was never anyone as good, and there will be nobody else as good, **ever!** It is intellectually incongruent because we do not know who and what circumstances will provide an athlete of greatness in the future. Therefore, conversation, ad nauseam regarding Tom Brady being the GOAT and then the continual banter along these same lines in the National Basketball Association about who is the GOAT is a waste of time and a conversation not worth having. A discussion pitting LeBron James or Michael Jordan as the recipient of GOAT is worse than frivolous. Considering the relativity of the "greatest of all time," it is wasteful to expend oxygen, nutrients, and brain power on the subject.

What if a young athlete upsets or dethrones the greatest of all time in his or her first year in the pros but has no body of work? This athlete might be amazing, however, they got injured and disappeared. Does the GOAT require comparison over a season, two years, five years, ten years, or a career? What does the "greatest of all time" require in terms of length of athletic participation? The questions are endless; the terms are, at best, arbitrary. We are dealing with criteria based on a constantly moving target. This constantly moving target is filled with opinion, prejudice, a lack of historical perspective, and difficulties.

Therefore, why are these terms used? The terms "The Best" and "The GOAT" are extremely inaccurate usage of words used during sports banter. Are sports' hosts genuine or are the terms just blather to create interest in television programming? It would seem clear these designations are elusive nomenclature without clear or even subtle realities of accurate comparisons. Simply put, they are nonsensical terms, creating an artificial standard that millions of children and adults seek to aspire to without the least chance of accomplishing something because it does not exist. Do we strive to reach these plateaus because they are real or because we need to believe they are real to drive our efforts to be the best, or to drive television ratings and money at worst?

ENDNOTES: CHAPTER 12

1. Barry Levinson, director. *The Natural*. Tri-Star Pictures, 1984. Based on Bernard Malamud's 1952 novel of the same name.

2. Associated Press. Tim Reynolds, "What Impending Scoring Record Means for James," *Las Cruces Sun-News*, February 7, 2023, 1B.

CHAPTER 13

REALITY CHECK #1: THE LIGHTNING STRIKE

N DEFINING HERO CRITERIA, WE FIND THIS AN ELUSIVE endeavor. What makes one truly outstanding enough to be a professional is a challenging conversation. Yet, the lure of sports stardom is so strong that many a young person dives into the deep end and pursues heroic sports greatness, hoping to be the next "best."

This was me. NBA, here I come! It started when I was four years old, playing the babysitter one-on-one in the garage. The game was so fun, it was thrilling, and I won. My basket was four feet in height, and the babysitter was five foot eight, and I won? I was hooked. I began playing basketball at recess whenever I could and went out of my mind when we could play indoors in the New Carlisle Elementary school gym. I loved the game. As I sat enthralled, watching the University of Dayton Flyers and Don May battle the mighty UCLA Bruins, featuring the amazing Lew Alcindor, my twelve-year-old passion for basketball ignited. (Lew later became Kareem Abdul-Jabbar.) Watching that game, I decided I would play at one of those two colleges and eventually turn pro. I had become a statistic. The driveway games became arenas filled with cheering, screaming fans, cheerleader adulation, scholarships, and significance.

Significance was important; I was not very significant in my day-to-day world. I rarely got to be with my dad as he worked long hours to provide for our family. I had few friends, and the girls did not notice me. I was extremely thin, wore glasses, had a mole under my nose above my lip, buck teeth, flat feet, a bad back, and was awkwardly uncoordinated. I was a real catch. Being a sports star would change all that and provide endless thrills and excitement. I was going to be a pro. Others did not agree. My best friend's dad once said, "I sure feel sorry for that Bailey kid. He wants to play basketball so bad, and he is painfully uncoordinated, just not very good." This appeared true as my heart was broken, in the seventh grade, when I went out for the eighth-grade basketball team and was cut. I pressed on, continuing to play. I worked hard, and amazingly, at fourteen years old, I grew six inches in about eight months. As a freshman, I had become a "big kid," six feet tall. This was amazing, as my dad was five foot nine, and my mom was five foot two. Around this time, I began practicing basketball, developing specific skills. I attended the University of Dayton basketball camp and learned from Don May how to shoot free throws. My free throws improved from 45 percent as a freshman to 80 percent as a sophomore. I diligently jumped rope every day, per the instructions of my freshman coach, and gradually, my coordination improved, as did my skills. No longer did the older kids and adults exclude me from their pickup games, as they had when I was a freshman. I was keeping up with my competitors.

One day, as a sophomore, I defeated my dad, my uncle, and my cousin in a game of one on three. Suddenly, there was a glimmer of hope. After years of hard work, this late bloomer cracked the varsity starting lineup as a senior and was one of the top scorers in our conference. Our team surprised everyone, and we became one of the top teams in the area. The Tecumseh Arrows were ranked locally and earned the best record in twenty-five years. But Randy Ayers and his Springfield North Panthers derailed our fairy-tale ending. They beat us in the opening game of the district tournament, deflating the hopes and dreams that our team had imagined. Our dream of playing in the finals of the district tournament at Hobart Arena had come to an end. Springfield North played in the finals. Randy Ayers played Division One basketball, and he received a tryout with the Chicago Bulls. He became the Head Basketball Coach at

Ohio State University and coached for decades in the NBA.

I received no scholarships, lettered at a small Division III school, transferred, and finally, at about twenty-one years old, gave up on "the dream."

My story is unique, and yet it is not. Whether one comes from a small town or the inner city, the glitter of NBA stardom shines brightly in the hearts of millions of young people. The question is, should it? Or should there be a backup plan? Motivational speakers exhort, burn the ships, storm the beach, be all in, and have no backup plan; that will bring success. I was all in! I worked harder at basketball than any young person in our community had ever worked, spending countless hours honing my game. Frequently, people talked about our local park and my name in the same sentence. I drove to neighboring communities in search of competitive games. If hard work would have done the trick, I would have played in the NBA. However, I should have been more well-rounded, I should have developed other interests, and I should have had a Plan B. Young people sometimes need perspective.

How reliably can we determine if a high schooler will play on a college team? Roughly 3.5 percent of high school basketball players will play at a four-year college, and about 2 percent will play at a junior college. Around 5.5 percent of high school basketball players will play college basketball. NCAA football weighs in at 5.8 percent, baseball 5.6 percent, ice hockey 12.9 percent, and soccer 5.7 percent. And other sports have numbers that are close to these statistics. Do these numbers necessitate a Plan B? Do professional opportunities give one pause? Should we have a Plan B? College players who play basketball have about a 1 percent chance of making the NBA, a 1.6 percent chance of earning an NFL roster spot, a 7.4 percent chance in the NHL, and 10 percent of playing on a major league baseball team; this includes the minor leagues. However, 90 percent of minor league players will never play in the big leagues. The NBA drafts about sixty players, but not all drafted players make an NBA team. To make an NBA team, a player must be one of the best players in their state in high school and one of the best four or five college players in a Power Five conference and/or be "lucky."

Making an NBA roster is roughly as common as the number of people being killed by lightning each year. A person has a remarkably low chance of being a professional athlete. A powerful Plan B would be an extremely wise decision. All sports mirror roughly the same odds. Decades ago, a *Sports Illustrated* author said, "If the odds were displayed on a tote board, no one would take them. Thousands and thousands to one against making the pros . . . He might well add that the colleges' willingness to participate in this fraud is, at best, shameful."

Being hit by lightning is rare and so is earning an NBA or other major league sports paycheck. Nevertheless, people believe we should follow the lemming in front of us. Disney, in the 1958 movie *White Wilderness*, created the belief that lemmings will follow each other right off a cliff to their deaths.[1] They do not, but the point is true. We often follow others to our own demise. Delusional, it will be me who gets the prize. We ignore the facts. Whether it's big-time sport zillionaires or playing the tables in Vegas, just enough people win to cause the average non-thinking citizenry to play and lose. And lose we do; millions of people play and lose the lottery every day, and millions of people play and lose in casinos. Thousands of young people disdain a high school or college education, mouthing words like, "What do I need to learn this for? I am going to be a professional athlete!" During my career, I have heard this refrain hundreds of times, frequently from a wisp of a kid five feet nothing and a hundred and nothing, arguing against learning. Education is a waste of time because I am going to be a professional. The professional sports factories love the hype, as it keeps a steady stream of talent pouring into their league and creates a voracious fan base.

Reggie Marra would add, "Most of us begin to speak very early in life, and very few of us make our livings as professional speakers. Even though we learn to write in elementary school, and even if we have an inclination toward complete sentences and coherent, unified paragraphs, very few of us make our living as writers. The talented, enthusiastic, hard-working student-athlete likewise cannot count on earning a living playing the game that he or she loves. Very few human beings make their livings as paid professional athletes, and this message, regardless of how many times or by whom it is delivered, does not ring true for those wide-eyed competitors who dream of careers playing the games they love.

"It is the job of coaches and parents to encourage those dreams and prepare the student-athlete cognitively, emotionally, physically, socially, and spiritually for the day that this message becomes real when a primary activity other than sport is appropriate-whether at high school or college graduation or at the end of a professional career."[2]

And even for professional athletes who have enjoyed the stardom of sports careers, the end comes; owners, general managers, coaches, and fans see only the last game. Legends of the past have said things like, "The ball player is only as good as his last game. No one remembers him after that." "There's nothing deader than yesterday's hero." Great players in the twilight of their careers are forced to come to grips with the need for other pursuits. Lightning did strike, but even they need to be prepared to move into another world, the world of non-athletes.

ENDNOTES: CHAPTER 13

1. James Algar, director/writer. *White Wilderness.* Walt Disney Productions, 1958.

2. Reggie Marra, *The Quality of Effort: Integrity in Sport and Life for Student-Athletes, Parents and Coaches,* From the Heart Press, 2013, 96.

CHAPTER 14

REALITY CHECK #2: PLAY, COMPETITION, AND RISK

HEN A YOUNGSTER PLAYS A GAME, THEY are not thinking of college scholarships, lucrative professional money, or being a sports legend. Generally, the joy of playing is and should be an end in itself. Play is an activity of leisure. Play is fun and stops when you're tired, it's not fun anymore, or when mom yells, "It's time for dinner." One should examine what it is that we are really discussing when we use the term competition, and we throw in the words "playing the game." Are we bantering about play or competition? We can say sports, competition, and athletics all grow out of the term "to play." Play involves "an activity characteristic of all ages occurring in a social setting. It is free and has more other than a self-directed aim; it is real only as a self-construct; it is happy, euphoric, rather than sad; it is structured, characterized by rules and regulations; it is meaningful activity."[1] Play is voluntary, and it can be terminated freely at any point. "Play is not athletics, though the instinct of play is undoubtedly one of their motives, and recreation is an important element therein. The child plays till he is tired and then leaves off. The competitor in a race goes on after he is tired, goes on to the point of absolute exhaustion."[2] He even trains painfully. The attitude of the participant is also an important factor in determining what it means to play. Attitude is so important that one may define an aspect of work as play. A task could be performed with sheer delight or simply for its own end. Some people experience this in their everyday jobs. Some professional athletes experience this in their work to play.

Sports and athletics both involve characteristics of play, but they add greater structure. A sport could be done simply as play, but often the attitude of the participant is keener and makes a greater planned effort. The structure of sports eliminates the option to cease at any time. Play ends at the whim of the participant, but sports involve an attempt to conclude the event successfully. Competition may be a part of both play and sport at its purest level, "competition exists when two or more people struggle for some common goal or object, if one individual achieves his or her goal, the others are preventing from reaching theirs."[3]

Gary Warner says, "Endurance may be the key factor that separates 'sport play' from 'sport competition.'"[4]

Reggie Marra states, "Athletes, parents, and coaches benefit when they recognize the difference between what goes on in the professional arena and what should be going on in the local high school gymnasium, on the Little League field, or at the elementary school fun-run. Not only are the rules of the games different from those in professional events, but the reasons for staging the games—for the games' very existence—vary by necessity."[5]

While we speak of playing the game even at the professional level, the words we use have misleading and misdirected meanings depending on the context. Professional athletes are not really playing; they are working. Most college athletes are working too, and in a perfect world, the payoff would be a four-year degree from a fine college institution. So, when we speak about playing the game, we really utter all kinds of confusing images. Intrinsic in this confusion is a hopeless morass of metaphors, hyperboles, and meaning misogyny.

Because competition involves enduring to the end, winning, or earning a successful outcome, injuries increase. During play, when a sprain or strain happens, the participant ceases the activity. But when competing for victory, people often push their bodies further, increasing the risk of injury. Sport carries the risk of injury, and too often, people do not weigh the cost of participation.

Evaluating risk factors is important for those who play or compete. For example, boxers are a high-risk group, with 90 percent of all boxers sustaining a traumatic brain injury in their careers. This makes sense as the target area is the head. Legendary Heavyweight Champion Muhammad Ali, at forty-two years old, suffered early Parkinson-like symptoms. Over the years, it clearly compromised his mind. MMA sport is so violent and injuries so frequent that combatants would be arrested if they behaved on the street or in a bar as they do in the ring.

In the NFL, programming goes to a commercial break when an injury occurs, and upon return, usually, the injured player has been removed as if nothing has happened, other than a mention that the player is receiving evaluation or treatment.

Lately, head injuries and concussions have been brought to the public consciousness. The NFL tried to downplay brain injury risk until they could no longer keep it quiet. A book, *Concussion*, brought brain injuries into the open and was so powerful and well-received that a movie by the same name was produced and aired. The revelation of dramatic brain injuries forever changed the way football is played. Interestingly, when the movie was first released, at its very end, the doctor who uncovered Chronic Traumatic Encephalopathy (CTE) warns if anyone tries to talk his child into playing football, he will sue them. This last statement or quote is removed from the Netflix version available for rental.

In discussing a settlement between the NFL and a lawsuit filed by players whose brains were injured by football, the judge wanted to know how many players suffered brain injuries. "One-third the report showed. One third of all NFL players were likely to develop football-related dementia, and at 'notably younger ages' than the general population. And that was by the NFL's calculations."[6]

Not only does football risk brain trauma, but it also contains risk for multiple other body parts; knees, ankles, spine, and shoulders are parts of the anatomy placed at risk by participation. These injuries and their long-term effects are chronicled by William Nack, who sarcastically wonders why orthopedic surgeons and specialist doctors aren't standing around NFL retirement conventions passing out business cards. He says everybody who played professional football has a lifelong injury. "They are the wincing, hobbling wounded: the man who played professional football, a notoriously joint-shearing, disc popping, nerve-numbing exercise that has grown only more dangerous . . . 'There are older retirees who walk around like Maryland crabs,'" says Miki Yaras-Davis.[7]

A Ball State University study from 1940 to 1990 found that of 870 players surveyed, 65 percent had a major injury, forcing them to miss at least eight games. Football has had as many injuries, if not more, since that study. Bigger, faster players playing on synthetic surfaces have increased injuries.

Other studies have found football injury rates, which keep athletes out of participation, i.e., practice or games during a season, as high as 100 percent. One hundred percent is not an unusual rate of injury during a football season.

This chapter's brief discussion highlights the need to understand the differences between play and competition and the increased risks when we compete at a high level. Thoroughly examining all aspects of sport, one must honestly examine the injury rate and type of injuries to make an informed decision regarding participation for oneself or loved ones. What are acceptable risks, and what types of problems are we willing to absorb? Our involvement at varying levels of sport requires an examination of why we play, the benefits, and possible hurdles or pitfalls. Tongue in cheek: is one death per one thousand participations an acceptable level? If so, then the adventure sport of hang gliding may be "your cup of tea."

ENDNOTES: CHAPTER 14

1. Robert Lee, *Religion and Leisure In America*, Abingdon Press, 1964, 4.

2. Norman Gardiner, *Athletics of the Ancient World*, Oxford: Clarendon Press, 1930, 5.

3. Bryant J. Cratty, *Social Psychology in Athletics*, Prentice-Hall, 1981, 7, 62–64.

4. Gary Warner, *Competition*, David C. Cook Publishing, 1979, 72.

5. Reggie Marra, *The Quality of Effort: Integrity in Sport and Life for Student-Athletes, Parents and Coaches*, From the Heart Press, 2013, 44.

6. Jeanne Marie Laskas, *Concussion*, Random House, 2015, 260.

7. William Nack, "The Wrecking Yard", *Sports Illustrated*, May 7, 2001, 62.

CHAPTER 15

REALITY CHECK #3: RISK'S REALITY, RISK'S REWARD

L IFE IS NEVER RISK-FREE! AFTER CHRONICLING injuries as a part of competition and play, it would seem that a call to boycott athletics would be reasonable. But this is not a polemic against playing a dangerous, risky sport; it is about evaluating risk and being sensible. An injury can limit or end a career. Injuries are the trap doors under the floorboards in a dark room of risk. The risk of injury is the "dirty little secret" or the "elephant in the room" that we would rather pretend doesn't exist.

Our world tries to brainwash us into believing that we can eliminate risk. If we eat right, sleep enough, don't smoke, drink, or use drugs, and behave responsibly, we can live forever. We obsess about risk: young children wear bicycle helmets when cycling, elbow and knee pads when skateboarding, motorcycle helmets when riding about town, lifeguards when swimming, face masks when catching in baseball, helmets in hockey, shoulder pads and helmets when playing football, mouth guards when playing basketball, shin guards when playing soccer, knee pads when playing volleyball, guard rails on mountains, warnings on cigarette packages, seat belts when driving, life jackets when boating and whitewater rafting, masks during COVID, and the "beat goes on." Lawyers, "helicopter parents," "bulldozer parents," regular parents, politicians, police officers, school officials, business professionals, and representatives from most walks of life seek to eliminate risks. This is impossible! We cannot eliminate risks. Living creates risks. From the moment we get up in the morning until we lie down at night, we are inundated with risk. Life is a risk; people die in their sleep. Everyone will die, life is risk, and we are mortal. On May 18, 2021, Kevin Pillar was struck forcefully in the face with a 95-mph fastball. Playing sports equals danger and risk. Danger lurks around every corner; tragedy hides in plain view, and death haunts our daytime nightmares. An old movie, *Brian's Song*, begins with the narrator being very honest, "All true stories end in death. This is a true story."[1] The spoiler alert at the beginning of the movie reminds us a life free of risk is a 100 percent impossibility. Risk cannot be eliminated. Vaccinations cannot eliminate illness. Staying indoors or wearing a mask does not remove risk. Risk is as much a part of life as the air we breathe. Suffering results from living in a world full of dangers, hidden disappointments, tragedy, problems, and risk.

When COVID hit, authorities ordered us to stay out of crowds, wear masks, maintain a 6-feet distance, regularly wash our hands, get tested for infection, and if we were infected, isolate in our homes . . . and people died! Hundreds of thousands of people died. No matter how diligent we were as a family, nation, or as a global community, COVID spread, and people died. Risk is everywhere. The authorities locked people down, and we could not do normal daily activities, even if we desired to pursue or do an activity. Why? Fear. We were seeking to live. People behaved as if to live, we must eliminate risk. Adults became phobic; children became "scaredy cats."

And it didn't work. We live in a world where it is impossible to remove risks. Remove suffering? Remove accidents?

Why do we try to remove risk? Control or fear! Control is important, and we are afraid. The parenting style of today is: protect our children, fix everything for them, do not let them suffer. We desire to control outcomes, all outcomes. Risks, accidents, and death remind us we are mortal and not in control. Suffering cannot be eliminated. But if we cannot eliminate suffering, then we will not be happy, and of course, we live to be happy. We do not understand values beyond the scope of the now or truth that transcends circumstances. Confused, we believe that eliminating risk will equal total happiness. If we extinguish failure and enjoy safety, success, and security, happiness will be our reward. This formula represents modern living and parenting, yet it has significant flaws.

Speaking on parenting, Brené Brown writes, "I spread my data all over my dining room table and asked myself this question: What do parents experience as the most vulnerable and bravest thing that they do in their efforts to raise Wholehearted children? . . . letting their children struggle and experience adversity."[2]

In a world of risk avoidance, in a world of fear, in a world that desperately wants to be in control of everything and eliminate ALL risks, truth rings out and quenches our thirst like nothing else. Though we live in the throes of fear, tragedy, death, and sorrow, hope is only found in the nature, being, and character of God. God may use struggles to birth hope. We mislead ourselves when we think we can remove all danger and adversity. A risk-free life is simply impossible.

As children and parents scrutinize their level of involvement with sports, important questions must be asked, is this a wise and profitable activity on a personal level, ethically, emotionally, and physically? Or are the dangers of competing in this activity not acceptable based on my values, goals, and dreams? Are the risks reasonable? Do they interfere with other life plans I may have in mind? Information, thoughtful perspective, and balance are essential in the "go forward" risk arena of sport.

ENDNOTES: CHAPTER 15

1. Buzz Kulik, director. *Brian's Song*. Screen Gems, 1971.

2. Brené Brown, *Daring Greatly: How the Courage to Be Vulnerable Transforms the Way We Live, Love, Parent, and Lead*, New York: Gotham Books, 2012, 238–239.

CHAPTER 16

LOSING OUR MINDS!

THROW CAUTION TO THE WIND. WHO CARES about physical risks? Who cares if an athlete has a lottery chance of playing professionally? Who cares if a child loses the joy of participating in a sport? Who has not "pulled out all of the stops" to squeeze out that elusive victory? How close to the line does someone tippytoe? Was the line crossed between good and bad, moral and evil, ethical and unethical? Who hasn't quipped that they would "give their right arm" to win an important championship game? The reward can seem so big that giving up a limb via an injury would be a possibility. To hold up the championship trophy, many would do anything. Forget that there are real risks. An all-important significant game may be a little league game or the championship of the world. And the tension in sport is to win. It often takes an all-in mentality to achieve victory, a "burn the ships" and go to "battle" with no retreat. Intensity of a freakish level is required, and the outcome must matter. And if the outcome doesn't matter, then one would really have to ask if the person is playing instead of competing. (Play was discussed earlier in Chapter 14.) There is a difference, and this difference can produce an incredible tension of values.

But do we lose our minds or souls in the process? Have we given up sanity? Have we given away morality? People often go too far in pursuing opportunities, especially when it comes to their children. Gary Warner recounts a story of parental over-emphasis when he describes Steven

Butler, living in Miami, Florida, as part of his birthday celebration, swam ½ mile with a toy boat in each hand. His dad said, "My son's a real star," and Fleet Peeples, his swim coach proclaimed "I don't plan to set any immediate goals for him . . . His potential depends on how much interest he shows.' Steven is two years old."[1]

It is difficult to combat the torrent of public opinion that pushes, prods, and demands that our child be developed to their "professional" capabilities. Parents enroll their daughters in gymnastics and cheerleading camps, pay huge fees, travel all over the United States, and enter them into national competitions at six, seven, and eight years old. Basketball teams for children travel from region to region and state to state, entering the children in tournaments at great financial cost and personal time. Parents will spend thousands of dollars to see that their child gets "the edge." Family togetherness is sacrificed, family meals are a thing of the past, and families that used to gather for Sunday morning church now join hundreds of sports league participants worshipping at the altar of Sport.

Rick Reilly, years ago, wrote a thought-provoking article detailing parental overemphasis. He mused the scenario was like reading from a science fiction novel, which could be entitled, *"A 2007 Sixth Grade Sports Odessey."* This true-life story is about a Dallas-based basketball team, the Texas Titans, sponsored by a billionaire who sends his team throughout the United States on a chartered 737 jet. The billionaire's son is a member of the team. The team travels with a large entourage of parents, coaches, and helpers. They stay in the finest of hotels, are provided the best of meals in luxurious banquet halls on food recommended by the team nutritionist, snack on desert delicacies, enjoy transportation provided by charter buses, and during downtime have the latest in video entertainment available. They have played games all over the country. Reilly concludes, saying, if your sports team is trying to attract the best and brightest talent, they would be well advised to find a billionaire benefactor; otherwise, your team may just be left in the dust on the tarmac.[2]

Parents spend thousands of dollars on athletic training, seemingly forgetting that their money could be saved for rainy days or for other worthwhile pursuits. Josh Peters wrote that the pandemic derailed countless young aspiring athletes' hopes of getting a college opportunity and scholarship. The article states that a Harris Poll between February 20 and April 16, 2020, found that 20 percent of athletic scholarships have been withheld or delayed. Forty percent of competitive athletes say their parents talk about how much they invest to help their kids excel. "Many families worry they will no longer be able to pay for elite sports if the economic downturn persists . . . One family estimated [they] had spent $200,000 on [their] son's basketball career. Now, he said, the family could have to pay up to $30,000 for Jordan's education for the next academic year."[3]

It sounds like this family can handle $30,000 in college costs. Should we feel sorrow? Four years at $50,000/yr. = $200,000. That would cover most college costs. What were the parents thinking?

This family is not alone in their headlong pursuit of sports sweepstakes. I have heard of many parents in the pursuit of high-level soccer competition, spending as much as $5,000 a month chasing challenging tournament opponents and investing in player development.

Further misplaced perspectives are seen in recounting a few true-life stories.

A coach's blood veins bulged out of his neck, and the sternocleidomastoid muscles were flexed. The coach's face was beet red and fumed, almost spitting as he spoke sprinkling choice curse words. There was good reason for this outburst. The very existence of the professional sports franchise was on the line, and millions, if not billions, of dollars were at stake. This does not account for a multibillion-dollar taxpayer-funded arena. The coach seemed justified as he berated his athletes; even numerous profanities were acceptable since so much was riding on this game. The megabucks were not the only spoils, but families' future careers and incomes, plus the sports franchise itself, were threatened. This scenario appears acceptable, especially if the team was on the verge of bankruptcy; this would be a make-or-break moment. Actually, all that was at stake was a game between two baseball teams, whose rosters were filled by six, seven, and eight-year-olds. Brubaker Elevator versus Deam's Auto, and the players, including myself, were looking up at their coach wide-eyed. Our eyes were full of fear, shock, and amazement as the coach breathed out his frustration on our Little League baseball team. Unfortunately, this scenario is repeated every day in Little League baseball parks, soccer fields, football fields, basketball courts, and other recreation centers across the country. This is an all too familiar scene; commonplace, the displeased coach confronts blundering athletes with tremendous anger. If this was the report of adult athletes facing elimination and a critical championship playoff game or the end of their careers, one where livelihoods were at stake, one might understand the zealousness or the extreme use of chastisement. But, to berate small children and exhort them to win a mid-week game on a Wednesday night for Little League, what's going on?

Years ago, one high school freshman basketball player was molded into a player who was motivated by anger. The coach would either tongue lash the player or place two teammates in a guarding position in practice who shoved, pushed, slapped, and harassed the freshman basketball player with the goal of a better performance. The performance improved, but the side effect was that the player played with anger. It became a vicious cycle in which the player needed to be angry to produce the best outcome. Ultimately, it reduced the performance it was meant to foster.

"An Indiana youth basketball game went off the rails over the weekend as a fan appeared to get into a fist fight with the referee . . . [the eighth-grade players] watched and tried to intervene in the altercation. Other bystanders at the game eventually separated the two."[4]

Losing our minds can be seen in youth sports across our nation. Methods to win are myriad. Youth coaches will play a "starting five" or make no substitutions as if the win is the supreme accomplishment. "[Dan Hinkle is the] commissioner of a youth football league who decided to fire [his] son's coach because the guy switched [his] precious 12-year-old, Scott, from defense to offense for *one* game. You got rid of a man, James Owens, whom the kids loved."[5]

This type of near-sightedness is all too common and sounds almost unbelievable. Yet, these scenarios are widespread. High school coaches suffer all manner of abuse from parents. Parents will abuse coaches, yell instructions and plays to coaches, berate officials, and even chastise their child's teammates, all to catapult their child to the status of "king of the hill." John Nicol, the coach of a lacrosse team in Yorktown, New York, coached lacrosse for five years. Many of his players earned opportunities to play in college. But Coach Nicol's had to step down because the parents were obsessive. He asked the parents not to call him at home, but they continued to call. He received "a nightly stream of phone calls from parents. They would call his home to ask what he was doing to get their kids scholarships or to nag about their kid's playing time. These parents, often took confrontational and accusatorial tones."[6]

Development takes a back seat to earning a name or featuring someone's little all-star. Youth coaches trying to make a name for themselves seek a way to make a living on the back of "success" at the youth level. They seek to win at all costs, overhyping the results and losing the process. Hyping the results and losing the joy of the journey happens despite research to the contrary. In an interview with *SportsBusiness Daily*, Ken Martel, the technical director of USA Hockey, stated parents know in their hearts something is amiss.

> "Why should my 9-year-old in Chicago have to travel to Boston to play in this tournament? All they hear is the loud voice of the youth coach who wants his piece of the glory of the business operation that's going to take their money."[7] The coach convinces the parents that their child is going to be great. The parents' ego or lust overwhelms

their good sense, and they believe the voice of the youth league gurus, who, most of the time, have no idea if their child is going to be the next superstar. But their fairy tale dreams burst the bubble of common sense, and parents spend the cash, put on pressure, and cross the country in search of the tournament that will fulfill the hopes and dreams of the sports mirage. All the while forgetting that the experts know "playing and loving the sport must come before excelling at it." The ADM model seeks to "get away from praising talent and start to praise effort . . . embrace what's best for their child and what their child most enjoys, versus 'Let's prepare my 8-year-old for his college scholarship.'"[8]

Tom Farrey, who launched Project Play in 2013, investigated "alarming stories from the front lines of the teams, leagues, academies, and camps that promote early sports specialization but often just result in early burnout."[9] It seems in today's marketplace, getting a lead on the competition drives all manner of shortsightedness.

Mike Sullivan at the USA Hockey High-Performance Symposium takes the pressure off by emphasizing simple goals. He "named the four characteristics that he looks for in an elite player prospect: competitive spirit, functional intelligence, puck possession skills, and speed, both physical and mental."[10]

Sidney Crosby, an NHL All-Star and owner of several Stanley Cup Championships, offers a different point of view regarding early sports specialization. "Growing up in Cole Harbor, Nova Scotia, whatever sport was in season, he was playing it. 'I played tons of sports in school: basketball, volleyball, track, cross-country, everything. I played hockey in the winter, baseball in the summer. I loved it.[11]

Brad Stevens, General Manager of the Boston Celtics, says, "I'm not a fan of specializing early, in large part because I think that you figure out what your passion is truly for as you get older. And then, when you start to specialize once you've figured that out, it becomes something that you are even more excited to work toward."[12]

Multiple sports leaders recommend the importance of basic running, jumping, balance, throwing, catching, and striking. These are introductory fundamental body activities that are the building blocks for all sports. These should be mastered and enjoyed through multiple youth activities. And maybe "wildly," just by being a kid and playing.

But insanity won't allow kids to be kids and to play for the sheer pleasure of sports activity. The parents are too busy developing their little heroes into professionals. However, the real professionals are the con artists who tell the parents what they want to hear: their child is special and has what it takes to be one of the truly unique players of his or her generation.

The parents pay. The coach fattens his bank account, and the parents have made little heroes, losing innocence and bowing before the all-powerful motivator "just win, baby."

ENDNOTES: CHAPTER 16

1. Gary Warner, *Competition*, David C. Cook Publishing, 1979, 220.

2. Rick Reilly, "What Money Can't Buy," *Sports Illustrated*, March 12, 2007, 86.

3. USA Today, Josh Peters, "Held Down," *Las Cruces Sun-News*, May 13, 2020, 1B, 8B.

4. "Indiana Youth Basketball Game Descends into Chaos as Parent, Ref Brawl," Fox News Indiana, May 23, 2023.

5. Rick Reilly, "Life of Reilly," *Sports Illustrated*, November 27, 2006, 84.

6. Rick Wolff, "Pesky Parents Can Push Quality Coaches To Quit," *Sports Illustrated*, March 3, 2003, insert.

7. Leonard Zaichkowsky and Daniel Peterson, *The Playmaker's Advantage*: How to Raise Your Mental Game to the Next Level, Gallery/Jeter Publishing, 2018, 18.

8. Leonard Zaichkowsky and Daniel Peterson, *The Playmaker's Advantage*: How to Raise Your Mental Game to the Next Level, Gallery/Jeter Publishing, 2018, 19.

9. Leonard Zaichkowsky and Daniel Peterson, *The Playmaker's Advantage*: How to Raise Your Mental Game to the Next Level, Gallery/Jeter Publishing, 2018, 27.

10. Leonard Zaichkowsky and Daniel Peterson, *The Playmaker's Advantage*: How to Raise Your Mental Game to the Next Level, Gallery/Jeter Publishing, 2018, 20.

11. Leonard Zaichkowsky and Daniel Peterson, *The Playmaker's Advantage*: How to Raise Your Mental Game to the Next Level, Gallery/Jeter Publishing, 2018, 23–24.

12. Leonard Zaichkowsky and Daniel Peterson, *The Playmaker's Advantage*: How to Raise Your Mental Game to the Next Level, Gallery/Jeter Publishing, 2018, 29.

CHAPTER 17

PLAYING THE BLAME GAME OR PIN THE TALE ON THE COACH

TO THIS POINT, IT HAS BEEN DISCOVERED THAT LIFE is not fair, hard work and refusal to give up do not guarantee success, most of us are average-a statistical demonstrative absolute, we are brainwashed by sports hype, there is more to life than money, numerically playing a professional sport has roughly the same probability as getting hit by lightning, sports contain risks, and we often fail to examine risks and live solely to achieve.

So, what do we do now? There is a certain gloominess to this discussion; too many facts, too much information (TMI); where do we go at this point? How do we handle the reality that our son or daughter may be average and will not play at the next level or any level? Blame, many of us look for a scapegoat someone, or something to blame.

We could blame the facilities or the conditions, but most of us realize the conditions have a way of being an inconsistent predictor. There are numerous examples of teams with poor or minimal facilities rising above their circumstances and accomplishing extraordinary feats. Movies based on true stories like *"Glory Road," "MacFarland, USA," "Seabiscuit," "Cinderella Man," "Cool Runnings,"* and *"Coach Carter"* point out that facility challenges can be overcome.

Money often produces wins or champions; money definitely increases opportunity, like facilities, but again, there are plenty of examples of teams with minimal financial resources enjoying amazing success. The movie *"Moneyball"* chronicles the successful struggles of a small market baseball team battling to win in professional baseball. The movies *"Queen of Katwe," "Hoosiers," "Invincible," "The Rookie,"* and "The Long Game" point toward success apart from tremendous capital. Without money, it is more difficult, but there is opportunity. Often, a small college or high school with a small gym or sketchy facilities, limited weight room, and minimal resources rises to defeat numerous opponents who have fantastic wealth in comparison. Blaming lack of money or resources could be the excuse anyway in a "pin the tail on the donkey" for losing. And it is done.

Often, the athlete, general manager, or fans are not willing to examine or accept that they may have shortcomings. It must be someone else's fault. The Coach. The Officials. The Venue. The Weather. The Distractions. It is someone else's fault. One author writes, "Our teams, athletes, and coaches, generally speaking, always have some sort of excuse. European athletes . . . accept defeat much better than we do."[1] The Brothers Osborne captured these sentiments in the popular country song, "It Ain't My Fault."[2] Blame must be affixed somewhere. Let's find a scapegoat.

Fire the coaches. Coaches getting fired for losing included Gary Patterson, a coach who by many was considered one of the best college football coaches in the country. "For a solid decade, a football program [was] right there with the blue bloods, winning big games and pumping players into the NFL. And then, on Sunday night, it ended . . . in his 21st season. The greatest coach in the history of the school had essentially been fired."[3]

Blame the coach. After the Philadelphia 76ers lost to Miami in the 2023 NBA playoffs, Doc Rivers was fired. Coach Rivers is the media darling scapegoat. The ineptitude of players in crucial situations did not factor in, we need someone to blame, let's blame the coach. This firing was decreed, although many consider him a "top fifteen" coach in the NBA and a former NBA champion (2008) and NBA Coach of the Year (2000).

Blame the coach. The week before Doc Rivers was fired, Monty Williams of the Phoenix Suns, the NBA Coach of the Year (20021 and 2022), was fired for apparently losing to the Denver Nuggets in six games. Both men are outstanding coaches and have received numerous awards, but our society looks for someone to blame. Why not the coach?

I have had parents who placed blame on me for their son's lack of opportunity. Typically, an AAU coach, trainer, and or family had sold a young man, who struggled in multiple aspects of the game, on the idea that he was a top player in the state. He was good, but the coach, me, was at fault for his lack of success. All too often, the overvaluation of an athlete's talents can, in the long run, be a deterrent to future skill development. If one expects privilege and receives a challenge, then frustration may result. This can interfere with the athlete's resolve and development. Many parents believe their child is the best athlete on the team, and the coach refuses to play him or her just to be spiteful. There are some coaches mean-spirited enough to pull such shenanigans, but due to the pressure presented in schools across the country to win, realistically, a coach is not really afforded that type of "luxury." They simply must play the talented players.

Coaches are doing their level best to make their teams exceptional. Coaches get an abundance of abuse because it would seem they are unfair, biased, unskilled, uncaring, lazy, or incompetent. There are differences for sure in a coach's sense of integrity and fairness. However, most are skilled, caring, hardworking individuals. These coaches are aware of the athlete's desire to play and excel, and it can be frustrating for the coach as well as the athlete when they do not get to play.

Blame is easier than taking personal inventory. People often find it easier to make excuses rather than engage in honest self-examination and seek areas for personal growth. We need an immediate answer, we need to appear seeking solutions, and we certainly are not going to challenge ourselves or the players around us to minimize suffering, just blame the coach. Naturally, winning is all that matters, not people's lives, not developing the skills necessary to be successful both on and off the court. Blame.

The athlete may not have the genetics needed to be a winner or perform at an outstanding level. The athlete may be too short, too slow, handicapped in some fashion, have poor eyesight, fatigue asthma, flat feet, allergies, laziness, the list goes on and on, but since my child is "special" and all children deserve equal treatment, then my athlete should excel and be made into a "Rock Star" or be given the opportunity to show the world that he is a "Rock Star."

But life is not fair. And we are not that special. Because life is not fair and a child may be average, he or she may get left behind. Years ago, a popular idea promoted in the political arena regarding education parroted, "No child left behind." This was a popular and crazy idea espousing that inherently, life is fair and that all children will be equal in education, sport, or life. This absurd mantra is illogical and impossible. "Should" no child be left behind depends on the activity. In a track meet, all the children are left behind but one. In a tournament, all the contestants "are left behind" except one individual or team. In a league, there is a league champion, leaving behind all other teams or contestants. Being left behind is most people's human condition. Statistically, only so many teams can win by sheer mathematical probability, and this forces a similar number of teams to lose. An example of this can be seen in the following make-believe story.

In professional basketball, if there were thirty teams, and all the teams had fifteen players and all 450 players were LeBron James, and they all played each other four times, and if all the players were coached by equally outstanding quality coaches, the outcome would still be roughly fifteen teams would win 50 percent or better of their games. The other fifteen teams would have losing records finishing lower than 50 percent. Were the players good? Yes, they were all LeBron James, one of the greatest basketball players in the history of the game, incredibly talented! Were the teams good? Yes, wonderful dream teams. Were the teams well coached? Yes, nearly identical. So, what was the difference? In statistical reality usually fifteen teams would have winning records, and fifteen teams would have losing records. Is this fair, is the wrong question? Should it be this way? Again, this is the wrong question. The right question is, is this the way that it is? Yes, teams will win and other teams will lose.

George Steinbrenner, whom I call the "Father of Firing the Coach," began an insane path of destruction promoting the idea that if a team is losing, the coach is to blame, and he must be fired. He hired and fired Billy Martin five times, and Lou Piniella twice, and in total, fired the head coach eighteen times in eighteen years.[4] Thanks to George Steinbrenner some fifty years later, not only are professional coaches fired with regularity, but so are college and even high school coaches. Today, this is the norm so often that newspapers run articles like "Coaches who may be in trouble," *USA TODAY*.[5] This article outlines five NFL coaches who will likely be fired and why. News outlets and beat writers talk about firing coaches like it is the solution to all things losing. The firing cleans everything up, and tomorrow will be a brighter day even though nothing substantive may have changed. In 2024, eight NFL coaches were fired and the attitude swirling around the firings was almost like it was fun, with a weird game show feeling.

Ray Ratto rightly rants that the blame mentality seems to just go off the rails in Texas. He says the University of Texas affixed blame at a weird new level, wasting astronomical amounts of money, $25 million, to remove Tom Herman and his staff. "Chris Del Conte [athletic director] must sleep comfortably at night knowing that $25 million in dead money isn't a deterrent to business . . . [this is an] unconscionable extravagance when so many actual teachers and support staff have lost their jobs in the time of 'rona."[6]

Toward the end of this rebuke, Ray Ratto said Clay Helton of the University of Southern California would soon be let go to the tune of over $10 million. And sure enough, Ray Ratto proved to be a prophet, as within nine months, the headlines read: "Helton ousted by USC after loss to Stanford." The change was announced in a "scathing" press release where Mike Bohn [athletic director] said: "Clay is one of the finest human beings I have met in this industry, and he has been a tremendous role model and mentor to our young men . . . [he] ran a clean program that inspired loyalty and love from his players."[7]

One should ask the question, who would want a fine human being, role model, and mentor who inspired loyalty and love in his athletes to coach anyway?

These are examples, and there are thousands more, of the misguided values and twisted thinking that goes into the evaluation of hundreds of coaches every day across our country, from professional teams to high school. The leaders set graphic examples of callousness, spinelessness, and incompetence, all the while being a marionette to public opinion.

Blame the coach. The coach is the source of failure and loss. Never mind that thirty teams all playing each other with exactly the same talent would result in 50 percent of the teams failing. Our thinking is so jaded that we look no further than the win-loss record, and as good old George Steinbrenner would say, "Fire the coach!" This screams out a fact made earlier with an exclamation point. Life is not fair!

Writer E. M. Swift offers compassion when entering the "firing" discussion. Swift says firings are incredibly painful and he chronicles heart breaking story after heartbreaking story of coaches who were fired. John Q. Public, sports analysts, and card-carrying members of the human race should know that being fired may be a sound bite on ESPN or a brief article in the local Sports section, but it is horrific! Firing may result in depression or even suicidal thoughts. Firing may be as traumatic as divorce, the death of a loved one or a serious illness. Being fired rips away parts of the coach's heart and soul. How does firing affect the coach? "[They] all feel the shame, anger, sadness, fear, and self-pity of people who have been fired from ordinary jobs. Except that in sports, the whole process is played out before millions of onlookers."[8]

Speaking of blaming others, what about the referees? If it is not the athletes' lack of talent, genetics, or skill, and the coach is okay, blame must be sifted somewhere. Why not shift it to the officials? The athlete fails and the game was lost because of the referees. Blame the refs!

At the outset, it needs to be clear that officials can influence outcomes, and unscrupulous officials can tilt a team to a win. I remember coaching high school basketball teams, when playing the teams on their home court, routinely received favorable calls, which often resulted in victories. There is documentation concerning home-court advantages. Jon Wertheim writes,

"As in all sports, the home team in the NBA wins the majority of the games. We argue it's largely the result of the officiating. It's the judgment calls . . . that go the home teams' way. This disparity is especially pronounced when there's a big crowd and when the games are tight."[9]

He writes in a separate article a more detailed explanation of numerous components: "Referee bias explains not only the home field advantage but also why the home team's success rate hasn't changed in more than a century. Although sports have altered their rules . . . the official's role in the game hasn't changed much."[10] The officials are human, people just like each of us, and they are affected by crowds, emotions, excitement, and all the normal psychological variables. Many fans demand AI to officiate, yet AI also possesses limitations and flaws. In summary, there is no ideal or perfect way to oversee sporting events.

The officials definitely affect the game. However, in the vast majority of games, officials do their level best to be fair and work hard to offer a well-officiated game. Many times, people perceive an official's weakness as unfairness, but at times, it is just a blind spot regarding certain player behaviors. But fans in the stands or, worse yet, parents blame officials and consider them terrible and out to get their team. The television sports machines that replay calls feed the public disconnect regarding referee mistakes, whether the replays show the competency or incompetency of the official. Network pundits can be vicious in their criticism and analysis of an official's ability. An instant replay frequently shows the accuracy of the officials. But let them make a mistake, and the entire world will be in crisis. When looking for someone to blame for a team or player's lack of success, the officials are easy targets. Ask Coach Calipari, who yelled at the officials for roughly three straight minutes during the Florida-Kentucky basketball game on October 2, 2021.

My personal philosophy regarding officiating centers on two points. First, the team needs a tough mindset. The team must become skilled enough and mentally tough enough to defeat an opponent regardless of the officiating. Coaches should not look for excuses. Officials are human beings and need to be treated with respect and dignity. It is never right to demean or publicly call out an official in front of the fans. Calls should be questioned respectfully and in the heat of the moment with passion. But at the end of the day, we must and should submit to their rulings and their work and appeal to a higher authority. Second, it was mentioned in Chapter 9, that what we build our values upon philosophically, affects how we think, make decisions, and reveals our motivation. Some people will turn to their own thoughts or logic. Others will look outside themselves. A healthy perspective could be found in answering the question, "What does God think?"

God thinks, "Everyone must submit himself to the governing authorities, for there is no authority except that which God has established. The authorities that exist have been established by God. Consequently, he who rebels against the authority is rebelling against what God has instituted, and those who do so will bring judgment on themselves" (ROMANS 13:1–2).

If more evidence is needed, these sentiments are echoed, "Submit yourselves for the Lord's sake to every authority instituted among men: whether to the king, as the supreme authority, or to the governors, . . . Live as free men, but do not use your freedom as a cover-up for evil; live as servants of God. Show proper respect to everyone." (I PETER 2:13-17a).

Since officials are our fellow men, and they give their best effort, and since God himself states we should submit to them, decrying the officials as responsible for all outcomes is wrong and unfair. Games are in the hands of God, not in the coach's hands or the officials and we are to perform to the absolute best of our ability, but we do not hold outcomes. If we think that's an unfair formula, we must take it up with God and put the blame there.

ENDNOTES: CHAPTER 17

1. Gary Warner, *Competition*, David C. Cook Publishing, 1979, 85.

2. Brothers Osborne, duo. "It Ain't My Fault, song. *Pawn Shop*, album, Nashville: EMI, 2016.

3. USA Today. Dan Wolken, "Patterson's Departure a Sad Ending," *Las Cruces Sun-News*, November 2, 2021, 3B.

4. Tim Kurkjian, "The Boss Strikes Again," *Sports Illustrated*, June 18, 199, 48–51.

5. Nancy Armour, "San Diego State does the whole country a solid by ousting Nate Oats, Alabama." *USA Today*, March 25, 2023. usatoday.com/story/sports/columnist/nancy-armour/2023/03/25/alabama-nate-oats-out-ncaa-tournament-thank-you-sdsu/11540433002

6. Ray Ratto, "Texas Has Discovered a New Level of F-U Money." Defector, January 3, 2021. defector.com/Texas-has-discovered-a-new-level-of-f-u-money.

7. Associated Press. Greg Beacham, "Helton Ousted by USC After Loss to Stanford," *Las Cruces Sun-News*, September 14, 2021, 2B.

8. E. M. Swift, "Up Against the Wall," *Sports Illustrated*, October 29, 1990, 76.

9. Jon Wertheim, "Truly Foul," *Sports Illustrated*, April 25, 2011, 30.

10. Tobias J. Moskowitz and L. Jon Wertheim, "What's Really Behind Home Field Advantage?," *Sports Illustrated*, January 17, 2011, 64–72.

CHAPTER 18

WHY TRY?
IT HURTS TOO MUCH

IF WE ACCEPT RESPONSIBILITY AND DO NOT PLAY THE blame game, coming to grips with a loss can be crushing, especially if a headlong pursuit of winning is coupled with resources and an investment of vast amounts of time. Intense, passionate, every fiber of one's being, the heartbeat of the athlete's total engagement and falling short cuts deeply. This may bring disappointment or failure and can feel as bad as a natural disaster. Floods can wipe out entire cities, destroying everything in their path; tornadoes spawn devastation beyond imagination; tidal waves can crush anything with terrifying power, and sports with a "winning is all that matters" mooring can be nearly as devastating. Hearts are broken, wounds unhealed for a lifetime, holes left in the soul, bodies broken, all crying for hope. Loss can cause an incredible depth of emotional pain, similar to natural disasters. We can lose virtue and decency in the pursuit. Is it possible to extract ourselves from the hamster wheel of the win-at-all-cost mentality? Can the jaws of life free us from carnage?

I remember numerous Monday mornings, where I wanted to hide my face and just disappear. I felt such humiliation and embarrassment. Our team had lost, and I felt like I had let our team, parents, and fans down. Upon returning to work or school, it was like there were leeches of shame attached to my face. Facing classmates or coworkers with leeches of shame all over one's face and body is painful and shameful. It was hard enough facing the media, friends, parents, and the crowd after the contest, but after marinating all weekend, it seemed unbearable.

Unbearable is the only word that floats through the brain. Where is the nearest cave? Where can one hide? Putting the proverbial foot in front of the other may be all the strength one can muster. One step. Keep moving forward, one step at a time. The outcome matters. The results have to matter. Otherwise, it isn't a competition or a contest. In fact, the outcome was all that mattered for a moment; during the last contest, the outcome was the size of King Kong. It mattered, and it should. When we put our whole selves into pursuing a challenge or goal, we spend ourselves. This cost is high. This expense compels our entire being to participate. We are "all in," so to speak, and anytime a person seeks achievement or accomplishment or elite excellence, it takes an "all in" attitude to attain levels of prodigious conquering. How can we be "all in" and be human? How does one accept the challenge of prodigious accomplishment without the obliteration of all that is sane, wholesome, or good? In a passionate pursuit, we're craving something irresistible, and no obstacle can stand in the way. This places the athlete on the precipice of a cliff. A cliff where one can sacrifice good. This intense quality of effort can set up a contrast found within the profundities of our struggle to be a "good human." And when we stand up with valor, we may still dash on the rocks of failure, pain, and suffering. Why take part if the cost is so deep and the risk so crushing?

The alternative could be to forget the effort or the risk. Just forget it, do not struggle; don't reach. How about hiding out or retreating from challenges. Some decide to live lives of quiet desperation. They do not stretch for the mountaintop or jump into the pool. Safety, status quo, comfort, steady state, these places of tranquility are the utmost goals. For some, living in the COVID bubble was pure bliss; it was breathtaking. Minimal risks, minimal obstacles, minimal discomfort. Everything vanilla. Sport holds this tension. How can one embrace sports and competition with all its missteps, wrong-headed moorings, and chasm of brokenness and still believe sports are a worthy journey?

It is a journey, even at the highest levels. Michael Jordan mentions in *The Last Dance* that maybe we could have won seven. It sounds like he wished he could have continued the journey with the Chicago Bulls. Sport holds a tremendous capacity for accomplishment and tremendous frustration. The trail may be a journey that involves always striving and never arriving. This seems to be man's plight. In commerce, it was said of J. D. Rockefeller, the world's first billionaire and the richest man in the world, when asked by a reporter how much money is enough, he famously replied, "Just a little bit more." The embrace of sports is such a journey; we never arrive. If that sounds like wrong thinking, listen closely to the talking heads, who, as soon as a championship is won, start talking about the next one or the possibility of a dynasty. It is never enough.

Why bother? Why pour oneself into the competitive contest?

Sports produce no goods or resources. Sports are wrought with pitfalls. What makes it a "worthy journey?" An answer could be the mountaintop moment with a view that sucks all the air out of the lungs. Challenge, thrill, exhilaration, pushing one's limits of mind and body, jumping, and feeling like for only a moment you are flying, scoring the winning goal, basket, or walk-off, doing something that sticks in one's memory for a lifetime. Moments rare, the rarity making them even more exquisite! But pain can lurk around the corner of exhilaration, the outcome of the journey may result in utter failure. Theodore Roosevelt's speech, "Citizenship in a Republic," delivered at the Sorbonne in Paris, France, on April 23, 1910, speaks to these opposite outcomes. His speech carries great life words, and a portion is important enough to repeat here:

> "It is not the critic who counts; not the man who points out how the strong man stumbles or where the doer of deeds could have done them better. The credit belongs to the man who is actually in the arena, whose face is marred

by dust and sweat and blood; who strives valiantly; who errs, who comes short again and again, because there is no effort without error and shortcoming; but who does actually strive to do the deeds; who knows great enthusiasms, the great devotions; who spends himself in a worthy cause; who at the best knows in the end the triumph of high achievement, and who at the worst, if he fails, at least fails while daring greatly, so that his place shall never be with those cold and timid souls who neither know victory nor defeat."

Life involves being in the arena. Mud, blood, pain, and suffering are the human condition. Parents today do everything they can to shelter their children from pain and suffering. Pain and suffering hurt intensely. Parents run interference for their deeply loved children and desperately seek to protect their offspring. Their child must not have it as hard as "I" had it; my child's life will be better than mine. So, fear becomes the emotion of the day. Years ago, a clothing line produced merchandise with the logo "No Fear," and terrified offspring proudly pranced around sporting their clothes, declaring "No Fear" all the while being terrified, just like their parents. And life can be frightening; shootings, drunk drivers, political unrest, war, cancer, the terror goes on and on.

Most sane people avoid pain. Who signs up for a car crash, drug addiction, bankruptcy, physical defects, learning disabilities, injury? Who signs up for suffering? No one! But by running away from and avoiding pain and suffering, we anesthetize. We become numb, feeling nothing. We use any drug to feel alive. The arena is too scary. Who wants to be "marred by dust and sweat and blood?" Who wants to "strive to do deeds" with "great enthusiasm," "spending [oneself] in a worthy cause?" Video games are close enough to reality; well, they are almost real. And with no risk, one can always hit the restart button. Protecting kids, practicing safe sex, and living safe lives.

The risks of life, and specifically sports, can birth authenticity found in truly living, wholehearted living! Living is not synonymous with recklessness. Living is not jumping out of planes with no parachute. Considering outcomes, living involves weighing the positives, negatives, and risks. Something may not be worth the risks; risk may be signing up for suffering. The question must be asked: is the suffering worth the activity? One must not forget: is it a worthy cause? Not all causes are worthy. To sound cliche, is it "God's will?" Processing the worthiness of a venture is critical. Not all activities are worthy cause[s], but sport and competition may be.

Sports can foster discipline, organizational skills, physical conditioning, determination, mental toughness, obedience, serving others, caring, committing, vulnerability, courage, perspective, and maturity. As has already been shown in this writing, sports are not without shortcomings and the seedy underbelly of human depravity, but they can be a wonderful complement to life. Sport can be a worthy endeavor and provide exhilaration. It can produce incredible gifts, one such gift I have named the "pull-up effect."

The "pull-up effect" can be an integral part of the journey. In fact, this process can turn the journey into something phenomenal. Reggie Marra expresses his thoughts as follows:

> "The dictionary tells us that serendipity is "an apparent aptitude for making accidental, fortunate discoveries." In *The Road Less Traveled*, M. Scott Peck describes it as "the gift of finding valuable or agreeable things not sought for." Dr. Peck suggests we take full advantage of these gifts because we don't recognize them or their true value when they come to us. Often, we are so consumed with what we want and are working toward we don't see what is essentially given to us.
>
> "What would you do if you gave your first love, middle-distance running (or whatever is true for you), everything you had, only to discover your real gift is on the golf

course? What if your goal is a NCAA Division I volleyball scholarship, but your best offer is "only" a four-year academic scholarship to an excellent university that has a Division III program? How will you respond when good things you haven't pursued or even considered come your way? The answer to this last question plays a major role in determining your views on success and justice, and the extent to which you believe they are present in your life.

"Not everyone gets to be a professional, or even a collegiate or high school athlete, or a movie star, recording artist, reality show contestant, or some other locally, nationally, or globally famous celebrity. When we have the courage to work toward our ultimate dream with a high quality of effort and we fall short, we really do need something to catch us. The love and support of family and friends are indispensable, but the safest net is within each of us—a truly integrated, balanced, and always expanding view of the world. The ability to recognize, appreciate and embrace serendipitous events and people can be a strong component of such a worldview.

"Sometimes we don't get what we truly (think we) want and we get lots of what we don't (think we) want. Just as often some very worthwhile, unexpected things come our way; we can enrich our lives by learning to recognize them and accept the good they bring."[1]

Chad Bladow, in his book *Seven Years Seven Ways* states,

"When I was in high school, I wanted to become an astronaut or at least work for NASA's manned space program. When I wasn't doing homework or playing music, I was usually reading about space. I read books about space, magazine articles about space, even free reports and literature from NASA that I requested through the mail from its public information office. I ate it up. I loved it. I often daydreamed about being an astronaut, imagining myself floating in space or walking on the moon or Mars. I imagined all the great and wonderful things I would do and the amazing things I would see.

"Was my dream realistic? Maybe, maybe not, but it doesn't matter. The dream energized and excited me. It helped propel me through the toughest times of my teenage years. My dream of becoming an astronaut was one foundation that supported me and helped me to keep going when I felt like giving up.

"Having a dream can provide an almost constant source of hope. It gives you something to look forward to—the proverbial light at the end of the tunnel. Your dream doesn't always have to be realistic or immediately achievable. It only has to be something you really want and enjoy. It should be something that brings a smile to your face and warmth to your heart when you imagine achieving it."[2]

Reaching for a dream and finding something new and challenging can provide the impetus to keep moving forward and stretching our abilities. "The new and challenging" along the way may be the very birth of a thrilling accomplishment, career, or stimulating path unknown to that point. The power of hope is chronicled in great literature and provides clear direction in fighting through being bloodied, dirty, beaten, and bruised. One book, the Bible, can give direction when suffering has gripped us. "He gives strength to the weary and increases the power of the weak. Even youths grow tired and weary, and young men stumble and fall; but those who hope in the Lord will renew their strength. They will soar on wings like eagles; they will run and not grow weary, they will walk and not be faint" (ISAIAH 40:29–31).

This kind of hope is found in the strength and dependability of God. He opens doors and provides opportunities; He redirects and sets us on a new path. God can build hope even in shattered dreams and especially in suffering. One takes the risk, and whether we win or lose, succeed or fail, God builds strength of character that stands one in good stead in life. God's work allows us to face all manner of difficulties, fears, and daytime terrors. A fresh and new outcome, a new journey may grow alongside or out of "being face down in the arena."

"And we rejoice in the hope of the glory of God. Not only so, but we also rejoice in our sufferings, because we know that suffering produces perseverance; perseverance, character; and character, hope. And hope does not disappoint us, because God has poured out his love into our hearts by the Holy Spirit, whom he has given us" (ROMANS 5:2b–5).

Our worthy cause may produce something remarkable, extraordinary, something truly wonderful. While in graduate school, I had an acquaintance who received an assignment to risk forming a relationship with someone unknown. We did not know each other well, but he asked me if I would like to meet regularly, talk, pray, have coffee, and develop a friendship. He acknowledged that it was a risk, requiring time and energy. I agreed to enter the experiment of getting to know each other. Three years later, we were now deep friends. He had graduated and prepared to leave town in his U-Haul. He visited the library to bid a heartfelt farewell to a close friend. We hugged, and he headed down the long sidewalk to the parking lot to drive out of town. That's when it hit me. We had taken an enormous risk getting to know one another. I scurried out the front door and down the steps. With all the drama of a Hollywood ending, I yelled, "Hey Doug! It was worth the risk!" This snapshot in my mind always brings a tear and a reminder that life contains risk, but there is reward in the risk.

ENDNOTES: CHAPTER 18

1. Reggie Marra, *The Quality of Effort: Integrity in Sport and Life for Student-Athletes, Parents and Coaches*, From the Heart Press, 2013, 50-51.

2. Chad E. Bladow, *Seven Years Seven Ways: Surviving Your Teen and Preteen Years*, Starrider Books, 2007, 169.

Part Three

Chapters 19–25

Planting Our Feet
on the
Highest of Mountains

CHAPTER 19

FACING REALITY
IS BRAVE

TO THIS POINT, GOD AND THE BIBLE HAVE BEEN mentioned briefly. Some critics may say the Bible has some inspiring words, but the Monday morning reality of loss and shame, the real devastation of a career-ending injury, or the gut-punch firing after giving everything possible, does not go away with some verses from an old book or pithy sayings of wisdom. And the critics would be right! But as we continue to struggle with suffering, pain, and failure, we will find there is hope.

The Boston Celtics felt a gut punch on May 29, 2023. That night, a storybook ending failed to materialize. The NBA's Boston Celtics had rallied from a 3-0 deficit, playing courageously to even the series with the Miami Heat. Boston was hoping to end the 0-150 record of teams falling behind 0-3 and winning the playoff series. The sports networks duly hyped the game. ESPN's Mike Greenberg even went on record stating Boston was the better team and they would emerge victorious, but Boston lost.

Jalen Brown, interviewed after the game, said, "We failed, I failed, we let the whole city down." He showed great courage and felt the enormity of the loss. The reporter asked some stupid questions, and Jalen added, "I expected to win today and move on, and that was what my focus was on, that's what my focus has been on. I failed, we failed, and it's hard to think about anything else right now, to be honest." After another poor question, Jalen Brown bravely said, "More pain coming up short . . ."[1] expressed his feelings. Failure at that moment was suffocating. Jalen Brown interviewed bravely.

Facing loss, facing all the ills that come with sport, facing all the Monday mornings, the firings, the disappointments, the heartaches, cannot be sugarcoated.

How does one handle failure and the antecedent shame? Do we succumb to fear and seek safety? Brené Brown suggests, "I'd say the one thing we have in common is that we're sick of feeling afraid. We all want to be brave. We want to dare greatly. We're tired of the national conversation centering on 'What should we fear?' and 'Who should we blame?'"[2]

We hunt for the worthy cause. "What's worth doing even if I fail?"[3]

Jalen Brown handled a remarkably difficult interview with tremendous poise. He did not run, hide, or deflect. He spoke well, displayed maturity, and showed grace. Examining ways to handle failure may cause many people to melt down. Most of us look for a way to escape the pain.

Escaping pain takes on many forms or expressions. Sometimes people "goldbrick" by pretending they were never all in or use a litany of excuses like being sick, succumbing to anxiety, or being depressed. We cannot compulsively overtrain or overdo it and then use the scapegoat that an injury is the reason one failed. We cannot argue that we missed our goal because of pressure or emotions that we just can't handle. Goldbricking does not let us off the hook. Read the multitude of articles and "sympathy masters" providing excuses for athletic greats who disastrously failed to live up to expectations. We must be honest, especially with ourselves.

We cannot "smokescreen" our way out of pain. We absolutely cannot use blame, or throwing a fit, or "it's not my fault," or "I don't genuinely care anyway." Hustling our thoughts and emotions and not examining how we really feel doesn't work. And we can't use the excuse that feelings and emotions are for sissies. We cannot cover how we feel with a smokescreen. No matter what we call it, we are twisting and deflecting reality. And if we are ruthlessly honest, we will find a big chunk of pride in the mix. Smokescreens love to lather over pain, adding a large dose of pride.

"Pollyanna" holds no place; playing the everything's OK game to navigate through failures is another weak strategy. Everything is not okay. Losing is disheartening and hurts. That's the point. That everything's OK, the world is filled with rainbows, butterflies, and unicorns is delusional. An insincere shrug of the shoulders, as if a magic wand erases everything, does not produce a happy-ever-after fairy tale. Pollyanna is cold-blooded denial. And denial always leaves a bitter aftertaste. Honestly, outcomes matter to us, we care.

Being a "Prickly Pear Cactus" doesn't work either. We cannot force everyone to just leave us alone, so we will feel better. People cannot walk on eggshells or act like anger and temper don't wound. Pushing others away and causing them to avoid us causes additional problems. We should not force those around us to hide and duck to avoid the wrath of the monster prickly pear.

An "Igloo with a fireplace" faces certain doom. Beating oneself to a pulp is extremely unhealthy and dynamically sick. The igloo will melt and implode upon itself. The fire of self-hate, saying things to oneself like, "I am a screwup," "I am a failure," "I can't do anything right," "I'm just no good at _____ ," all smack of humility. It is not humility; it is sick and damaging to ourselves and everyone around us. It may even act as a misguided reversed pride. We play these mind games for pity, comfort, and validation. A steady diet of unhealthy self-talk stokes a fire that will melt the igloo of misdirection and damage our hearts.

Finally, "escapism" never, never, never works! The heart-pounding dance party to end all parties doesn't remove the pain and suffering.

No drug or amount of alcohol can sufficiently numb the deepest depths of agony. Sex brings another person into one's sorrow and ultimately resolves nothing and cheapens intimacy. Food, shopping, gambling, obsessive exercise, and workaholism can all be used to produce the dumb numb. Escapism is always ineffective.[4]

Facing our pain is healthy and requires strength. When we peer deeply into ourselves and seek to discover what is really going on in our inner being, we find power and strength. Brené Brown offers, "Daring greatly is not about winning or losing. It's about courage. In a world where scarcity and shame dominate and feeling afraid has become second nature, vulnerability is subversive."[5]

Vulnerability, admitting failure, mistakes, and deep disappointment begins an incredible walk into strength and courage. Experiencing hurt and feeling pain and sorrow is being human. The agony of defeat, despair of pain and suffering can call us to "live on a new plane."[6] "Suffering is one of God's most precious gifts,"[7] writes Tim Keller.

We put loss and pain in the proper place when we engage in authentic self-evaluation. When we realize we are not that special, we cannot be anything we aspire to be. We honestly hold ourselves accountable. We are realistic. We do a pride-humility check. We honestly and fairly embrace our strengths, abilities, and weaknesses. Self-evaluation neither underappreciates the gifts and talents we possess nor exaggerates the qualities we seek. We "get to a place where we can give ourselves permission to both be imperfect and to believe we are enough."[8]

We defeat shame and suffering when we recognize our worth is not based on performance! We are normal people. Suffering does not label or define us. The things we suffer do not erase our value. Oddly, confident strength and power grow out of this revelation. Winston Churchill famously proclaimed, "Success is stumbling from failure to failure with no loss of enthusiasm." The problem with so many "failure-to-success stories" that populate the motivational genre is they list hundreds of people who have failed, worked hard, never gave up, and climbed the ladder to success after failure. This distorts the point. Sometimes, one blinks, looks around, and realizes the event that just flew by will never be repeated, marking the end, a failure, and the end of that opportunity.

At thirty-two years old, as a second-year head basketball coach, I found myself in the state playoffs, losing to the eventual state champs by one point. Even though it hurt to lose in the semifinals by one point, there was cause for hope, as we had all our players back for the next season. The future looked bright, and the playoffs felt like our yearly pilgrimage. The following year, as a third-year head coach, we lost a playoff bid by the erasure of a bucket with ten seconds left on a traveling call during a league finale of two 8-0 teams. But again, we were confident we could get into the playoffs by going to the district tournament finals. We did not go. A team we had defeated earlier in the season tipped the ball in from ten feet on a missed shot one tenth of a second prior to the buzzer. And as the ball rattled in as the buzzer sounded, we exited out of our potential playoffs by one point. This stung all the worse as those two teams finished first and second in the state playoffs. I never realized at the time that it would take twenty years to make a playoff return, and sadly when we did return, we never had a realistic chance of winning a state championship. A "Hoosiers" story that wasn't! The opportunity for the second and third seasons never materialized. We blinked, looked around, and the moment was gone.

A popular movie in yesteryear found a moon-landing mission aborted because of a damaged spacecraft. Key space officials boldly declared the mission was going to be a "successful failure." The astronauts would return to Earth safely. And they did! It made for a spellbinding movie, but none of the Apollo 13 astronauts EVER walked on the moon.

Finding successful failures is challenging, as most of them either disappear or perish. The hero that bravely storms the beach for God and country winning the battle gives her life for the victory. She failed by dying, but success reigned. Successful outcomes like this make it difficult to find successful failures.

Successful failures are rare gems with an emphasis on rare. Exponentially multiplied failures surround one's success, and torrents of grief wash over these individuals and their extended families. It is real pain. It is real suffering. It is real loss. And it never goes away! It's not like the superhero genre of movies where hundreds or thousands of people die, but we exit the theater happy because the hero saved the world. That is fiction, and it's a movie. In real life, thousands of extras died.

Failure, loss, and pain do not have to own us. We can break the grip of sorrow and shame. Pain still drips from the brokenness, but removing the trappings of self-hate and unhealthy habits starts with the courage to admit the loss. See the suffering and stumble forward. It is healthy to acknowledge the devastation and admit all that failure entails. At the same time, we should recognize that even in the most devastating of failures, we can add richness to our hearts and lives, just like nutrients. The grip of shame is broken.

When we bravely face and accept our losses, what is our next step? The suffering bubbles to the surface, and we scramble to make sense of it and survive. Fortunately, there is much more to mine. Diamonds, after all, are formed deep in the earth under incredible pressure.

ENDNOTES: CHAPTER 19

1. Asylum Interviews. *"Jalen Brown Postgame Interview | Boston Celtics Lose to Miami Heat 103-84,"* NBATV Live, May 27, 2023. https://www.youtube.com/watch?v=TPvyZ0ceNZI

2. Brené Brown, *Daring Greatly: How the Courage to Be Vulnerable Transforms the Way We Live, Love, Parent, and Lead*, Gotham Books, 2012, 30.

3. Brené Brown, *Daring Greatly: How the Courage to Be Vulnerable Transforms the Way We Live, Love, Parent, and Lead*, Gotham Books, 2012, 42.

4. Brené Brown, *Rising Strong: How the Ability to Reset Transforms the Way We Live, Love, Parent, and Lead*, Spiegel & Grau, 2015, 59-65. Dr. Brown's excellent book heavily influenced my thinking. Her ideas provided clarity and depth as I formulated my thoughts in the grouping of pain escaping strategies.

5. Brené Brown, *Daring Greatly: How the Courage to Be Vulnerable Transforms the Way We Live, Love, Parent, and Lead*, Gotham Books, 2012, 248–249.

6. Timothy Keller, *Walking With God Through Pain and Suffering*, Dutton, 2013, 280.

7. Timothy Keller, *Walking With God Through Pain and Suffering*, Dutton, 2013, 283.

8. Brené Brown, *Rising Strong: How the Ability to Reset Transforms the Way We Live, Love, Parent, and Lead*, Spiegel & Grau, 2015, 213.

CHAPTER 20

SHAME AND MENTAL HEALTH

THE GAME IS ON THE LINE, THE UNDEFEATED league leaders are battling it out. Franklin has the ball, he makes an incredible move, takes the shot and it ripples through the net. Our team has just won the game and he hit the game-winning basket. The whistle blows and the official states that our hero has traveled. In an instant the hero turns into a loser. Self-hate creeps in and he says to himself, "I am so stupid, how could I make that mistake? It cost us the game! I am bad." He looks for a way to crawl under the boards on the court. In an instant he says to himself, "I am such a loser, I blew it." In the pain of that moment, he forgets that he is made in the image of God. We are never really a bad person except when compared to a perfect God. In front of God, we are bad, and of course we feel shame in his presence. But a mistake does not make a person bad. People may feel guilty, pondering "how could I have made such a critical mistake?" This may create a deep sense of guilt. But as an image bearer of God, I am never bad except when compared to His perfection. God provides the pivot point in healing from loss, failure, and suffering. God pivots the story. He is healing and hope. God completely breaks down the walls of shame. Digging deeper into shame and pain will birth incredible power, strength, and healing.

Dr. Curt Thompson states,

"The mind—where shame originates and lives—is neither limited to nor should it be understood merely in terms of what or how we *think*. Instead, it is, in the language of interpersonal neurobiology (IPNB), a fluid, emerging process that is both embodied and relational, whose task is to regulate the flow of energy and information. It is a fluid process in that it is literally never completely at rest. We are always sensing, imagining, feeling, thinking . . . or acting out something, whether consciously or unconsciously, while awake or asleep . . .

"From the day we enter the world, our neurons are firing not only out of the depths of genetically influenced patterns but also in response to the myriad of social interactions we sense and perceive when we encounter other people. Not only this, but data from the field of epigenetics now suggest that human experience has the capacity to turn genes on and off. In this way, our relational interactions can actually influence our lives at the most basic biological level."[1]

This is why finding health in our relational lives both horizontally and vertically (God) is critically important. Thompson chronicles the damaging effect shame has on our mind and body. He points out that guilt is what we feel for doing something bad, and shame is what we experience for being bad.[2] Dr. Thompson says repeatedly, at shame's heart is the statement, "You are not enough."

Thompson lists shame's disruptive mental health processes:

1. Shame starts when "I find it virtually impossible to turn my attention to something other than what I am feeling."

2. "I am not able to think coherently."

3. "My memory is inundated with old . . . recollections of other times I have felt this, and I am unable to marshal

the necessary memories of strength and confidence I desperately need at the moment."

4. "I then begin to . . . construct a bleak and pessimistic future. I am unable to tell the whole story, certainly not one in which I am loved by God unconditionally and life, in the end, will be okay."

5. "I can only see myself as intolerable to others, and I sense . . . this feeling will never end."

6. This damaging process "follows a predictable, inevitable trajectory, one that begins with separation and ends in the hell of utter isolation."[3]

So many mental health issues inside and outside of sports relate to processing suffering. We get abused; we twist it around in our heads and end up blaming ourselves. We make a mistake; we beat ourselves up because we buy an idea of perfection. We behave differently from those around us; we feel like outcasts. We have a handicap; we believe we are different and less than others. This is self-talk. And it can be destructive. But where do we go to learn to talk correctly to ourselves? Do we visualize success? Do we speak positive self-image words into a mirror? Do we find a self-help book that tells us how to fix all our shortcomings? Do we find the book that seeks to convince us we are not bad?

Mental health begins with being honest and admitting I am bad, and bad things have been done to me. As a result, we have made misguided vows and evaluations, and we respond at times with bad recourse. So, a cycle of dysfunction starts to swirl until we have a tornado of problems. Sometimes, these problems reach such a great magnitude we mentally are no longer healthy; we need help.

Many books offer practical hands-on, helpful advice, and some counselors provide growth through interaction. Medicine can calm things down long enough to begin healing. But the words and stories we say to ourselves carry tremendous power and provide the soil for growth or desert wastelands. Words within our mind can produce growth or destroy us. Words can be words of life. They do not have to destroy. Words can bring healing, wholeness, and hope.

Healing starts with wrestling with what God says about us. What are God's standards? He says we are all messed up. He says we all fall short. He says we all fail. We are born bad. We feel shame. But He has a solution. He has fixed it.

How? Jesus loves us, making us worthy. Jesus offers us forgiveness for our inherent badness and all the bad stuff we have done. Jesus heals our pain and suffering. Jesus prepares a place for us in eternity. People who know these truths have God's power within, they know they have worth, deep worth and value. They matter. "Those who feel lovable, who love, and who experience belonging simply believe they are worthy of love and belonging."[4] This produces individuals who operate from health and wholeheartedness. Therefore, we know we have worthiness founded in God's view of us through Jesus. Jesus forgives our badness and makes us good. God loves us!

In fairness, we should state that Dr. Thompson alluded to mental health issues rooted in brain development and neurological conditions, which may require intensive medical intervention. However, even in these cases, the Holy Spirit, God, can bring healing, sometimes miraculously.

Suffering embraced bursts basic organic failures that we have as a people and lays the groundwork for hope.

"And the day of death better than the day of birth. It is better to go to a house of mourning than to go to a house of feasting, for death is the destiny of every man; the living should take this to heart. Sorrow is better than laughter, because a sad face is good for the heart. The heart of the wise is in the house of mourning, but the heart of fools is in the house of pleasure. It is better to heed a wise man's rebuke than to listen to the song of fools" (ECCLESIASTES 7:1b–5).

God challenges us, he seeks to correct us, and brings a different perspective to winning and losing and all of life. For us to grow and to enjoy good mental health, we need feedback. Strength grows out of suffering. God provides feedback, He tells us that we have shortcomings and woundedness, and even in God's feedback, there may be suffering.

Brené Brown says, "The problem is straightforward: Without feedback there can be no transformative change. When we don't talk to the people we're leading about their strengths and their opportunities for growth, they begin to question their contributions and our commitment."[5] She insists that disengagement is an outcome and limits accomplishments. Brown notes people are not comfortable with confrontation, and they don't know how to offer or accept constructive, challenging conversations. People need feedback and everyone wants to grow. But we let our fears and discomfort rule the day and too often, there is no conversation and no growth. She says we need the "confidence to look at myself and assess the behaviors I'd like to change . . . Vulnerability is at the heart of the feedback process. This is true whether we give, receive, or solicit feedback . . . it's worth the risk."[6]

God provides feedback to all men; just like the Biblical character Job, who endured horrific suffering, God's feedback brought him to "naked faith," says Timothy Keller. Keller quotes Francis Anderson, "Job is brought to contentment without ever knowing all the facts of his case . . . to learn to love God for himself alone. God does not seem to give this privilege to many people . . . suffering itself [is] one of God's most precious gifts."[7]

This raw growth from God sometimes brings woundedness and produces freedom where development can grow unhindered. Failure, guilt, and shame are seen for what they are, and we are changed.

Don Clifton says, "A revision to the "You-can-be-anything-you-want-to-be" maxim might be more accurate: *You cannot be anything you want to* *be—but you **can** be a lot more of who you already are.*"[8]

Job's ordeal allowed him to become "more of who [he] already [was]," a man who wholly walked with God. God gave feedback, and Job, in humility, experienced profound growth, healing, and importantly, wholeness. He and we are "enough" by the grace of God. God makes us good, and our shame is removed. I may have lost the game, but I am enough, God still loves me.

ENDNOTES: CHAPTER 20

1. Curt Thompson, M.D., *The Soul of Shame : Retelling the Stories We Believe About Ourselves*, InterVarsity Press, 2015, 39–40.

2. Curt Thompson, M.D., *The Soul of Shame : Retelling the Stories We Believe About Ourselves*, InterVarsity Press, 2015, 63.

3. Curt Thompson, M.D.,*The Soul of Shame : Retelling the Stories We Believe About Ourselves*, InterVarsity Press, 2015, 66.

4. Brené Brown, *Daring Greatly: How the Courage to Be Vulnerable Transforms the Way We Live, Love, Parent, and Lead*, Gotham Books, 2012, 220.

5. Brené Brown, *Daring Greatly: How the Courage to Be Vulnerable Transforms the Way We Live, Love, Parent, and Lead*, Gotham Books, 2012, 197.

6. Brené Brown, *Daring Greatly: How the Courage to Be Vulnerable Transforms the Way We Live, Love, Parent, and Lead*, Gotham Books, 2012, 200–201.

7. Timothy Keller, *Walking With God Through Pain and Suffering*, Dutton, 2013, 283.

8. Don Clifton and Tom Rath, *StrengthsFinder 2.0: Discover Your CliftonStrengths*, Gallup Press, 2017, 9.

CHAPTER 21

DEEP WRESTLING WITH FAILURE AND SUFFERING

LIVING REQUIRES SUFFERING. LOVING REQUIRES suffering. Winning requires suffering. Dying requires suffering. We can't live, love, win, or die without suffering. These ingredients are the mixture one finds in life that make healing and wholeness so challenging.

To live, one must be born; being born, one must die. There is suffering from crying at birth to wailing at death. "Tears and cries are not to be stifled or even kept under strict limits-they are natural and good."[1]

Love unequivocally requires suffering. Upon the loss of love, in his case after the passing of his wife, C.S. Lewis said, "The pain I feel now is the happiness I had before. That's the deal."[2]

Failure, pain, and suffering are joined at the hip, producing great emotional trauma. "The past couple of years have given rise to failure conferences, failure festivals, and even failure awards . . . But embracing failure without acknowledging the real hurt and fear that it can cause . . . is gold-plating grit . . . *the death of our expectations can be painful beyond measure.*"[3]

In the realm of sports competition, to win, one must suffer. The will to use our talents in the context of the discipline of one's body will produce suffering. (Training alone embraces voluntary suffering of a high magnitude.) Physical discipline, training, and practice hold hands with pain and suffering. One must bring their body into subjection during the course of training. The discipline of the mind finds resolve when obstacles hit us head-on, like a car crash. Many call this mental toughness or grit; it is facing pain and suffering.

Our newspaper featured a front-page article titled "Pain Is Optional." Unfortunately, she writes: "While suffering is an inherent aspect of life, what most of us do not fully realize is that most suffering is a choice. In both Hinduism and Buddhism . . . being aware of the *kleshas* (ignorance, ego, attachment to pleasure, avoidance of pain, and fear of death) may help you end your suffering."[4]

Suffering and pain are not optional! Suffering is integral to what it means to be human. And suffering has the capacity to release infinite blessings. "Suffering was not to be dealt with primarily through the control and suppression of negative emotions with the use of reason or willpower. Ultimate reality was known not primarily through reason and contemplation but through relationship."[5] Your relationship with God and your relationships with others creates the wonder of sharing life. "Connection is why we're here. We are hardwired to connect with others, it's what gives purpose and meaning to our lives, and without it there is suffering."[6] And in our life's journey suffering cannot be escaped!

Enlightenment, reducing attachment to pleasure, redefining pain, and changing the sorrows of death to celebrations are not realistic thinking processes for handling suffering. When we live our lives with genuine honesty and see reality for the exhilaration and darkness that is part of being human, we are able to charge to the finish line in first place or come in last with a whimper. It is in the pursuit and process of extracting accomplishment from our endeavors in life and particularly in sports that we find indescribable growth, in embracing pain and suffering, not in spiritualizing them away.

In a book about minor league baseball, by John Feinstein, he marvelously details several baseball players, coaches, and referees who battled in the minor leagues. Minor leaguers: "Defines the struggle of people who are extremely good at what they do-but *not* as good as they want to be . . . when Triple-A players do finally get to the majors-or back to the majors-it is so overwhelmingly meaningful that tears, not words, explain how they feel."[7] Being a minor leaguer is not on anyone's bucket list, Buck Showalter, a manager, said, "Managing at that level is the worst job there is in baseball. Why? Because no one wants to be there." When a player gets called up . . . "that guy leaves with a big grin on his face, you have to deal with the five who didn't get called up. That's the hardest part of the job."[8]

An outstanding pitcher for the Chicago Cubs, after an injury, was working his way back through the minor league system when he was called upon to relieve the starting pitcher. However, nobody noticed his big opportunity because the crowd was too busy cheering for the fans trying to "Whack the Intern." The crowd was treated to the "Whack the Intern" game, a game designed for the lulls in the contest. "A large box with four holes cut in the top is brought out to the third baseline. Four of the summer interns crawl beneath the box. Two fans are selected and handed plastic bats. Each time an intern pops his head out of one of the four holes, the fans attempt to whack him."[9] Fans were more attentive to "Whack the Intern" than the comeback of super star pitcher Mark Prior. The grind to achieve in anonymity, with loneliness, low pay, relentless travel, and the reality one has to outperform teammates, creates a strange mix of suffering and pain not uncommon in all sports.

This is why, when discussing suffering and pain found in sports, it is imperative that we acknowledge and recognize the pain of failure. When an athlete feels disengaged or finds that his performance creates disengagement, it can create a vacuum. The disengagement vacuum all too frequently ends up in an attempt to fill the empty space with the "dumb numb" response. We compulsively look for a way to anesthetize the hurt. This is done in a variety of unhealthy ways.

Instead, when we lose a game or when we fall short of our goals, we must embrace the deep hurt and suffering. If we try to overlook it, or use mind-play or enlighten it away, we miss the opportunity for growth and what it means to be fully human. To be fully human, we must risk failure, engage in pain, and endure suffering. So, to that end, we cannot minimize or devalue the impact agony has on us when we compete in sports and experience the beat down. We can be beaten down by losing, by self-talk, by other talk, shame, firing, injuries, or shattered dreams. These agonies need to be felt. We must engage with the hard stuff. This requires being honest, sincere, genuine, and vulnerable. Health flourishes and we are then able to move forward to seek and create solutions.

The goal is to be fully human. The goal is to be whole and mature. The goal is to uncover the depths of pain and still get out of bed and put one foot in front of the other. The goal is to rise out of the arena covered in dust and blood with people mocking, jeering, spitting, and hating. "*Yes, I am imperfect and vulnerable and sometimes afraid, but that doesn't change the truth that I am also brave and worthy of love and belonging.*"[10]

Failure is real.

Failure hurts.

Failure and suffering cannot be avoided.

ENDNOTES: CHAPTER 21

1. Timothy Keller, *Walking With God Through Pain and Suffering*, Dutton, 2013, 44. There is hope, and it is powerful!

2. Richard Attenborough, director. Richard Attenborough and Brian Eastman, producers. *Shadowlands*, based on book *Shadowlands: The True Story of C. S. Lewis and Joy Davidman*, Brian Sibley, author. Price Entertainment, Spelling Films International, and Shadowlands Productions, 1994.

3. Brené Brown, *Rising Strong: How the Ability to Reset Transforms the Way We Live, Love, Parent, and Lead*, Spiegel & Grau, 2015, xxiv–xxv.

4. Ashton Graham, "Pain is Optional," *Las Cruces Sun-News*, April 14, 2023, , 1A

5. Timothy Keller, *Walking With God Through Pain and Suffering*, Dutton, 2013, 44.

6. Brené Brown, *Daring Greatly: How the Courage to Be Vulnerable Transforms the Way We Live, Love, Parent, and Lead*, (New York: Gotham Books, 2012), 8.

7. John Feinstein, *Where Nobody Knows Your Name*, Anchor, an imprint of Knoph-Doubleday, 2014, 7.

8. John Feinstein, *Where Nobody Knows Your Name*, Anchor, an imprint of Knoph-Doubleday, 2014, 46.

9. John Feinstein, *Where Nobody Knows Your Name*, Anchor, an imprint of Knoph-Doubleday, 2014, 2

10. Brené Brown, *Daring Greatly: How the Courage to Be Vulnerable Transforms the Way We Live, Love, Parent, and Lead*, Gotham Books, 2012, 10.

CHAPTER 22

SURVIVING FAILURE AND SUFFERING

WAS I ALL IN? DID I DO ALL I COULD? DID I DO my best? These words have haunted me throughout my life both as an athlete and as a coach. "If you can look back during your rumble and see that you didn't hold back—that you were *all in*—you will feel very different than someone who didn't fully show up. You may have to deal with failure," but you won't have to wrestle . . . with the feeling that you betrayed yourself."[1]

These words, though true, were my demons, was I all in? Watching *The Last Dance*, Michael Jordan said, "My focus is to win the game, it drives me insane when I can't."[2] Welcome to insanity, Michael. There are millions of young men who can't win, granted some did not do their best, and they will wrestle with their poor effort, but most did their best. Most who fail will not be driven to distraction or insanity. I was. I grew up in a home where absolutely everything was a competition. Who was best at checkers, Chinese checkers, cards, Monopoly, ping pong, Yahtzee, croquet, running, baseball, football, and basketball. The only black eye I ever got playing basketball was received playing my dad. I pushed hard in academics, work, money, and sports. I competed at everything. It did "drive me insane." My white suburban life did not detract from the work, interest, passion, and desire to become a college athlete, with wild youthful dreams of playing pro. I did *everything* I knew to do, went to camps, lifted weights, ran all over town dribbling a basketball, brushed my teeth with my left hand, wore out dozens of Converse basketball shoes while playing at the park, and looked for games in neighboring towns. High school was classes, two to three hours of homework every night, and sports. I was driven, and it worked. This paid off by earning me membership into the National Honor Society. High school went well, and I was an outstanding student and a top player on a top team.

I had to win! In college, I knocked guys around in practice in my obsession with being the best, never letting up, playing hard, staying after practice, and working out. I played in the gym on weekends during the season. I did everything! Think the old football movie "*Rudy.*"

But as a sophomore in college, I broke down. After months of giving it my all and believing I deserved to start, I asked my coach on our bus ride back to our college, "Why am I not starting?" He gruffly dismissed me with, "I was going to start you next game, but not now." This crushed me. I cried deep, soul-wrenching tears. If desire, hard work, and the will to win were enough, I would have battled all comers. Stardom would have been mine. I had held nothing back. (Later, I transferred from that college.)

When I couldn't play any longer, I pursued coaching. I coached with the same intensity with which I played, as if my life depended on it. In my first season coaching freshmen, we practiced for three to three and a half hours a day. I bashed a chair on the blackboard, smashed clipboards, chased refs down the hall after games, winning meant too much. I knew this was too much, I stepped back, but I still pushed and worked at it too hard. I was "all in," but it eventually imploded. Coaching at a small college, I broke. It wore me out. It wounded those around me, and it simply was not sustainable. My pursuit of winning finally got to me and at thirty-five years old, I was very depressed, contemplated suicide, lost my wife through divorce, and spent five years wrestling in counseling, trying to unravel my misguided priorities. I questioned God in many ways. This began a deep quest for me to understand what it means to be genuine, healthy, and uncover real winning. Should winning be the ultimate goal? How does one look at oneself and handle it when things fall apart or when one does not win, especially when one has "been all in," putting everything into it?

How do we recover from that kind of body blow, one day realizing the dream has ended? What if an injury forces the end of one's sports aspirations? What if the firing ends the coaching ladder climb? Pain and disappointment cannot be described. It is like a white-hot poker burning the soft tissue of one's soul. The sought-after prize is lost, and the opportunity or person is never going to walk back into one's life. It is over. Failure and suffering have struck a mighty blow. The water is over the dam and whatever was held in that moment in time has now become past. There is no capture that moment, no more chances. The door shuts, it is even nailed shut. Whether it is losing, death, distance from loved ones, divorce, doors shut that will never be opened, that moment, event, person, is gone forever. "We must therefore feel the soul-piercing pain of disappointment . . . Hurt openly in the presence of God . . . Feel your pain. Regard brokenness as an opportunity, as the chance to discover a desire that no brokenness can eliminate but only brokenness reveals."[3] "I've come to believe that only broken people truly worship,"[4]declared Dr. Crabb.

Brokenness forces us back to the pivot point, God. God is where everything pivots. And we dive into a depth of life where answers are only found in Him. God's person and his creative acts may bring exhilaration. God's light is most brilliant in the dark, in the sorrow, in the brokenness.

Nebuchadnezzar, king of Ancient Babylon:

"Now, driven from his palace by insanity, he gains a new perspective: 'I . . . raised my eyes toward heaven' (DANIEL 4:34). In this 'look' he is like the young man in the story told by Jesus in Luke 15, who also 'came to his senses' (v. 17)."

"When Nebuchadnezzar thinks seriously about God and his glory, he is able to come to terms with himself and his need. Calvin says, 'Man never achieves a clear knowledge of himself unless he has first looked upon God's face,'"

In looking to heaven to a personal God, "in that moment, the King's sanity is restored."[5]

When we are face down in the arena, fully invested, covered with dust, bloodied, beaten, and we look around; this is where we find hope and truth. It is in giving the "all-in" effort that Brené Brown challenges each of us to pursue—being wholly present. Larry Crabb, at the tension between life and death, declares, "God is pleased with people who suffer terribly, whose lives never straightened out, but who keep trusting. We call them fools . . . my cancer came back, I just lost my job, and my wife filed for divorce; I feel angry, discouraged, and miserable. But I intend to keep trusting God."[6] This perspective is only possible by holding onto the gift of love available in knowing Jesus. Jesus unites us with himself, God. "The cause of all suffering is separation from God . . . Nothing but God satisfies our most profound desire. The way to handle suffering is to discover your desire for God, this moves us toward God. We enter our thirst. Feel the ache . . . eventually, we will seek God"[7] for forgiveness, life, love, and hope. Intimacy with God produces gratitude, and we find discovering God brings us a life and love that no shattered dreams can destroy. "Problems don't disappear . . . It did not come from anything I did or didn't do. Hope comes not in the solution to the problem but in focusing on Christ, who facilitates the change."[8] The pivot, the turning point in wrestling with shame, suffering, pain, and failure is found in a relationship with God, His perspective, His love. Life will not always be as it is now.

Someone may argue, "Enough already! Don't go getting all religious on me. Don't try to sugarcoat pain and suffering using God. Why is life so full of suffering if there is a God?"

If God is integral to facing failure, pain, and suffering, one might ask, "What is the point of God allowing failure, pain, and suffering in the first place?" Far greater minds than mine have wrestled with this problem for centuries. The best short answer provided by Tim Keller is that if God is infinitely brilliant, He may have a reason that I might not understand for allowing it. If He is infinite and I am finite, then he is far superior to me and I might not be able to understand everything about Him. If He has good reasons for allowing it, then evil does not erase His existence. It is possible that He allows pain to bring greater happiness into our lives.[9]

Once we discover that God holds a position of authority far above us and is also infinitely more intelligent, then we must decide how we are going to relate to this power beyond ourselves. There can only be three basic positions. (Look back to Chapter 9 to understand different philosophical positions that explain life and epistemology.) The three basic positions for us to examine are:

1. There is no God.

2. There is a God who is impersonal and does not involve himself or herself in human affairs.

3. There is a God who is personal and who is involved in human affairs.

If there is no God, then I have no framework outside of myself or my society with which to explain things. Therefore, the idea that "winning is all that matters" is a valid position, especially since it is held by so many.

If there is a God, but he is impersonal and not involved in our daily lives, then it does not matter if I adopt the "win is all that matters" philosophical position. God would be aloof. He just wouldn't care if we won or lost, as he is not involved in the affairs of mankind.

If there is a God who is involved in our lives on a personal level, then logically, how He views winning and losing, success and failure, may be defined differently than what "I believe" or the culture at large. God does not see as man sees; His ways are above my ways.

"For my thoughts are not your thoughts, neither are your ways my ways,' declares the Lord. As the heavens are higher than the earth, so are my ways higher than your ways and my thoughts than your thoughts" (ISAIAH 55:8–9).

"But the LORD said to Samuel, "Do not consider his appearance or his height, for I have rejected him. The LORD does not look at the things man looks at. Man looks at the outward appearance, but the LORD looks at the heart" (1 SAMUEL 16:7).

"As for those who seemed to be important—whatever they were makes no difference to me; God does not judge by external appearance" (GALATIANS 2:6a).

Carl Trueman quotes philosopher Phillip Rieff, "No culture has ever preserved itself where it is not a registration of sacred order. These cultures have not survived. The notion of a culture that persists independent of all sacred orders is unprecedented in human history."[10] Trueman states that the loss of sacred pillars or moral absolutes creates a culture without any foundations. Cultural confusion happens as Trueman goes on to say, "Human beings may still like to think they believe in good and bad . . . In practice, it is we who decide our own preferred ends and shape our ethics to that purpose. Any greater sense of purpose, any transcendent theology, is now dead and buried."[11]

There is a clear line, a clear choice: either God is involved intimately with us and places value on failure, pain, and suffering, or "it is we who decide our own preferred ends." We (and others around us) decide what has value. And it is here that "winning is all that matters" finds its philosophical zenith or nadir.

At this juncture, one may recognize that God sees pain and suffering from a different vantage point. It can have hidden, miraculous, and subtle value. It is by no means always understandable. Failure, pain, and suffering force us to examine whether there can be meaning via God's perspective or whether God simply is not plausible. One must wrestle with the question, does a personal God exist or not? For the purposes of this writing, from this point forward, we will declare that a personal God absolutely exists. This personal God impacts heavily a philosophical position offering hope, wholeness, healing, and sanity in suffering. God provides the resources that allow us to believe being human includes deep purpose amid all manner of heartache. Therefore, God's existence, as found in the *Holy Bible* is our presupposition.

ENDNOTES: CHAPTER 22

1. Brené Brown, *Rising Strong: How the Ability to Reset Transforms the Way We Live, Love, Parent, and Lead*, Spiegel & Grau, 2015, 208–209.

2. Hehir, Jason, director. Jason Hehir, Michael Tollin, and Peter Gruber, producers. *The Last Dance*, a ten-part documentary. ESPN Films & Netflix, 2020, episode 2.

3. Larry Crabb, *Shattered Dreams: God's Unexpected Path to Joy*, WaterBrook, 2001, 72-73.

4. Larry Crabb, *Shattered Dreams: God's Unexpected Path to Joy*, WaterBrook, 2001, 57.

5. Alistair Begg, *Made For His Pleasure: Ten Benchmarks of a Vital Faith*, Moody Publishers, 1996, 151.

6. Larry Crabb, *Shattered Dreams: God's Unexpected Path to Joy*, WaterBrook, 2001, 39–40.

7. Larry Crabb, *Shattered Dreams: God's Unexpected Path to Joy*, WaterBrook, 2001, 72.

8. Timothy Keller, *Walking With God Through Pain and Suffering*, Dutton, 2013, 109.

9. Timothy Keller, *Walking With God Through Pain and Suffering*, Dutton, 2013, 97–98

10. Carl Trueman, *The Rise and Triumph of the Modern Self: Cultural Amnesia, Expressive Individualism, and the Road to Sexual Revolution*, Crossway 2020, 76–77.

11. Carl Trueman, *The Rise and Triumph of the Modern Self: Cultural Amnesia, Expressive Individualism, and the Road to Sexual Revolution*, Crossway 2020, 88.

CHAPTER 23

HOPE EXPLORED, GOD'S PERSPECTIVE

WHO SHOULD WE LISTEN TO?

URING THE 2023 NBA PLAYOFF RUN, A VERY unlikely team found its way into the NBA finals. The Miami Heat lost a play-in-game opportunity to the Atlanta Hawks; consequently, in their first attempt to make the playoffs, they failed. However, somehow in a last-gasp effort with no more losses allowed, they defeated the Chicago Bulls, thus entering the NBA tournament as the Eastern Conference's eighth seed. One of my favorite NBA players, Jimmy Butler, was the subject of a lengthy article written by *USA Today* writer Jeff Zillgitt. This is a typical article whose content could have been written by hundreds of sports writers across our country about dozens of different players. This article speaks of general thoughts on sports and life echoed from sea to shining sea. Sportswriters enjoy and use plenty of hyperbole in their articles, and there was a generous sprinkling of such in this writing. Miami Heat Coach Eric Spoelstra and Jimmy Butler shared ideas about what they had accomplished and what they hoped to achieve as they marched into the NBA finals. The editorial concludes with these thoughts, "Nobody is satisfied. We haven't done anything. We don't play just to win the Eastern Conference. We play to win the whole thing." "If you didn't before, believe Butler when he speaks."[1]

This article critiqued here is an example of a sportswriter's philosophy and perspectives. The critique offered dissects the typical verbiage heard so regularly in the sports world with the following points to ponder:

1. There is mention of the great culture in Miami. The culture is great because they are winning! Pure and simple, we are singing their praises because they have had success. We would hear nothing of this "great culture" if they had lost to Chicago. Also, one should note there are great cultures in other organizations that did not win.

2. The franchise has been steady, patient, and kept and developed good people, all to be commended.

3. Butler says I am here "to win championships." What elite athlete doesn't think and talk in this fashion? Every single NBA player has dreamed his whole life about winning a championship.

4. "I'm just confident," he said. "I know the work that we all put into it." Wait a hot minute, do all NBA teams not work? It is safe to say NBA teams put A LOT of work into their efforts to be champions. Are the Golden State Warriors lazy? How about the Milwaukee Bucks, Boston Celtic, Phoenix Suns, or the Dallas Mavericks? All top teams work hard; all top teams put everything into it, and all top players are confident.

5. Butler says, "Nobody is satisfied." True nobody! Nobody is ever truly satisfied in life, especially in sports. There have been ample hit songs chronicling the woes of being unsatisfied. Rhythmically set to music, singers croon over and over that we are not able to find satisfaction. Satisfaction in this life is always out of reach.

6. "We haven't done anything." A below-eighth seed makes it to

the NBA finals with a key player hurt and they "haven't done anything?" Only one other eighth seed has EVER made it to the finals. They defeated a more talented team, Boston, on their home court; Boston had won three games in a row and had all the momentum, and they "haven't done anything?" They have found, developed, and utilized seven or eight undrafted players in the playoff run, and they "haven't done anything?" Their accomplishments were the stuff legends are made; gratitude is needed.

7. "We play to win the whole thing." . . . "If you didn't before, believe Butler when he speaks." What wonderful superlatives of nonsense. Why does the writer suggest that we should listen to Jimmy Butler? What are Jimmy Butler's credentials? How many championships has he won? Is he NEVER wrong? Is he God? Of course no one would suggest this.

Who should we listen to when they speak? Our rapt attention should be fixed like a team in a photograph in *Sports Illustrated* on December 15, 2008.[2] A photograph capturing an incredible moment forever! A legendary coach, who had lost his leg and almost his life in an automobile accident, speaks from his wheelchair. He has returned to coaching and is on the sidelines exhorting his team. All eyes are glued to this elder statesman. Every eye to the man, including assistant coaches, managers, and every single player is riveted, watching, and listening to the one-legged miracle, Don Meyer. It appears as if he is imparting the most precious knowledge man has ever had ears to hear. The team is holding their collective breath as their coach turns each heart to his message of strategy and motivation. The photo has an urgency, a riveting attention and awe reserved for the rare legends that have respect that moves the soul. It is this kind of raw wonder and awe that we wish for as we peek behind the proverbial curtain and see the inner workings of truth and knowledge almost too wonderful for words. Someone far greater than Don Meyer is speaking. Maybe we should listen when God Speaks. God has spoken. What does God have to say?

WHERE ARE GOD'S WORDS FOUND?

When God speaks, His ideas are not found in great literature, like the *Iliad* by Homer, even though there has been an incredible number of archaeological recoveries, 643 copies of this book written around 400 B.C. God's ideas are not found in the book by Demosthenes, which has uncovered 200 copies from the year 300 B.C. Ultimate knowledge is not found in the *Annals* by Tacitus, even though twenty copies have been located. To hear the words of God and His speech, words that stand winning and losing on its head, words that bring hope and healing, words begging for our wide-eyed breathless rapt attention, are found in the Bible where 5,366 copies of the New Testament have been uncovered and have been quoted in other works of ancient literature 36,289 times.[3]

In addition, thousands of Hebrew manuscripts, confirmed by the Greek Septuagint, the Samaritan Pentateuch, and numerous other sources, validate that God speaks from the Old Testament. One source alone, the attic of Cairo, revealed 10,000 Hebrew manuscripts (portions of the Old Testament).[4] These sources, the Old and New Testament are more widely validated than any other work of literature in history. This offers credibility to God's thoughts and points out that God is real, and He speaks. When God speaks, we should listen. The words of God, who shows us all truth provide understanding and explanations of any aspect of life. This truth found in the Bible produces gold nuggets, diamonds, rubies, and pearls of wisdom, allowing us to see the events of this world, specifically losing, winning, failure, and success, through the lens of a teacher far greater than Don Meyer, Vince Lombardi, John Wooden, Gandhi, Confucius, Siddhartha Gautama, or anyone else.

God's writings are His credentials and words, He has spoken the universe and all creation, the Earth and all its plants and animals, and mankind into existence (GENESIS 1–3). God's speech calms a storm (MATTHEW 8:23–27, MARK 4:35–41, LUKE 8:22–25). Lazarus was brought back to life by God's words (JOHN 11:1–44). God shows repeatedly that He is in control of all things. He is the one we should listen to and who deserves our single-minded collective focus, like the team pictured in *Sports Illustrated*.

When examining the thoughts of God, we should not offer any apology because His words are not second-rate in any way due to their faith-based nature. All too often, when we try to explain events in the arena of life, we behave, think, and speak as though any word outside of humanity is irrelevant. But these words of God, which are truth, declare that in evaluating all of life's activities, there is a wisdom and a standard that is otherworldly. Again, we cannot emphasize enough that no apology is necessary, and no apology is needed when introducing God into a philosophical discussion on any topic. God, who is the truth, always factors into the equation of life. Therefore, we need to turn to the Word of God in the Bible when attempting to examine the minefield of life. His Word provides truth to all aspects of life, including winning and failure.

HOW VALUABLE IS GOD'S PERSPECTIVE?

- "Wisdom is supreme; therefore get wisdom" (PROVERBS 4:7a).

- "The fear of the Lord is the beginning of wisdom, and knowledge of the Holy One is understanding" (PROVERBS 9:10).

- "The fear of the Lord is the beginning of knowledge, but fools despise wisdom and discipline" (PROVERBS 1:7).

- "Blessed is the man who finds wisdom, the man who gains understanding, for she is more profitable than silver and yields better returns than gold. She is more precious than rubies; nothing you desire can compare with her" (PROVERBS 3:13–15).

- "By wisdom, the Lord laid the earth's foundations, by understanding he set the heavens in place; by his knowledge the deeps were divided, and the clouds let drop the dew" (PROVERBS 3:19–20).

These facts are not manmade ideas that are spoken out of the profundity of our intellect. These ideas did not originate in books by great thinkers. They are expressions of the Word of God, and apart from these truths, there is no basis for winning, losing, success, failure, victory, defeat, or understanding life.

"Your word, Oh Lord, is eternal; It stands firm in the heavens. Your faithfulness continues through all generations; you establish the earth, and it endures. Your laws endure to this day, for all things serve you" (PSALM 119:89-91).

When we know that truth and wisdom can be found in God, and His writings enable us to accurately evaluate life events. There are answers.

VICTORY IS IN GOD'S HANDS

All outcomes are in the hands of the Lord. Victory, defeat, success, and failure ultimately are under the control of God alone. God "causes his sun to rise on the evil and the good and sends rain on the righteous and the unrighteous" (MATTHEW 5:45b).

"There is no wisdom, no insight, no plan that can succeed against the LORD. The horse is made ready for the day of battle, but victory rests with the LORD" (PROVERBS 21:30-31).

Isaiah repeats this refrain "The LORD almighty has sworn, "Surely, as I have planned, so it will be, and as I have purposed, so it will stand . . . For the LORD Almighty has purposed, and who can thwart him? His hand is stretched out, and who can turn it back?" (ISAIAH 14:24–27).

"It was not by their sword that they won the land, nor did their arm bring them victory; it was your right hand, your arm, and the light of your face, for you love them" (PSALM 44:3).

"See now that I myself am he! There is no god beside me. I put to death and I bring to life, I have wounded and I will heal, and no one can deliver out of my hand" (DEUTERONOMY 32: 39).

We see God is in control of all events. This shifts the narrative from me to Him. Alan Goldberg says, "In essence, once an athlete steps out onto the field or court, winning is totally out of his or her control."[5] (He is speaking regarding what is in our control, but his point is correct.)

We frequently see the truth of these statements in sports. One team is undeniably not equal to or the quality of the other team, yet somehow, they pull out the victory. During the winter of 2023, the National Football League playoffs showcased a clear example of this when the Cleveland Browns faced off against the Pittsburgh Steelers. The Browns and the Steelers had just played each other the previous week, and the Browns only won on their home field by two, 24 to 22. The Pittsburgh Steelers had rested key players and their quarterback, so when the Browns had to travel to Pittsburgh to play the mighty Steelers in their home stadium, the "experts" had all but written the Browns out of the playoffs. The narrative seemed to suggest that playing the game was pointless. The smart "money" was on the Steelers. To worsen matters, COVID illnesses rendered the head coach of the Browns and several of his assistants unavailable, and the team was prohibited from practicing the week leading up to the playoff game. The Browns could only practice forty-eight hours before kickoff. To add insult to injury, a couple of key Browns players suffered injuries. Therefore, the Cleveland Browns were going to lose! The game began, and to everyone's shock, Cleveland led the Steelers 28 to 0 at the end of the first quarter and cruised to an easy 48 to 37 victory. It cannot be explained why this happened, but it was clear on that day the Pittsburg Steelers could not win. The power of victory seemed to be in the hands of someone outside of the game.

Another example of the "victory is in the hands of the Lord" occurred during the 2021 NCAA March Madness Basketball tournament. A team new to Division I, the Abilene Christian University Wildcats men's basketball team scored a remarkably unlikely upset of in-state power the University of Texas Longhorns. The Longhorns had established themselves with the usual big-time pedigree and had proven their mettle in the strong Big 12 conference. They faced an unmistakably undermanned Wildcat team. The scrappy Wildcats hung with the Longhorns only down five points at the half and played close throughout the second half. Oddly, going down the stretch, Texas could not score. They failed to get key stops, and they turned the ball over repeatedly. Going into the final minutes, the Wildcats found themselves ahead by five points. But Texas battled despite dribbling off their own leg and missing free throws, with under a minute to play, Texas had the lead. However, ACU ended up at the free throw line behind by one point and their worst free throw shooter at the line. He could win, lose, or tie the game. Earlier, some of the Longhorn's shots rattled out as if being blocked by an unseen hand, and with the game on the line, the worst free throw shooter on the Wildcats team made both free throws to secure the incredible upset; maybe one of the most unexpected upsets in tournament history. These types of events happen in life frequently.

A Biblical perspective on matters of the underdogs is found in the battle between David, a shepherd boy, and a nine-foot-tall Warrior named Goliath. David boldly declares before the battle that he would win, but instead of the routine trash talk, David says, "All those gathered here will know that it is not by sword or spear that the Lord saves; for the battle is the Lord's, and he will give all of you into our hands" (1 SAMUEL 17:47). It is clearly unconventional thinking. David possesses humility and dispenses his own importance and prowess as a necessity for genuine success or victory. This humility gives God the honor and the jubilation for the outcome. We are not as omnipotent as we often think. God must always sign off on all outcomes.

TWENTY-TWENTY VISION

Many writers have examined the subject of winning and losing and have concluded there is more to sport and more to life than winning. Alan Goldberg suggests, "Too many athletes, coaches, and parents walk around mistakenly feeling like a failure just because they didn't win. Truth be told, in any given competition there is only one winner and a ton of 'losers' . . . They are NOT failures."[6]

"The more we make sports a life-and-death matter and the more we concentrate on a youngster's needing to win or to succeed in order to feel worthwhile, the more we will undermine the contribution that sports can make."[7]

We are able to uncover a different reality when examining failure, because God's realm is different from our finite ideas and thoughts. God says, "As the heavens are higher than the earth, so are my ways higher than your ways and my thoughts than your thoughts" (ISAIAH 55:9).

"How great is God—beyond our understanding!" (JOB 36:26a).

As the oldest son of the family was brought before Samuel, the prophet heard God say, "Do not consider his appearance or his height, for I have rejected him. The LORD does not look at the things man looks at. Man looks at the outward appearance, but the LORD looks at the heart" (1 Samuel 16:7).

A Bible hero named Elisha illustrates a different perspective, in a different dimension, thinking God's thoughts, when being surrounded by a hostile king's army. "Go, find out where he is,' the King ordered, 'so I can send men and capture him.' The report came back: 'He is in Dothan.' Then he sent horses and chariots and a powerful force there. They went by night and surrounded the city. When the servant of the man of God got up and went out early the next morning, an army with horses and chariots had surrounded the city. 'Oh, my Lord, what shall we do?' the servant asked. 'Don't be afraid,' the Prophet answered. 'Those who are with us are more than those who are with them.' And Elisha prayed, 'O LORD, open his eyes so he may see. Then the Lord opened the servant's eyes, and he looked and saw the hills full of horses and chariots of fire all around Elisha'" (2 KINGS 6:13–17).

God's perspective creates understanding by virtue of wisdom found only in His eyes. We can rightly frame winning and losing or success and failure by looking through the lens God provides. Dale Ralph Davis declares, "Yahweh's [God's] . . . reverses the conventions of men, overthrows the human cannon of what ought to be ... he turns human standards on their heads, causing us to wonder and cheer. Without this God who ignores our proprieties, most of us would have no hope."[8] Therefore, the lens by which we evaluate our results conceives a different outcome! Winning becomes another dimension with unorthodox markers. The final score, the adulation of the hero, the sound bites on ESPN all fade to nothing in the light of true victory. Our world commonly defines winning as the fastest time, most points, best score, and knockout punch. In short, victory in an event. But God declares, "I decide who wins." God declares the value of the outcome. In recognizing God's place in our affairs, we experience an enlightenment of meaning as He interprets our life events through His eyes, with His values, for His purposes.

GOOD'S ORIGIN

Another other-worldly thought is the idea that God is good. If we were not told this, we could not discover that God is good through our experiences, even armed with the truth that God is good. It takes faith to see that God is good. Tears of pain blur our vision. In chapter one of Genesis, God tells us seven times in thirty-one verses that His creation is good. In fact, at the conclusion of this chapter, He says, "it was very good." His creative work is excellent! Jesus walks on Earth and changes the world for good wherever He goes. Jesus miraculously creates the best wine at a wedding, heals the sick, raises the dead, brings peace to the tormented, sets prisoners free, offers life out of death, all exceptionally good outcomes. Outcomes that are so good we call them miracles. The otherworld nature of these events can cause the best of us to refuse to believe that they were real and part of historical fact.

God "sustains all things by his powerful word" (HEBREWS 1:3).

"By him all things were created: things in heaven and on earth, visible and invisible, whether thrones or powers or rulers or authorities; all things were created by him and for him. He is before all things, and in him all things hold together" (COLOSSIANS 1:16–17).

God creates an all-good world/universe, and he sustains the same. He moves every event in this world toward redemptive outcomes in both humanity and creation (ROMANS 8:21). In the events of his children, He makes all events totally good. No other being in the entire universe wants our total good and no other being in the universe can bring that about!

God has a formula for bringing good into our lives in all circumstances. This produces joy and hope. God's formula bridges despair into hope and sorrow into joy.

How do we deal with the narrative that we are all miserable failures? How do we deal with a heartbreaking loss, firing, divorce, missed goals, and being mistreated? The "failure" creates a posture of humility; we no longer see ourselves as all-powerful. Birthing out of humility and respect for God, we deal with suffering, defeat, and failures by realizing that this kind of suffering is the fertile soil for all positive future development. This is hope.

Failure, loss, and suffering forces us to look within. When we look within, we don't always like what we see. The death of dreams, the impossible recovery from the loss of honor, the loss of value as a person, and the loss of identity all strip away the masks of pretense. Winning bolsters us up on the outside. Winning makes everything appear good. Losing embarrasses us and exposes our weaknesses, stripping away the layers and forcing us to confront our true selves. What do we find? Greatness is not born out of avoidance of pain and always winning, but true victory is birthed by suffering rightly.

C.S. Lewis wrote a book where he explores the truth that in suffering, God gets our attention. "Pain insists upon being attended to. God whispers to us in our pleasures, speaks in our conscience, but shouts in our pains; it is his megaphone to rouse a deaf world."[9] We need to suffer to really grow as a person.

Paul speaks a profound truth when he espouses, "I want to know Christ and the power of his resurrection and the fellowship of sharing in his sufferings, becoming like him in his death and so to somehow to attain to the resurrection from the dead" (PHILIPPIANS 3:10–11).

The fellowship of sharing in his sufferings goes beyond the trials of being persecuted for being in Christ. It is sharing in the frailty of being human with all its pain, sorrow, groaning, disappointments, grief, and despair. "Perhaps we're meant to learn that the richest hope permits the deepest suffering, which releases the strongest power, which then produces the greatest joy. Maybe there is no shortcut to joy."[10]

We have events happen in our lives, and we try to make sense out of them, but we cannot. We see the present through a glass darkly. We cannot see the future unequivocally! And because even with the benefit of hindsight, we see the past dimly, as it is not fully illuminated. Understanding the mind or plan by the hand of God is impossible, looking forward or backward. It is foolish to suggest we understand all events in the past, as if we can understand God's mind in totality. It looks to us like a lesson or an outcome but ends up being a dead end or misinterpretation of the motives, events, or facts in the unfolding drama of life and its pathos. Suffering creates in us a need to look outside of ourselves. Pain drives us to look deeply at the meaning and purpose of life. Therefore, suffering that moves us to look to the cross and God's love and mercy produces true value. "The way to power, freedom, and joy is through suffering, loss, and sorrow." This is not conventional thinking, says Tim Keller. "If we know he [Jesus] loves us unconditionally, despite our flaws, then we know he is present with us and working in our lives in times of pain and sorrow."[11]

Allowing ourselves to believe in him and turn our pain over to him during suffering produces perseverance, character, and hope through the love of Jesus. Of course, this is not conventional thinking or even conversation in our culture, much less in the arena of athletics . . . but that does not make it untrue. In fact, just the opposite; this truth can turn a heartbreaking loss into a springboard of growth in the life of an athlete.

A season-ending ACL tear can begin a pathway to deeper wholeness and a journey into those things that hold profound value. A setback, an injury, a defeat, may produce strength of character. Resilience, which is integral to real "Grit," may grow in the athlete. A person begins a journey into true education; leaders throughout history have recognized the value and need for virtue and morality in educational development. Suffering can educate an individual and move a person toward being someone of true character.

Will this happen apart from a Biblical perspective? Unlikely, but seeing through God's lens, it can happen. Seeing God's hand in disappointment and suffering creates a person who can thrive. God's ways are truly unconventional and genuinely encouraging, even in the face of a powerfully unwanted outcome. A person intimately connected to Jesus will find that "we know that in all things God works for the good of those who love him, who have been called according to his purpose" (ROMANS 8:28). This makes an athlete fail proof! This removes the fear of winning or losing for an athlete, and the results will bring about good in their life. No outcome is ultimately considered a failure because God will bring about growth, maturity, character, and untold qualities that prove more valuable than silver, gold, rubies, or diamonds.

MOTIVES–THE FINAL FRONTIER

The other dimension or looking at things with a different lens deepens as one drills down, recognizing God looks into our heart. He judges the inside as well as the outside. An infinite number of factors matter to Him, resulting in a complex grid that often stands traditional outcomes on their collective heads. God digs into the motives of a man's soul. He sees the attitude of the heart. He has a different scorecard. He asks, "What is going on in the battle?" What is the core value from where the power and life force emanate? Courage places us in the battle, uncertain whether we can win, and sometimes fully aware we probably will not win. But courage takes us into the arena. "Winning is doing the really brave thing." Brené Brown Netflix special.[12]

In an old classic movie, *The Wizard of Oz*, we meet a character who lacks courage. Throughout the movie he runs from everything, including his own shadow, and he has the courage of a flea, not of a lion. His love for Dorothy, a character who is trying to get home, alters all his fears and ultimately bestows upon him courage, resulting in him being crowned.[13]

God's love, His directives in our lives, His working all things out for our ultimate good, creates courage. Courage is what makes heroes, but the pathway that has been discussed so far is not the locker room motivational speech genre. There are no posters in football locker rooms with God empowering us with courage. God's pathway is a path seen from a different perspective with different light. Winning becomes another dimension with unorthodox markers. He would also say, "sometimes winning is losing and losing is winning," because His criterion differs from ours.

This "God grid" will find us fearlessly engaged in a struggle to win, succeed, try with our whole heart, while the whole time wrestling with our core motives and values amid the contest. This intensifies the stakes. As one strives for victory, a new level, a new triumph, and a new challenge emerges. Competing in the new arena changes the outcome, turning a win into a mere fraction of a point. It makes a win at all costs a failure. How did we get to the victory? If the journey does not make us better people, if this battle does not delve into the depths of the Marianas Trench, then what's the point?

Motives are a "slippery fish." What is the attitude in the heart of the assailants in battle? Sport brings out the best in us when, in its purest sense, contestants move from a self-motivating purpose to a joyful participation for altruistic reason, the greatest being: enjoying all that God has created, including the aspects of competition or sports. Sports do not have to produce tantrum throwing, spoiled egotists, self-seeking narcissists, or characterless buffoons. Sports can be an act of personal expression. For some people, it can express itself as glory to God. Others may find it in the joy of exploring the depths of personal dedication while striving to reach the pinnacle in an activity. Whatever reasons an athlete competes, the attitudes or motives of the heart colors everything.

I recall two fine teams locked in a basketball contest: Ohio State, highly ranked fourth nationally, battled Michigan State, a team desperately stretching to make the March Madness Tournament. The game was very physical, especially in the paint, which is nothing new in the Big Ten. This is where it became interesting. With the score for both teams around forty, the Ohio State coach became angry because he believed Michigan State was making too much contact and his team was not receiving foul calls.

The coach went wild, yelling, flailing, being restrained by his assistant coach and making sure he received the technical he earned. However, he may have gone too far in reaching for victory. He may have stained his heart; I think the coach went too far. I can sympathize, having done the same thing myself. A question needs asking, "What are the motives of our heart during an athletic contest, or in life for that matter?"

The motives are the watershed, and they will color everything. No one will ever completely tame them. The inner workings of our heart are the truest of battles and take the greatest courage. Anyone can use exterior motivational obstacles, the final score, performing to the roar of the fans, the vendetta, the personal affront.

The latter, the personal affront, was comical in *The Last Dance*.[14] By his own admission, Michael Jordan created an affront to motivate himself to play his best. He would stir up a real or imagined offense that he would use as fuel to create maximum performance. But where does this mental gymnastics place the heart and the motives?

Greater courage is summoned by cultivating the power of the heart offers Brené Brown, "rather than protecting and hiding our heart behind bulletproof glass, wholeheartedness is about *integration*. It's integrating our thinking, feeling, and behavior."[15] She says, this integration of the full aspect of our person brings us to the best of performance in the best of methodologies. Without whole person integration, "We imprison the heart, we kill courage."[16]

Instead of reaching greater maturity, greater strength, greater courage, true victory, the opposite occurs when motives are damaged by "tricks." Only when the inner man and his motives are aligned with an ethic built on higher values can an athlete truly perform to their maximum and be at peace in the process.

A practical application of the principles being discussed can be found in observations made a few years ago regarding a couple of losing football teams. The Indianapolis Colts were at midfield. Their first win of the season was within their grasp. It was fourth down and about a yard to go. The game was tied, and momentum was necessary to pull out a win. They had faced injuries, setbacks, and even the sidelining of their star quarterback, Peyton Manning. On fourth and a yard, with the game possibly on the line, they elected to punt. Why?

The New Mexico State Aggies had defeated a Big Ten opponent the previous week and were playing their archrival, the University of Texas, at El Paso, on their home field. They were playing well and needed another score to ice the game. They were one yard from the end zone on 4th down. A score would give them a likely victory, a field goal would give UTEP hope they could still defeat the Aggies. The coach elected to kick a field goal. Why?

In both games, the Colts and the Aggies eventually succumbed to defeat. Both teams were in the throes of losing seasons. (The Aggies were enduring many losing seasons.) What caused the coaches to choose safety rather than risk? Both teams had nothing to lose, they already had losing seasons.

I believe we can find the answer in a peculiar place. We avoid the fear of heartbreak by allowing heartbreak or failure. By scoring the touchdown or picking up the first down, we find out what kind of strength we truly have or do not have. Knowing that God holds the outcome, God looks at the moment through His lens, knowing suffering can bring hope, hope can produce courage and courage can birth victory, regardless of what happens next. When we fully invest in the moment, check our motives, explore our abilities, trust in God, and make the most of the moment, we emerge victorious. We have the satisfaction of having reached for what we truly desire, putting it all on the line with passion, rather than compromise, by grasping a watered-down version of what we're willing to accept. The safe option causes the very thing to occur that we are avoiding. By taking the risk which carries serious consequence, we teach those that we care about, our team or loved one, that they can score the winning touchdown, get that critical first down or overcome the life obstacle. This shows, "We believe in you." This is a real victory. Real victory is in their grasp. They are fully human and capable. By saying we believe in you enough to risk everything dear at the moment, we impart strength.

When we allow someone to test their limits and dare greatly, even if they experience deep wounds and feel the full brunt of pain, we say that we believe God will supply the strength to find those ingredients necessary to overcome. We offer them dignity in their humanity. As humans, we know we are frail. We know we are failures. But dignity is found because we are created in the image of God. Solace and comfort are available in Him. We will meet God, He will be found, He will be good, and He will be enough. In moments of profound weakness, this knowledge generates power, strength, and hope. Virtues cannot be accomplished with shortcuts and without pain. Strength is found when my life is on the line full of fear, but God's abilities and powers will intervene in a way that truly qualifies as the miraculous. A standard higher than who wins, a standard that plumbs our motives, our heart, the bowels of our courage, our very life. It is here in this context that we find that the game and life is evaluated from God's perspective.

COMPELLING LOVE

God's heartbeat is love. We are loved by God; this is a game changer!

We must know who we are. We are people formed in the image of God himself. The creator of all things, the creator of the universe made us like Him. When he came to Earth, he looked, walked, talked, and acted like us. Not the us who are pretty. Not the us who are winners. Not the us who are talented. Not the us who are perfect. The us who are ugly. The us who are losers. The us who are failures. The us who are incomplete or challenged in some fashion. That is God, in us, human.

"So God created man in his own image, in the image of God he created him; male and female he created them" (GENESIS 1:27).

"For you created my inmost being; you knit me together in my mother's womb. I praise you because I am fearfully and wonderfully made; your works are wonderful, I know that full well. My frame was not hidden from you when I was made in the secret place. When I was woven together in the depths of the earth, your eyes saw my unformed body. All the days ordained for me were written in your book before one of them came to be. How precious to me are your thoughts, O God! How vast is the sum of them!" (PSALM 139:13-17).

"For God so loved the world that he gave his one and only son, that whoever believes in him shall not perish but have eternal life" (JOHN 3:16).

Being made in God's image gives us an identity far more precious than anything in all creation. And being cared for so much that He laid down his life to fix us, warts, and all, leaves us breathless without words! This truth must be fused into our heart and mind. This truth provides the foundation for all evaluative narrative regarding our personhood. My wife, Karen, points out, "If we understand who we are in Christ, we will not seek more, there is 'no more.' We have everything, we are complete in Him. How He sees us is as His Bride, fully perfect."

We move forward knowing we are complete. We have everything. How He sees us; we are His bride, His beloved-fully perfect! If we are incomplete, we must win to be accepted, our accomplishment will make us significant, then we do not know who we are. It is this other-worldly value that we possess which changes the standards by which we measure winning and losing. When we see our worth, we see that our efforts hold a grander meaning, a higher court, a greater worth. Suddenly, we realize that our lens and God's lens provide a grid by which to measure our results, and they differ from what we are told by sports media magnets. Winning is not everything, and life is not divided into winners and losers. We are no longer defined by the world's standards but by the one whose thoughts are not our thoughts whose ways are not our ways, we are free to win and lose, love and cry, dance and crawl.

Whatever our task, the endgame is to find a performance devoid of the standard of those around us. Speaking about our jobs, Dallas Willard states, "You must be a person . . . who finds his personal sufficiency in God. If you don't have this one down . . . you will be torn between pleasing people and pleasing God. You will be torn between your own integrity and what people who don't understand are saying about you. You won't be able to lead like this."[17]

The late Rick and Dick Hoyt, the son with cerebral palsy and his father, epitomized the victory found in the inner man by participating in Iron Mans, marathons, 10Ks and various other events, including a run of 3,735 miles across America. Rick was pushed and pulled by his father a total of 1,130 times. They showed a father and son whose lives were love wound into each other's dreams, hopes, and accomplishments. Living and winning is measured by a standard unknown to most of us, but by a higher standard, a standard of love. Amazing! Their lives make it evident that they aspire to stand on a different podium. This podium is where victories are not found in the typical sports pinnacle, the win at all costs. This is a finish line far too low. Many strive to stand at a podium that says it is all about us. Winning and losing validates us. We create the standards to base success and identity, a gold medal around our necks. This is shallow. Along with the Hoyts, I would suggest there is a podium of far greater value. We possess deep value and our lives have profound meaning.

It is not about us.

Trophies, gold medals, and victories do not derive our meaning. We don't remember the heroes. It's not all about us. The world does not know us. For that matter, who is the world, and no, they don't really care! "The World" is the ultimate hyperbole; there are over 8 billion people in the world, and most have never heard of _____ . Billions of people have never and will never hear of you or me. When a celebrity walks into our living room and implies that everyone in the world recognizes them by their first name, they are stating an intellectual incongruity.[18] The entire world does not know them by any name, let alone one name. These sloppy syrupy sentiments about a person's worth set up an artificial standard to measure validation. We do not know Milo of Croton, a wrestling legend in 536 B.C., who was the Olympic champion six times. The world forgot his name, even in the past fifty or so years, the world has long since forgotten heroes like Jim Ryan, Bob Pettit, Jim Brown, Branch Rickey, Edwin Moses, Jimmy Connors, and Mario Andretti. Ultimately, it is not what the world thinks of us that matters. It is what God thinks of us. His evaluation of our performance is *all that matters*.

"In the presence of God and of Christ Jesus, who will judge the living and the dead, and in view of his appearing and his kingdom" (2 TIMOTHY 4:1-2a). He is the judge of all the world, living and the dead. He sets the standards for success and failure; He judges with different lenses. He knows who we are. And because he knows who we are, we matter. We reach for accolades upon a different podium and with our identity fixed. We have an identity in His eyes grounded in love, and that makes more difference than 1,000,000 hits on X (TIKTOK).

ENDNOTES: CHAPTER 23

1. USA Today. Jeff Zillgitt, "Butler Did It," *Las Cruces Sun-News*, June 1, 2023, 1B-2B.

2. David E. Klutho, photographer. Don Meyers, subject. *Sports Illustrated*, December 15, 2008.

3. Josh McDowell, *The New Evidence, That Demands a Verdict*, Thomas Nelson, 1999, 38, 43.

4. Josh McDowell, *The New Evidence, That Demands a Verdict*, Thomas Nelson, 1999, 72.

5. Alan S. Goldberg, "Is Losing And Coming in Second Really Failing?," *Competitive Advantage* (website), October 5, 2018. https://www.competitivedge.com/is-losing-and-coming-in-second-really-failing/

6. Alan S. Goldberg, "Is Losing And Coming in Second Really Failing?," *Competitive Advantage* (website), October 29, 2018. https://www.competitivedge.com/is-losing-and-coming-in-second-really-failing

7. Thomas Tutko and William Burns, *Winning Is Everything and Other American Myths*, Macmillan, 1976, xiv.

8. Dale Ralph Davis, *Joshua: No Falling Words*, Christian Focus, 2000, 135.

9. C.S. Lewis, *The Problem of Pain*, Macmillan, 1962, 93.

10. Larry Crabb, *Shattered Dreams: God's Unexpected Path to Joy*, WaterBrook, 2001, 45.

11. Timothy Keller, *Walking With God Through Pain and Suffering*, Dutton, 2013, 52.

12. Sandra Restrepo, director. *Brené Brown, The Call to Courage* (documentary), Netflix, 2019.

13. Victor Fleming and King Vidor, directors. *The Wizard of Oz*. Metro-Goldwyn-Mayer, 1939.

14. Hehir, Jason, director. Jason Hehir, Michael Tollin, and Peter Gruber, producers. *The Last Dance*, a ten-part documentary. ESPN Films & Netflix, 2020.

15. Brené Brown, *Dare To Lead : Brave Work. Tough Conversations. Whole Hearts*, Random House, 2018, 72.

16. Brené Brown, *Dare To Lead : Brave Work. Tough Conversations. Whole Hearts*, Random House, 2018, 73.

17. Dallas Willard, *Renewing the Christian Mind: Essays, Interviews, and Talks*, HarperOne/Harper Collins, 2016, 430.

18. Gatorade Bolt24. *Keeping It Real with Serena: One Name* (television commercial). USA: Multiple Media Outlets, 2021.

CHAPTER 24

HOPE DEFEATS FAILURE AND LOSS

IT'S OVER; THE TOOTHPASTE IS OUT OF THE TUBE

T HUS FAR THIS WRITING HAS ESTABLISHED THAT when we pour our totality into the pursuit or achievement of a goal and miss the expected or hoped-for results, it hurts. We suffer in pain and anguish. We often refer to missing our objective as failure. This may cause a loss that is unrecoverable. Failure may result in pain so deep that one feels like throwing up. It can hurt so bad that we give up. Suffering may be so bad that pain is all we see, and death looks attractive. Physical bodily failure like a terrible illness or paralysis, marital collapse, career shipwrecks, or unrecoverable loss begs healing. Where is hope? How do we look in the mirror when our eyes look back and all we view is a sickened soul?

"I am a failure," my friend said, as he talked about the way his children had turned out. "My kids failed to respond to the life lessons and values that were instilled over their young lives." The dejection in his voice, the disappointment in his eyes, the hopelessness in his countenance stunned me.

Douglas K. Erlandson echoes this same refrain, "I'm a failure." After teaching philosophy for eight years at the college level, I lost my job. I was a pastor for six years and left my second church, totally burned out. Between those two careers, I tried being a salesman. I quit after a few weeks."[1] How many other men have looked back over their lives and uttered those same devastating words? I am a failure!

Looking back over my life, I've said the same words: I am a failure. Career outcomes that fell desperately short, crushing my soul not once, but many times. Each time I coached another season with gusto, only to watch a strange turn derail the pursuit. The pain was devastating.

The truth is, we are all failures, dismal, underperforming, poor-excuses-for-men failures. We have failed to live up to our potential, our dreams, expectations, even our God. Failure is a guarantee that everyone will "enjoy." All of us will fail miserably! Failure is something we work desperately to avoid, even avoid at all costs, but something impossible to elude. Failure is so much a part of human existence that courses should be taught on the subject. It should be expected. It should not be a surprise to anyone. It will appear with absolute certainty, inexorably certain, as day is followed by night.

I saw failure up close, watching my sister fight for her life. Her crippled and often epileptic body, surgery riddled, fought to live another day. After numerous surgeries over the years where her large intestines were removed, then 90 percent of her stomach, then 75 percent of her small intestines, then 5 percent more, followed by more surgeries including a surgical site, a five-by-seven wound, left open never to heal was too much for her seventy-five-pound body to withstand. She gave way to respiratory failure. This woman and this battle could not have a happy ending. This battle she would lose. All of us stared failure in the face. Failure of her body to be healthy, failure of her doctors to stop the insidious death of her intestines, failure to find any solution to bring healing and even failure of prayers to spare her life. This was a front-row seat watching failure in living horrific color day after day. My sister gasping for life, gasping for air, battling moment by moment until failure reached up, grabbed her by the throat and took her away. Her failure in life marked my failure, I was helpless! Utterly and totally helpless. I shared the love of Jesus, but there was nothing humanly, nothing, I could do but love her to the end.

Failure grabbed a good friend of mine in a very different arena. My friend lost a good job only to replace it with something equal or better. Working diligently for years and seeing marginal success he battled on, he sought to be a good employee with outstanding work ethic and provide value to his company for their confidence in his hire. Then, like a flash of brilliant light bursting through a dark storm, he landed a huge victory. He landed a sale that had taken years to cement. Jubilation and thrill would be the understatement of this victory. He got fired the following day! Failure crashed into his life unexpectedly, unreservedly, and underhandedly. Failure dashed his accomplishment with all the ferocity of a cage fighter thrashing an opponent to the mat, he was done!

People speak of failing their way to the top, or failing to success, or failing forward, or failing as fast as one can, as a reverse inverted mantra for success. But for the brokenness of failure to carry the true weight and heaviness of being a failure, the definition must be very clear. Failure must be the death of an outcome that cannot go either way. For failure to truly be failing it carries with it a do or die, all or nothing component, it cannot be a motivational tool to "see you at the top" or "I failed repeatedly before I became a great success." Failure in its ultimate sense, to be truly failure produces death. The objective or subject of the task matters, and it matters so deeply that by not achieving it the very life and marrow is sucked from our soul. Therefore, books, lectures, and magazine articles that trumpet how great it was to fail two or three times and then finally achieve victory; are to be lightly regarded. Authors, thinkers, professors, and leaders must stop sugarcoating failure! They must stop using pyscho babble such as looking for the pot of gold at the end of the rainbow and making failure into a warm cuddly little furball. If a book seeks to explain failure in the context which results in success, it has missed the point. Success often does not come out of failure! That is why they call it failure! Failure is incorrectly defined by most self-help gurus as the step needed to succeed or the necessary process to recover or the magic bullet to self-revelation. It may be none of those things. Success is not falling forward or failing until you get it right. Failure is the end, collapse of hope, the destruction of a desired outcome. Failure is the loss of something deemed dear, finding that entity vanished to vapor. The moment falls into a past that has sealed the gates on that point and place in time.

The failure to prevent death from swallowing a loved one hurts beyond words. There is nothing in the failure to cancer, gross disease, bodily shutdown, and ultimately death that has a "happily ever after" ending. Real failure kicks you when you're down, keeps kicking you until you succumb, and then kicks you one more time for good measure. That is failure! A couple desperately seeking a child only to have interrupted pregnancy after interrupted pregnancy followed by a stillborn child does not do a happy dance. A parent who has a child killed by a senseless drunk driver or one who sees their offspring overdose and die, doesn't jump up and down and say, "what have I learned that will make me successful?" Failure is a moment of abject pain wrapped in finality. To truly fail is the end of a dream. Failure causes the death of a dream.

Failure to be true failure, by my definition, must destroy the hope and the goal. It parrots the nursery rhyme that "all the King's horses and all the King's men couldn't put Humpty Dumpty back together again." Failure's outcome swallows up the desired moment forever, forever lost. There is not always a "big lesson" or "let's plumb the lessons of this tragedy" or "how do I use this to reach a better place?" It is history. Failure is the end.

We are all failures, even our heroes are failures!

In the very beginning of the book, the first man and first woman are failing. Adam stands by and lets his wife be seduced and then participated in her horrible prideful decision. Adam's wife, Eve, actively pursued a prideful eternity-changing-decision and ate food that she had been told, by God himself, not to eat. To make matters worse, their first child eventually flies into a jealous rage and murders his brother Abel. The beat goes on. A man named Lamech turns from God's model of one man and one woman, like Adam and Eve, and marries two wives. Lamech follows the family lineages of murder by killing a man.

By the time we get to Genesis chapter 6, in just a few pages, God states, ". . . every inclination of the thoughts of their heart was only evil all the time." The Lord said, "I will wipe mankind, whom I created, from the face of the earth." The failure of humanity had reached the place where God himself decreed the end of the very creation he had formed. However, Noah found favor in God's eyes, so we think we have finally found that successful hero, but no. After Noah is miraculously spared from a worldwide flood, he becomes drunk and is lying around his home naked. Ham, his son, commits a sexual impurity with his naked dad and his ancestors suffer as a result. By Genesis 11, people have built a structure that will reach the heavens, linking their accomplishment to a unity of immortality and a monument to their human greatness. God sees this as wickedness and forever mixes up the languages and scatters the people.

After reading a few more chapters, we find Abraham telling his wife to lie to the ruler of all of Egypt, Pharaoh. To make matters worse, Abraham lies again to the King of Gerar. Abraham has a nephew named Lot, who moves into a town called Sodom. The town is 100 percent homosexual. A visitor comes to see Lot and the men of the town bang on Lot's door demanding that he allow them to have sex with this visitor. Lot offers his daughter to the men, as a sex slave, and the men reject this offer. Finally, the wickedness of the men is so vile that God strikes them blind. Eventually Lot, his wife, and their daughters flee Sodom, but his wife looks back longingly and dies. Living in caves, Lot's two daughters coax their father into drunkenness and have sex with him for the rationalization of producing offspring.

Remarkably, the amount of tragedy, sin, lying, and deceit found in just a small portion of the book of Genesis, the first book of the Bible, is shocking. One might think failed characters in the Bible were the exception, but they are the norm. These stories of ancient lives demonstrate man's repeated propensity to fail.

This theme and mantra strike a heavy beat as the names and faces change, but the undeniable evidence keeps pounding upon our minds like a relentless surf. Evidence surfaces in the popular character of King David. This King of Israel is mentioned as part of the family lineage of Jesus. In fact, this man who was king, was held in such high regard by the people of Israel that his name is mentioned almost as often as the scriptures are discussed. He was given the nickname of a "man after God's own heart." However, David was an abject failure. David killed 200 Philistines to provide the bridal price to Saul for his daughter, which just happened to be 200 men's penises. Year's later David has sex with the wife of one of his mighty men, then tries to cover it up by having the man, Uriah, go home from battle to spend time with his wife. When Uriah refuses to go into his home because his comrades are in battle, David gets him drunk and sends him home to be with his wife. When he still does not spend the night with his wife, David sends him back into battle to have him killed at the front lines. Scandal surrounded David because of these horrific decisions.

David's failure is revealed, confirming the worst of fears. Who could call this man a winner? Who could call this man a success? Yet throughout history, people have trumpeted him as one of the greatest men in history, a man after God's own heart. God calls him a success. Therefore, instead of combing the pages for heroes, let us search from a different perspective. Gradually, in the death of a dream, God shows up, the real hero to all stories, good and bad. It has been stated that God is the starting point for all truth. This truth is in the Bible. God's word gives us fresh eyes.

Therefore, there must be an important principle in the formula for success that is not intuitively obvious as one looks for the so-called winner. For a person to be called a success, there must be a criterion that is not observable on sports talk shows or in most teen locker rooms. For us to recognize we are failures and to maintain any human dignity, to crawl out of bed and go to work, to hold one's head up among his peers, to actually believe there is dignity and worth in being a part of mankind, we realize that there has to be another formula for success. As Thoreau shows in context of one of his writings, the mass of men do not have to lead lives of quiet desperation. One does not need to read the Bible for very long to realize mankind is deeply flawed. When we finally reach the point where we are honest enough to recognize that we fail at every turn, there is a balance wherein we dangle and we are found wanting, only then can we realize there is something greater.

INTIMATE LOVE

Jesus. "Jesus loves me this I know for the Bible tells me so," says the old spiritual song. We may only think of futility in our failure and pain. "The Lord knows the thoughts of man; he knows that they are futile" (PSALM 94:11). But in our humanity, God delights, "The Lord your God is with you, he is mighty to save. He will take great delight in you, he will quiet you with his love, he will rejoice over you with singing" (ZEPHANIAH 3:17).

God made us in His image. "Then God said, 'Let us make man in our image, in our likeness, and let them rule over the fish of the sea and the birds of the air, over the livestock, over all the earth, and over all the creatures that move along the ground.' So God created man in his own image, in the image of God he created him; male and female he created them" . . . after finishing the creation of man, "God saw all that he had made, and it was very good" (GENESIS 1:26–31).

Humans are worth being loved by God and He has declared this to be the case. He loves us this we know. He has made us in His image, given us dignity and He finds us interesting. We offer something marvelous, unique, and extraordinary even to God. Therefore, He values us infinitely and with great interest and passion. Sometimes, we behave as if God owes us protection, deliverance, victory, marriage, etc. But He owes us nothing. We are here because He allows it. He brings us life. We owe Him everything. He owes us nothing. However, there are so many promises of God for health, healing, power, deliverance, success, wealth . . . that today we have what is called a "prosperity gospel." We sacrifice for God-He blesses us, like a formula. But this is not how God works. He works all things, good and bad, for our good to those who love Him. Satan desires to steal, kill, and destroy all the good that God has created. Satan is the father of lies and his endgame is to bring us to a place of cursing God. His goal is to make us curse God and become utterly useless and die. Our pain can blind us to all the good in God. We may never see God's goodness and we may question His very existence. Why does the course of our lives unfold as they do? What part does our choice play in the existence we enjoy? If we make real decisions in real time that result in real outcomes, there will be pain, failure, and suffering as well as accomplishments, victory, and success. How is it that God lets us be free moral agents and yet he controls all things and works all things together for our good?

We are dead in our sins and trespasses. Dead. Yet life is offered us in Jesus Christ. How can life be offered to a dead person? Choose! The people of Israel were given a challenge "then choose for yourselves this day whom you will serve" (JOSHUA 24:15B). The choosing was a pre-fall garden command. Do "not eat of the tree of the knowledge of good and evil, for in the day you eat you will die." (GENESIS 2:17). Death did not occur instantly, but it was in comparison to eternal time. The intervening time between life and death allowed for humanity to wrestle with evil, sin, and death in horrific measure. And in this intervening time, God seeks our willing "yes" to him like a suitor. As a suitor, He wants our relationship and intimacy, and the outcome is already known but not accomplished.

What's at play here? There is something in us that God wants to know. We have value and are worth love. All people are worthy of love. God wants to know us. The Holy Spirit blows where it will, and life is always available by the Holy Spirit's omnipresence. Therefore, through the Holy Spirit, God, touches all people, yet not everyone enters into this relationship. Is God ineffectual? Impossible, but is a man without real choice? Equally impossible. Another dimension of reality is in play. A dimension that is unseen and yet just as real as this reality. These actualities intersect infinitely, but not in totality, which is where both the regeneration of the human by the Holy Spirit comes into play and yet the reality of human autonomy exists. Two dimensions equally real, equally true, resulting in life. This is just like the reality of God being three persons, and yet one. Jesus was equally God and man; He was fully both.

In all of this, God's revealed plan is that He desires to have a love relationship with us. This relationship is one of mutual enjoyment and is prefigured in his relationship with the two other parts of the Trinity. God's greatest desire is to share his love with us. He also desires intimacy, which is why we pray and why prayer is so vital. The act of prayer brings the transcendence of God into the human experience. This action, praying, connects us to God in a supernatural connection. This is not something we have to beg for or implore, it happens when we pray. The transcendence of God enters our life and builds imminence all at once. We can recount His attributes and nature as an appreciation of gratitude or a statement of his character, but His transcendence is immediately available the moment we pray. This elevates our communication through prayer infinitely, and is therefore not just a function of duty, but a thrill and joy of hanging out with God, like a best friend or lover. We communicate with this person in a special relationship by prayer. Prayer is us talking, sharing, and being intimate with God. Group prayers are equivalent to a party where we include God, and it is one of great joy, satisfaction, and power. Parties usually bring a deeper level of pleasure and happiness, a party of piety.

LIVING FREE

Because of this fact that God loves us, He wants a relationship with us. He views life from a different dimensional perspective. He works in our lives, and He desires to redeem the ashes of our lives' brokenness. Processing life simply put; we trust Him. Then, His expectation is that we serve Him with our talents and gifts with all our hearts as an offering to Him, but the endgame may not be what we desire. We may label our life a failure, and we may experience pain and suffering. But the results do not substantiate, validate, or prove whether what we have been doing is what God created us to do. The results are not the issue, but rather, are we serving God? Are we seeking His glory and His joy? Are our eyes fixed upon Him? The failure we experience may reap tremendous spiritual benefits while crushing the participant. Phillip Yancey says, "Saints become saints by somehow hanging on to the stubborn conviction that things are not as they appear, and that the unseen world is as solid and trustworthy as the visible world around them. God deserves trust, even when it looks like the world is caving in."[2]

Yancey says we look around and life doesn't always make sense. We find ourselves in doubt, and doubt must be present for faith to exist. Faith flourishes in difficulties, confusion, and uncertainty. God often shows up in dramatic fashion but refuses to explain everything or bend our lives to go the way "we" think they should play out. This births faith.

Results and "success" do not determine the value and worth of a life. Accomplishments, accolades, herodom, notoriety, wealth do not equal a winning endgame! Results are not an "ends justify the means" mantra. Just because we "look" like "we are on top of the world-successful" does not mean the way we achieved the pinnacle was accomplished through a journey that brings us closer to God. This other dimension sees success differently. Success is an achievement accomplished through a journey that brings one closer to God. The process matters! Closeness to God matters more than winning! It is true that how we play the game, or how we go about living our lives . . . DOES matter. It matters to God!

Keller exclaims, "Remember this—if you don't live for Jesus you will live for something else. If you live for career and you don't do well it may punish you all of your life, and you will feel like a failure. If you live for your children and they don't turn out alright . . . you feel worthless as a person."[3]

Chris Watkins writes, when abandoning idols of this world, we are free. We are free because we have "a Lord who loves and serves his worshippers."[4] This is true freedom, a God who truly loves. What other master would operate on this basis? Because of this love, it is therefore not the event or the outcome of the event whereby we measure greatness, but the one for whom we toil. Did I please the creator of the universe? Did I bring joy to His heart? Was He pleased that it was my hope and goal to glorify Him? We may have had enough failures to last many lifetimes, but God can take failures and turn them inside out to reveal the knowledge of Him which is more brilliant than a million diamonds.

LIVING WITH A WHOLE HEART

The information in this chapter checks off all the boxes that the popular author and sociologist Brené Brown declares for being a wholehearted person. In her phraseology, she states we need to pursue wholehearted living. To find wholehearted living we must know we cannot generate our true worthiness by establishing our own worthiness, by parenting, involvement, admiration of peers, or personal strength. Personal worthiness must come from outside ourselves. It is found in unconditional love, our giftedness, and in being clean and restored.

These qualities will establish our worthiness, and I believe they are all accomplished in Jesus. We know God establishes our worthiness. We are worthy because of Him, otherwise King David could have been nothing but a scoundrel. It is God's perspective on events and His work in our lives that builds real life and a whole heart, not in what we accomplish.

Let's review what we know to this point:

1. Suffering, failure, pain, and sorrow are a part of life.

2. Another dimension exists.

3. This dimension factors in God.

4. God made us in His image.

5. Since God made us in His image, we have intrinsic incredible, indescribable worth. God loves us.

6. He desires a relationship with us. This includes vibrant prayer.

7. We can choose to be in a relationship with God or not. We can choose to love Him or not.

8. How we see life and what is important is different from how God sees life and what He considers important.

This information turns everything on its head. We can have hope in pain, peace in suffering, comfort in sorrow, joy in difficulties. Tim Keller says Paul, the apostle, asks us to accurately examine how God changes everything. We are to "reckon," ponder, count, "that our present sufferings are not worth comparing with the glory that will be revealed in us" (ROMANS 8:18). He says people may argue that this is doctrine and not very comforting. But Keller says, wait, is God really alive, now? Did he endure infinite suffering for you and me? Does He really promise to heal all our problems and illnesses? "If not-if none of these things are true-then we may be stuck here living for seventy or eighty years until we perish . . . and if some trouble or suffering takes that happiness away, you have lost it forever. Either Jesus is on the throne ruling all things for you or this is as good as it gets."[5] If our day-to-day life is as "good as it gets," then just be happy and win, baby!

But if God loves us, then winning is not all there is. We not only have peace and comfort, we have hope. Paul states,

"Therefore we do not lose heart. Though outwardly we are wasting away, yet inwardly we are being renewed day by day. For our light and momentary troubles are achieving for us an eternal glory that far outweighs them all. So we fix our eyes not on what is seen, but on what is unseen. For what is seen as temporary, but what is unseen is eternal" (2 CORINTHIANS 4:16-18).

Suffering suddenly takes on a different shade of color. Suddenly it is not all grays, blacks, and darkness. God takes suffering and transforms it, He provides restoration which we need to possess to know worthiness and embracing worthiness is essential.

"Yet it was the LORD's will to crush him and cause him to suffer, and though the LORD makes his life a guilt offering . . . After the suffering of his soul, he will see the light of life and be satisfied; by his knowledge my righteous servant will justify many, and he will bear their iniquities. Therefore, I will give him a portion among the great, and he will divide the spoils with the strong, because he poured out his life unto death, and was numbered with the transgressors. For he bore the sin of many and made intercession for the transgressors" (ISAIAH 53:10–12).

Isaiah refers to Jesus. God intervenes on our behalf through infinite personal sacrifice. He held nothing back and felt the full brunt of the suffering that we caused. He felt the pain that has been described earlier and in previous chapters, He feels the depth of loss, tragedy, and disappointment. All our failures caused by sin are removed in our relationship with God/Jesus. Our failures, disappointments and suffering regardless of origin are meant to cause us to look to things that are unseen for the unseen reality. These things are meant to change our perspective and the course of our life. "He [God] has also set eternity in the hearts of men; yet they cannot fathom what God has done from beginning to end . . . I know that everything God does will endure forever; nothing can be added to it and nothing taken away from it. God does it so that men will revere him" (ECCLESIASTES 3:11–14).

Our lives need an eternal perspective. This gives us a different viewpoint on suffering, failure, and disappointment. Instead of despair, we have hope. Instead of sadness, we have joy.

PURE JOY

"Consider it pure joy, my brothers when you face trials of many kinds, because you know that the testing of your faith develops perseverance. Perseverance must finish its work so that you may be mature and complete, not lacking anything" (JAMES 1:2).

"In this you greatly rejoice, though now for a little while you may have had to suffer grief in all kinds of trials. These have come so that your faith—of greater worth than gold, which perishes even though refined by fire—may be proved genuine and may result in praise, glory and honor when Jesus Christ is revealed" (1 PETER 1:6).

"Let us fix our eyes on Jesus, the author and perfector of our faith, who for the joy set before him endured the cross, scorning its shame, and sat down at the right hand of the throne of God" (HEBREWS 12:2).

These other world truths produce maturity, making us complete, and bring us joy. These qualities are things that trophies and winning can never produce. Dr. Paige Cunningham, past President of Taylor University once wrote:

"Don't confuse joy with happiness. Happiness is a fleeting emotional response to an external circumstance. Someone gave me a gift. The DTR went as I hoped. I aced the test. Those emotions can vanish in a moment. But joy is God-given, and it is a reality into which we as Christ's followers are called to live. Our trials threatened to undo us. *But God* offers a life of joy. God's word is filled with joy. In the English Standard Version of the Bible, the word 'joy' is referenced more than 200 times!

"Joy is grounded in our relationship with God, arises from a response to Him, and as a gift of the Holy Spirit. *While I know that the Lord is always with me* (PSALM 16:8), joy goes beyond that awareness. Joy can arise when we experience by faith the presence of God when we join in corporate praise and worship . . . Joy also grows in suffering. When we face trials, we count them as "pure joy" (JAMES 1:2) . . . I challenged our students to anticipate the joy that lies ahead: 'When you get on the other side of suffering—when you get on the other side of a terrible breakup with your boyfriend, the death of a parent, emerging from debt, or coping with the learning difference, you will have a treasure, something that you can share with others.' . . . May we each love the Lord with all of our heart, mind, and strength. And may we be filled with that joy that is inexpressible and can never be taken from us."[6]

Genuine joy arises out of the Lord and looking at things through His eyes. We are to mature our thinking in that we no longer fear suffering but embrace it as a boost to bring us to see reality and eternity in a different light. This light causes change.

THE MAKING OF MATURITY AND CHARACTER

"Not only so, but we also rejoice in our sufferings, because we know that suffering produces perseverance; perseverance, character; and character, hope. And hope does not disappoint us because God has poured out his love into our hearts by the Holy Spirit, whom he has given us" (ROMANS 5:3–5).

This is the place of character. Sports, discipline, winning, or education, does not forge character. It's born out of a relationship with God and by embracing Jesus. Jesus has provided the pathway for true character. Schools want to build character with no basis for it. Character must flow out of something. Character flows out of a relationship with God and His work in our suffering, loss, and struggles. Jesus produces character and maturity. He is the only one who has suffered on our behalf and can transform our suffering. Schools use a slogan, "character counts" but they cannot build it apart from an eternal perspective found in the Bible. To say "character counts" without a standard for character produces contradictions and impotence. Character must have a basis, and that basis is Jesus. He will produce it in our lives, and when he does, we will have real true character!

Open eyes, open minds, and open hearts require a different orientation. Clear thinking, quality of life, and a healthy perspective require a different life lens. Real love, real character, real life requires new values. How can we get to a place where "winning is not the only thing," and that God is not a vending machine built to meet our needs? How do we understand failure and suffering and awaken to loving God as the only thing? Tim Keller offers, "How can you get there? How can you move from loving God in a mercenary way toward loving God himself? I'm afraid the primary way is to have hardship come into your life . . . you could adjust and focus on him in a way you had never done before."[7] In the Book of Job where Job goes through horrific suffering, Satan looked to destroy Job. Satan wanted to prove Job did not love God. "God knew that Satan was ultimately wrong about Job. But he also knew that Satan was penultimately right . . . God was going to enable" Job to love God solely and deeply for who God is forming in Job a path "to attain that kind of greatness the only way it can be attained—through adversity and pain."[8]

"Shonda Rhimes . . . of 'Grey's Anatomy and Scandal,' . . . When asked about her role of struggle in storytelling, she said, 'I don't even know who a character is until I've seen how they handle adversity. On screen and off screen, that's how you know who someone is.'"[9]

Cynthia Cooper, during a Q & A at a lecture on Economics and Ethics at New Mexico State University, September 4, 2021, when asked how she knew she had to be the "whistleblower" against WorldCom, who had committed $3.8 billion in fraud, said, "When we reach a big crossroad, how we respond is a result of character forged decision by decision, brick by brick, over time."

The bricks are best built in the decisions over time recognizing that "nothing but God satisfies our most profound desires."[10] My sins, my failures, my inadequacies are all healed by the cross. My bitterness, anger, invisible failings are all emptied into Christ and His blood. His sacrifice has given me joy, made me whole, deeply worthy, deeply loved, deeply healed. I am not a zero. I am superabundantly loved, an infinitely blessed person growing in character and maturity. In short, there is real, true, honest, hope.

ENDNOTES: CHAPTER 24

1. Douglas K. Erlandson," Are You a Success?", *Confident Living Magazine*, April 1991, 28.

2. Phillip Yancey, *Disappointment with God*, Zondervan, 1988, 244.

3. Timothy Keller, *The Reason for God: Belief in an Age of Skepticism*, Dutton, 2008, 172.

4. Christopher Watkins, *Biblical Critical Theory*, Zondervan Academic, 2022, 312.

5. Timothy Keller, *Walking With God Through Pain and Suffering*, Dutton, 2013, 299.

6. Dr. Cunningham, P. C., "Letter from the President" [editorial]. *Taylor University Alumni Magazine*, Spring 2021, volume 121.

7. Timothy Keller, *Walking With God Through Pain and Suffering*, Dutton, 2013, 274.

8. Timothy Keller, *Walking With God Through Pain and Suffering*, Dutton, 2013, 275.

9. Brené Brown, *Rising Strong: How the Ability to Reset Transforms the Way We Live, Love, Parent, and Lead*, Spiegel & Grau, 2015, 42.

10. Larry Crabb, *Shattered Dreams: God's Unexpected Path to Joy*, WaterBrook, 2001, 72.

CHAPTER 25

LOOKING FOR HEROES: MUST HAVE CHESTS

HOW DOES BEING DEEPLY LOVED AND WORTHY, filled with hope, and profoundly blessed translate into success? What is the recipe for a true hero, G.O.A.T., and "The Best?" How can the idea of heroic be explored? Money does not make a hero. In fact, to make an obscene amount of money and lose it could make someone a villain, anti-hero, or scoundrel. To be blessed with millions of dollars, and squander a fortune is something that usually births disdain and disappointment. Even if one wins an indescribable number of games, wins championships, sets records, and is a Hall of Famer, squandering resources historically has been shameful in the eyes of the public. Naturally, with great wealth and privilege comes great responsibility and when that responsibility is marginalized then there are usually consequences.

Webster's New World Dictionary provides five definitions for hero, only numbers three and five apply to this writing. "#3. Any person, esp. a man, admired for qualities or achievements and regarded as an ideal or model." And #5. "The central figure in any important event or period, honored for outstanding qualities."[1]

Only definition five can be used for the athlete consistently. Definition three could be used if the person is viewed by most people as someone who is an outstanding model or ideal. This person would typically be referred to as a role model. However, most athletes today do not want to be considered role models and Charles Barkley famously stated, years ago, "I am not a role model." Many athletes apparently agree they are not seeking role-model status. An infamous recent non-role model incident occurred at a strip club March 4, 2023, around 5:00 a.m. where Ja Morant of the Memphis Grizzlies was suspended for waving a gun around with his shirt off. It is common for professional athletes to attend strip clubs, apparently that is not problematic. The issue is that he waved a gun, and this was not his first offense. Unfortunately, many famous athletes are not role models and there is plenty of material supporting this thesis. A strip club is ripe with non-heroes and finding athletes at a strip club is common. Researching this sadness of heroes and strip clubs, (If a person can stomach researching it.) one source called "TheSportster" compiled a list of the "Top 15 Athletes Who LOVE Strip Clubs Way Too Much." The "winners" or the top 15 were household names, many recognizable to most anyone.[2]

One does not have to look far to find infamous role models. It is obvious that real role models or heroes are few in all walks of life regardless of era. Wilt Chamberlin, one of the NBA's greatest basketball players famously bragged that he had slept with about 20,000 women.

Pete Rose, one of the all-time best baseball players in history, owner of the all-time hit record, breaking Ty Cobb's record on September 11, 1985, was banned from baseball for life for gambling and associating with drug traffickers. He received a prison sentence for filing false income tax returns. However, his ego stayed intact as he frequently sells memorabilia and autographs.

News articles are plentiful that expose athletes who can find multiple ways to get into trouble.

The lack of role models goes far beyond the playing field, Chuck Colson, a political leader during the Watergate Scandal, writes about malfeasance stating the FBI implicated Richard Miller as a spy, indicted Sharon

Scranage of the CIA on eighteen counts of espionage and revealed that FBI and West Point graduate Wayne Gillespie sold weapons to Iran. Colson bemoans that the traditional values disappeared and were replaced by, is it good for me? Colson writes, "C.S. Lewis did not live to see the America of the 80s . . . when he argued in 1943 that mere knowledge of right and wrong is powerless against man's appetites. Reason must rule the appetites by means of the "spirited element" . . . the essential connecting link—to the chest."[3] Colson argues that without the spiritual element we will have no honor, courage, or virtue. We will ask men to have chests or behave admirably without their possessing the foundational anatomy.

C.S. Lewis saw it in 1943, Chuck Colson saw it coming in 1985. Do we see it is here now, today?

Today, sports betting is legal to the public and is advertised on all major sport outlets. Fraternizing with drug dealers is fashionable and popularized by numerous TV shows, the biggest recent hit being "Breaking Bad." Music, generally as seen on MTV and VH1, glorifies sex and drugs so frequently that examples would be a nano-sampling not worth placing in print. And strip clubs are now a staple in American culture and are featured in many movies with the obligatory scene set at such club. Even "family-friendly" movies, like *The Proposal*,"[4] feature nudity and a male stripper.

Christopher Watkins states:

> "To live and die by the dynamics of 'making a name for ourselves' is to submit to a court of a public opinion which only allows certain achievements to count, and it is to give a warped view of life in which value is ascribed to our words and deeds according to the fickle tastes of the crowd. God's judgment, by contrast, cuts across these perverse and changeable hierarchies of importance, 'for the Lord sees not as man sees: man looks on the outward

appearance, but the Lord looks on the heart' (1 SAMUEL 16:7 ESV). There are no meaningless actions, meaningless words, or meaningless thoughts, for our witness is also our judge.

"Whatever you do, work heartily, as for the Lord and not for men, knowing that from the Lord you will receive the inheritance as your reward. You are serving the Lord Christ" (COLOSSIANS 3:23–24). We all tend to erect a hierarchy of significance among our actions, placing certain deeds at the top (getting that promotion or visiting a sick friend in hospital) and relegating others to also—ran status (praying the prayer no one will ever thank you for or sweeping the floor). Whoever made the front page of the newspaper by caring for an elderly relative or bringing up a normal child in a normal way? I have often wondered whether the front-page splash on heavens broadsheet, so to speak, will be the anonymous elderly lady who, perhaps unbeknownst to her church friends, persisted for years in private prayer for God's world, never having preached a sermon, never mind led a revival. She is the unspectacular spectacle of God's glory."[5]

The anonymous elderly prayer warrior is a real hero found. But in our culture, people laugh, mock, ridicule, and degrade those who define heroes in this way. God doesn't exist! So, how could we define heroes according to His standard? "The theme of mediating our identity through displays of greatness perhaps characterizes our age more than any other."[6]

A true hero from a bygone era was Eric Liddell. Eric Liddell's decision not to run on Sunday, being given an opportunity to run a different race and winning the gold medal in that 400-meter race, was portrayed in the movie "*Chariots of Fire.*" This movie pointed to a man who lived by standards and values derived outside himself.[7] Liddell later became a missionary to China where stories of heroism abounded. One such story recounts him rescuing a wounded man despite the risk to his own life. If during the rescue attempt, he had been caught by the Japanese, he would have certainly been punished severely. However, he found a man who helped him load a wounded man into a cart for rescue. As they were leaving, Eric Liddell heard of another man who was to be decapitated, but the executioner had missed, and this man had fallen severely injured and left for dead. Eric Liddell and the cart owner rescued this man too. They traveled eighteen miles to get these men medical help, using an old wooden cart. This action and others led to wonderful outcomes. Some years later, Eric Liddell died in an internment in Weihsien, Shantung, North China before World II ended. Eric Liddell was truly a man with a chest.

Another man with a chest was Gary Bradds; he was one of our assistant coaches while I was in high school, and several years later he passed away. He was an outstanding basketball player who was an All-American at Ohio State University and later played professionally for the ABA Champions Oakland Oaks. A letter to the editor praising Gary Bradds after his death at the age of forty concluded with the praise, "He told us that the only two things more important than basketball during the season were God and our families . . . Long after we forget about squaring up to the basket, cutting off the baseline, or boxing out under the boards, his daily lessons in living will be making us better human beings."[8]

Another person cut from heroic cloth was Earlie Thomas. He was an NFL player not defined by being an NFL player for the New York Jets and Denver Broncos. Instead, he spent his free time studying bugs. He eventually earned a doctorate degree in entomology at Colorado State and wrote his doctoral thesis on a species of parasitic wasps. Thomas would study feverishly in his lab, then go to football practice, and then continue studying sometimes until midnight. His goal was to specialize in agriculture or medical entomology. Thomas was a man not defined by stereotypes; he worked hard to make the world a better place through diligent research and study.

Dave Hartsock, a skydiving instructor demonstrated heroic resolve, when his parachute did not open properly on a tandem jump with a client. As he fought to stop their fall, thinking of his responsibility to Shirley Dygert, his client, he had her thrust her legs upward as he pulled on the straps, causing the two of them to invert, ultimately saving Shirley's life. The cost for saving Shirley's life was Dave lives as a quadriplegic. Heroism with a price, heroism always has a price.

As Christopher Watkins stated, today heroes are people who display their own greatness. The four men mentioned in this chapter followed different paths, providing substantive leadership. Today, heroes are the winners, the wealthy, the opulent and famous, the celebrities. We are told who the heroes are, and we are told how they qualify to be heroes. Heroes are who and what we are told they should be. An influencer with two million followers makes someone, well, an influencer! They get rich. It does not matter how they influence, what they influence, or who they influence, just get "greatness." Be noticed! Get rich! The end justifies the means. They are influential; therefore, they are a "hero."

The new "hero" machine started its engine when the NCAA passed a rule which affords athletes the opportunity to profit at the college level using one's name, image, and likeness. Today, it is referred to as the NIL rule. There is a formula for funding of the NIL, but at the end of the day, athletes can make money using their "star power." This creates wealthy college players playing alongside athletes who "only" receive a scholarship. And other athletes, who walk on with the hope of earning a college scholarship. Even high school athletes have cashed in on the NIL sweepstakes. Sean Labar writes in "Outkick" how young people can profit from NIL. "LeBron James's son, Bronny James . . . has 12.4 million social media followers [earning] . . . $7.5 million, followed by Mikey Williams . . . who has six million social media followers earns

$3.6 million . . . Oliva Dunn, a gymnast from Louisiana State University . . . 9.3 million social media followers and earns $2.7 million."[9] She is a good gymnast, but her appeal is in the marketing of her pleasant appearance. Image has afforded all three of these young people wealth, fame, and influence . . . whether merited or not. These young people are representatives of a whole class of modern young people earning large sums of money using their Name, Image, and Likeness (NIL). Today, does anyone separate themselves by quality of personhood. NIL is all about the external appeal and the media image created.

Frank DeFord lamented years ago, "Does anyone in sports stand above the crowd? Not likely . . . You can't become a hero the same way you can become a Dallas Maverick . . . merely by putting on a new uniform . . . the status of hero in the past represented something more than just themselves."[10]

NIL is shallow. And its hero status quickly fleeting. Professional sport figures must prove they are heroes by winning the grand prize, not just their conference crown, or a playoff game; sport figures are gods by winning "The Championship"! Just like the NIL stars "the ends justify the means." It doesn't matter how they win the ultimate prize, just get it done. The NIL aggrandizes achievements and ability and show a little skin; professionals' step on someone's chest, humiliate a rival by stepping over them, desecrate the work of a lifelong athlete by uttering disrespectful epithets, stare down the opponent after a home run, stare down a player after a powerful dunk, yell at an opposing team's bench, bite, kick, and punch one's way to the top. "I am not a role model" anyway, I am a hero, I am the central figure in THIS contest, look at my "greatness." It is obvious we need "men with chests."

ENDNOTES: CHAPTER 25

1. Victoria Neufeldt and David B. Guralnik, editors. *Webster's New World Dictionary of American English, Third College Edition,* Prentice Hall, 1991.

2. TS Staff, *Top 15 Athletes Who LOVE Strip Clubs Way Too Much,* TheSportster (August 15, 2015)
   https://www.thesportster.com/
   search/?q=Top+15+Athletes+Who+LOVE+Strip+Clubs+Way+Too+Much

3. Chuck Colson, "Men without Chests," *Christianity Today,* November 22, 1985, 72.

4. Anne Fletcher, director. *The Proposal.* Touchstone Pictures, 2009.

5. Christopher Watkins, *Biblical Critical Theory,* Zondervan Academic, 2022,218.

6. Christopher Watkins, *Biblical Critical Theory,* Zondervan Academic, 2022,214.

7. Hugh Hudson, director. *Chariots of Fire.* Allied Stars Ltd. and Enigma Productions, 1981.

8. From an anonymous former basketball player, Letter to the Editor, *Springfield News-Sun,* August 4, 1983, 15.

9. Sean Labar, "Top 10 NIL Earners Include Bryce Young, Olivia Dunne And Three High School Ballers Making Absurd Money." Outkick, January 6, 2023. Outkick. com/sports/top-10-nil-earners-include-bryce-young-olvia-dunne-and-three-high-school-ballers-making-absurd-money.

10. Frank Deford, "No Longer a Cozy Corner," *Sports Illustrated,* December 23, 1985, 44–61.

Part Four

Chapters 26–31

So What?
Applications
&
Common-Sense Ideas

CHAPTER 26

PARENTS THINK!

N THE *WASHINGTON POST* ARTICLE "OVERZEALOUS parents are ruining youth sports. It's past time to sit quiet and let the kids play." Randi Mazzella wisely makes three important points:

1. "Youth sports are a different game than what many adults experienced as children.

2. Today, youth sports are a $15 billion industry.

3. 'Initially, the focus of youth sports was developmental. But now there is an overemphasis on competition and winning.'"[1]

And if the truth were known, too many parents have professional expectations, including a Brinks truck full of money. As a result, many parents also seem to confuse youth sports with professional sports. This creates a fantasy for parents who pretend or visualize this moment in time as a "professional sport" and it will produce professional benefits now or very soon. This challenge has been magnified by the new NCAA NIL ruling, where riches can appear much sooner than ever before, dwarfing the college scholarship.

Parents hire professional coaches and trainers to "work" with their child. They send their children to games, camps, and tournaments all over the country at an incredible cost. Many parents seek a competitive edge and place their children on teams where they can gain that competitive edge or playing advantage. Their competitive aggression can turn into hateful and hurtful insanity toward anyone who stands in their way. The professional coaches and trainers that are hired to work with children may or may not be outstanding, but one thing they know, the child better want to attend their training, and the child better like them. So, paid for hire coaches and trainers are in the big business of building athletes' skills, egos, and making money. Of course, they are going to butter up the child and his parents, they need proteges and proteges means money. So, the little baller is going to be the greatest, he has loads of potential, and let's take him to the $2,000 tournament in Las Vegas. The coach and trainer need that child to return for the next lesson; a man's got to make a living. And Vegas is fun!

Kelly Treleaven says, 2023 is a whole different ball game and it can be hard to pin down the myriad of reasons why. She blogged her ideas concerning the difficulties associated with coaching, utilizing an email from a parent to a coach. She notes:

- "People on the sidelines think they're the expert . . . observing something endows them with the ability, permission, and expertise to critique it. Clearly . . . being a fan . . . has bestowed upon them coach-level knowledge. You know, the same way that watching *Grey's Anatomy* makes you a surgeon.

- Their perception is reality."[2]

No longer should parents be referred to as "helicopter parents" or even "lawn mower parents." They are "bomb parents." An example of "bomb parents" was seen in a commercial for a phone carrier. The commercial shows several young boys preparing to run a dash. The mother is filming the race on her phone and runs adjacent to her son as he runs his hardest to the finish line. The whole time she is filming the child, she is knocking everyone out of her way to capture this moment on her phone video. "Bomb" parents will destroy everything or anyone to see that their child gets the position he or she deserves. These parents will do anything to get what they want.

This type of behavior happens all too frequently, a recent headline provides another example of "bomb" parents, "Umpires walk off field, quit after little league parents, players threaten them" Taunton, Massachusetts. (WBZ). Paul Nadeau the umpire behind home plate said parents were threatening to meet them in the parking lot, "As soon as we got off the field, we started to be confronted and accosted by numerous parents continuing to yell at us and get in our faces." The parents allowed their children "to yell at us and say we suck . . . They won't officiate another game, and now, the league has no umpires."[3]

This behavior is not limited to one section of the country. It is everywhere. This could be the headline in any town in America. "Two coaches punished, another sent to the hospital after brawl at youth football game," "Parents, players and coaches punched, choked and hurled helmets at each other for about three minutes until the affray subsided . . . while the fight might have started between children, witnesses and authorities said that adults took it to a new level."[4]

Parents can lose perspective and get completely carried away. The following is an example of a text which was sent to me after a game.

"I have held my tongue the majority of this season. 'Adam' had never received so many technical fouls in his whole basketball career. This come from much frustrating with lack of coaching, lack of plays, and horrible substitutions. I will be talking to athlete about quitting this team as his skill level n confidence is only decreasing! Failure for you to resign as a coach who is not helping those boys in any way should do the right thing n resign your position!"

This text was followed by three more texts every half hour, all equally charged with anger and emotion. This example is a torrent of texts poured in from one parent after one game, without any comments between. This parent poured out emotional commentary in rapid text fashion, without stepping back and thinking. The anger and vitriol are seen in the misplaced words, misspelled words, and poorly thought-out ideas.

Emotional barrages were sent throughout the season by a variety of parents, but sadly many were so much worse that they would not be appropriate to print. Texts, negative comments, haranguing from the stands was common behavior from parents. Parents frequently yelled who to substitute, plays to run, who should finish the game, along with derogatory put downs to coaches and players. Sadly, this is common behavior across sport venues in America. Coaches are frequently yelled at, receive threats, ugly comments, emails, and texts. Why do parents behave so irrationally? Bissinger writes, "The people in the stands lost all sight of who they were and what they were supposed to be like, all dignity and restraint thrown aside . . . their boys, their heroes, upon whom they rested all their vicarious thrills, all their dreams"[5] was their sole focus.

Parents jockey for advantage for their son or daughter, some have gone so far as to purchase "DNA test kits to help moms and dads choose the perfect athletic careers for their children. 'It's disturbing,' says Dave Czesniuk, the director of operations at Northeastern University's Sport and Society center. 'It plays into the [obsession] some parents have with accessing a pot of gold—a college scholarship or pro contract—through their children.'"[6]

What is the underlying motivation? The endgame goal for parents is:

- They want more playing time for their child; "look at my girl."

- Hero status. They want everyone to see that "their child is special."

- It must be recognized that my child is outstanding and the recipient of due accolades.

- The child and the parent need validation they are worthy human beings.

- They want their child to get a sport scholarship and/or megabucks. This will produce validation for both athlete and parent as being better than others.

They have bought the mantra mentioned in our local newspaper last fall, by two of our four big school football coaches, "You are what your record says you are."

They do not want to win. They have to win!

Parents need to examine their core values just like athletes. We all operate from core values that have been formed over a lifetime. Everyone has a philosophical starting point. Parents need to determine if their philosophical starting point is healthy and creating wholeness in their life. Parents should think and not just jump into a cultural river which flows downstream trumpeting all things sport. Think through ultimate values. Why is this activity important? What do we want to see accomplished? Is this a good fit for their child? Can the child handle the rigors of the sport? Can the child handle the discipline of the activity? Is it a "worthy endeavor?

Healthy guidelines will improve parents' judgment on all things related to their children's involvement in sports. As a parent, being willing to be wrong is huge. Maybe our child isn't the next coming of "generational player X." A parent's willingness to learn and consider their motivation is critical. Parents may need to ask, "Am I a good parent or am I blowing up everything around me and my child?" One must ask oneself the hard questions. What is the price for success? What are the parental and moral compromises that are acceptable based on one's values and beliefs. Parents need perspective, and they must examine their own choices. Where are the core values found? What constitutes success?

Parental behavior often goes off the rails. When winning must happen, careers are destroyed, parental "bombing" occurs, referees are harassed, unnecessary DNA testing is used, youth training is embraced, $15 billion a year is spent to achieve and win. And of course, the pressure to win distorts the judgment of organizations, schools, and universities. The resulting tragic consequences are seen in our youth, who following the adults' lead, lose their way with no means of extracting themselves from the confusion. This confusion is found at all levels. A popular phrase credited to Theodore Roosevelt, could easily be stated in relationship to training the successful athlete "To educate a person in the mind but not in morals is to educate a menace to society."

ENDNOTES: CHAPTER 26

1. Randi Mazzella, "Overzealous Parents Are Ruining Youth Sports. It's Past Time to Sit Suiet and Let the Kids Pvlay." Washingtonpost.com, March 2, 2020, NA. Gale OneFile: New (accessed August 23, 2024). https://link.gale.com/apps/doc/A616025546/STND?u=nm_a_nmlascr&sid=bookmark-STND&xid=bd6bf321.

2. Kelly Treleaven, "This Email to a High School Softball Coach Pretty Much Sums Up Teaching in 2023. And Honestly, It's More Respectful Than a Lot of What Teachers and Coaches Get." We Are Teachers, April 12, 2023. www.weareteachers.com/high-school-softball-coach-email/

3. CNN Newsource. Mike Sullivan "Umpires Walk Off Field, Quit After Little League Parents, Players Threaten Them," *WBZ-TV Boston*, June 9, 2023.

4. Justin Garcia, "Two Coaches Punished, Another Sent to the Hospital After Brawl at Youth Football Game," *Las Cruces Sun-News*, November 15, 2021, 1B.

5. H.G. Bissinger, *Friday Night Lights*, Boston: Addison-Wesley, 1990, 14–15.

6. Selena Roberts, "Gift Ideas for the Meddling Parent," *Sports Illustrated*, December 15, 2008, 76.

CHAPTER 27

THE EDUCATION SPORTS MILIEU— WHAT DIRECTION?

JOHN FEINSTEIN DECLARED IN HIS BOOK *The Last Amateurs* that amateur athletes were apparently gone. The subtitle was *"Playing for Glory and Honor in Division I College Basketball."* If the last amateurs were gone in 2000 and if they played for glory and honor, then there are no more amateurs and there may be no one playing for glory and honor. Today, is anyone playing for honor?

Youth and high school sports chronicle the tragic results that crescendo in the degradation of college and professional sports. If the university must win, and today let it be clear they must, then graft and money are the rulers of the college kingdom. Money has long been the ruler, but we have tried to convince ourselves, since college athletes were not being paid, that there were still young people playing for the love of the game. But our naivety should have long since been burned away by the scorching sun of money and winning. Revealing bare empty hands declaring the truth, we play to win and enjoy its benefits.

The University of Alabama, during the NCAA basketball tournament in 2023, lost their way as depicted in this article by Nancy Armour: "San Diego State does the whole country a solid by ousting Nate Oats, Alabama," "If Oats and Alabama athletic director Greg Byrne had even the slightest shred of conscience or integrity, they'd have shut the program down two months ago, when at least three players were present during a shooting that left a young woman dead." Armour, with great passion, argues that it is a moral failing on the part of the University of Alabama and college athletics when they put winning above someone's life. She believes that Brandon Miller was in the midst of a murder and losing playing privileges was a minimum consequence and she argued the university and Coach Oats failed in their leadership.[1]

This character lapse cost Brandon Miller little, as he became wildly rich as the second pick in the 2023 NBA draft. This is one example, and there are hundreds, where character and honor matter little, but glory and money are the pinnacle endgame of sport.

A parallel situation which made national news in 2023, occurred at New Mexico State University, where during a football game, fans which included some NMSU basketball players, fought with fans from the University of New Mexico. Consequences were minimal and the University of New Mexico students decided to mete out their view of justice. A couple of months later at 3:00 a.m., a more serious fight broke out where a NMSU basketball player was shot and returning fire killed a rival from UNM in the altercation.

During this same time period, unbeknownst to the public, NMSU basketball players were hazing younger athletes on the team. It was later learned that several basketball players had been sexually harassing and abusing a player or players during the season. The University demonstrated a breakdown of discipline throughout the entire basketball program, resulting in the eventual firing of the head coach and shuttering of the basketball season.

In July 2023, Northwestern University fired the head football coach for a continuing lack of oversight into hazing that had been a part of the football culture for at least a decade. Hazing was not dealt with for years and the coach failed to demonstrate healthy leadership. Northwestern University sports programs were toxic and sick. It was revealed that the baseball and softball teams were also infected with hazing and the baseball coach was fired as well. Northwestern University sport's program is in deep trouble and yet it continues forward with only mild slaps on the wrist.

These are just three examples of institutions and people being willing to bend rules, look the other way, and rationalize criminal behavior. Problems and examples like this could seemingly be written about endlessly. Simply put, we have lost our way and distorted our values. Or worse yet, we have no values, honor, or real glory.

But people will do anything to win, they will destroy everything in their path. To win. The out-of-kelter emphasis and perspective starts in youth leagues and ends up in college atrocities with people wringing their hands wondering, what happened? College sports are now professional sports. The transfer portal and monies offered to athletes have made a mockery of the student athlete. There are athletes pursuing a career in professional sports any way they can make it. A college degree is so devalued as to be almost laughable in the modern sports world. College sports are now professional sports.

"Professional sport is for-profit business. It is entertainment marketed to fans . . . winning the title is the only satisfier . . . parents and coaches benefit when they recognize the difference between what goes on in the professional arena and what should be going on" in youth sports from high school to the children playing soccer, baseball, and other sports all across our country.[2]

Education is "caught," often more by example than by what is taught. Therefore, in the educational milieu the leaders and especially the parents need to build a healthy philosophy of sport. Parents and educators need perspective; they need a moral high ground. Parents and educators need to embrace values, which can be found in *The Bible*. A statement like this may sound old-fashioned or archaic, but where else do we look for healthy direction? Values are not born out of a vacuum. Does directional character grow from media, politics, opinion polls, or education? All venues without a framework for right and wrong or philosophical underpinnings are vacuous. It is time to be honest and admit we have been adrift culturally, and without a biblical perspective, we do not have a reason for why we do things. So, with no reason, "dog eat dog" "winning at all costs" becomes the default position in sports and life. I am what matters. My kid is what I value. What I believe is right and there is not a standard beyond my opinion. Autonomy has become the quintessential "good" and I behave as god.

Leaders of sports and parents should reach for greater understanding and build a perspective beyond a cultural definition, or "I" as the start point. Life cannot be based exclusively on results or performance. "The performance narrative is prominent in contemporary life, shaping our attitudes to almost everything and creating divisions between those who are justified (considered in the right or to have 'made it') because they meet a certain threshold of performance and those who are condemned for falling short of it."[3] Outcomes cannot define life. Perspective is critical.

All leaders, especially educational and parental, need to see the differences between youth sports, college, and professional. When educators and parents think deeply, forge a road that may be less traveled, and evaluate living life with open eyes, they can grow. Wisdom is found by investigating sports in the light of Jesus, who provides "true north." Without a "true north," everyone will just do as he or she pleases. Let's just win! Anarchy anyone?

ENDNOTES: CHAPTER 27

1. Nancy Armour, "San Diego State Does the Whole Country a Solid by Ousting Nate Oats, Alabama." USA Today, March 25, 2023. usatoday.com/story/sports/columnist/nancy-armour/2023/03/25/alabama-nate-oats-out-ncaa-tournament-thank-you-sdsu/11540433002/.

2. Reggie Marra, *The Quality of Effort: Integrity in Sport and Life for Student-Athletes, Parents and Coaches*, From the Heart Press, 2013, 43–44.

3. Christopher Watkins, *Biblical Critical Theory*, Zondervan Academic, 2022, 412.

CHAPTER 28

COACHING 101

THE FOLLOWING IDEAS ARE BORN OUT OF MY LIFE in sport, as both participant and coach. It is primarily a brief first-person account of my thoughts regarding coaching. I did not choose coaching because it was easy, but because of the challenges and the way it enabled me to grow. Here are some of my life lessons. I start with seven general coaching principles, followed by keys to motivate, the place of "Grit," balance, and knowing when to quit.

SEVEN LESSONS

In my first year of high school coaching, due to the rapid improvement of our team, I was selected "Coach of the Year." This was quite an honor and in our second season we missed defeating the eventual state champs by one point, two successful years. In the third year, we missed the playoffs in two playoff opportunities by one basket in each game. In our fourth season, we had to rebuild, and I was not rehired. I was the victim of a political coup. But over those first four years, the wins were easier than they should have been, and my ego became inflated. I went on to coach at a small college and we enjoyed outstanding success. However, I should have realized the trap door of early success. It can lead to pride and a sense that one has the "it" factor. Early success can swallow up normal cautionary flags and foster a belief that "I am really special." Athletes and coaches who are good begin to think that they are above the rules and deserve privileged treatment. The rules apply to others, not me. The attitude of entitlement is easy to contract. **Lesson One: A person can be too good too soon. Be humble.**

If a person coaches for very many years, the chances are very high that they will be fired or run off by angry parents. Parents blame coaches and push school boards around. They also push administrators around who want to keep their jobs; coaches are disposable. **Lesson Two: Firings are common. Learn perspective. Be resilient.**

A coach or athlete may lose, they are not a loser. A coach or athlete may fail, they are not a failure. An outcome does not define a person. A person lost a game and a person failed to reach their goals. **Lesson Three: People are not defined as failures or losers; an outcome may result in loss or failure.**

Enjoy activities and foster activities outside of coaching. Coaching is a black hole and can swallow all of one's time, energy, and thoughts. **Lesson Four: Passionately protect balance.**

Success, fame, riches are fleeting; they can sprout wings and fly away. A friend of mine, an assistant Division One coach, in the midst of a stellar season, used to blow into his hand and say it could all disappear as quick as dust is blown from one's hand. Gone in an instant. **Lesson Five: Hold things loosely and don't take oneself too seriously.**

When we are young, we are constantly asked, "What do you want to do when you grow up?" We have the question wrong. It should be, "Who are you becoming as you grow up? **Lesson Six: Life is a journey. Seek values of substance.**

Jesus is important; get acquainted; go to a good church. **Lesson Seven: Eternity matters more than what is seen.**

MOTIVATION

The issue of motivating athletes is extremely important. Some general principles for improving communication in athletics and enhancing motivation in all arenas of life are listed below. These ideas were rigorously compiled during graduate school. The results included outstanding principles, but the biggest and best motivator was left out of the discussion. (What was left out?)

- Create curiosity and ask for attention.

- Establish points of contact, observe the needs of the listeners, and ask questions.

- Set a challenge, express a reason for the importance of the objective.

- Be enthusiastic and use illustrations.

- Review.

What was left out of this motivational list? There is one motivational ingredient more important than all other principles combined. Love. Love is the strongest motivator known to man, it is greater than all other techniques. It is greater than abilities, greater than education or positive thinking, even greater than sacrifice. Love is the most powerful and profound motivator available. Love toward athletes should be offered even in the face of poor performance or loss, especially in the face of poor performance or loss. This information is well-discussed in the Bible in the book of 1 Corinthians 13:1–13.

GRIT

Besides motivation one could ask at this juncture, "What place is Grit?" And do its tenants carry any weight? Grit is the combination of passion, persistence, and consistent effort over a very long time. It has been said in articles about Grit that it is not directly correlated with intelligence, but it can be a more powerful factor in determining success, than intelligence alone.

Dr. Angela Duckworth says Grit is more important than talent. Grit embodies consistent effort over time akin to a marathon, not a sprint. Grit has powerful passion, a commitment to something, focus, and tolerating and learning from setbacks. She teaches that a growth mindset sees failure not as terminal; failure is OK. These broad headings were born out of twenty-four character-building blocks, with the top seven being: zest, grit, self-control, social intelligence, gratitude, optimism, and curiosity.

The basic building blocks of Grit overlap with other researchers and experts, who teach methods to improve one's abilities when developing skills in sport or other activities. Many select expert testimonials found in the Harvard Business Review titled *On Mental Toughness* suggest singular focus, setting benchmarks, analysis of success and failures for each activity, brutally honest feedback, and celebrate victories without over doing it. Bonus advice in the HBR advocates to stay curious, be passionate and don't dwell on failure, dust off and move on. Finally, there is tremendous value in lifelong learning.

But coaching is not all about motivation, Grit, and the objectives of mental toughness.

BALANCE

Coaches and athletes need balance. We need to know when to hold'em, fold'em, walk away, and when to quit. Too many coaches and athletes think that if one hour of training is good, two is better, if two hours is good, four is better, and if we lose, keep increasing the work. But working harder is not always the answer. We discussed this in Chapter 5. Balance is critical to both coaching and athletic success. When do we stop? When do we rest? God created the heavens and the Earth in six days and on the seventh day God rested. Was God tired, worn out, exhausted? No, He knew we needed to rest, recalibrate, and worship. He gave us an example. We need to know six days of turning the hamster wheel is enough. He wants us to rest and worship. Sometimes we need to step back and evaluate, walk away from the game and gain perspective. In my opinion, when Michael Jordan transitioned from basketball to baseball, it served as a pivotal moment of recalibration and rejuvenation that remarkably propelled him to win three more championships and achieve greatness.

During my own coaching career, we had a team that was completely drained both physically and mentally; at practice we shot a few shots and then went to Dairy Queen. The next day, we played with rockets on our feet. A stop can be a turning point. When we are grinding it out, up close and personal, "we miss the forest for the trees." At points, stepping back, resting, and thinking is life giving.

HAMSTER WHEEL DISENGAGED

Sometimes we must cease entirely, a challenging feat in sports and one that should be infrequent. Nevertheless, there are moments when halting and allowing the "hamster wheel" to come to a natural end is imperative. A step back can reinvigorate, recalibrate, refocus, and redirect.

If one is quitting, the most difficult piece is knowing when. This is made harder by thousands of voices crying out, "Never give up." But there are times when it is time to give up. There are times when giving up is brilliant. We quit and look for a new direction and kindle an alternate path. No one can ever finish every journey on this planet and say they have done everything possible. This is the nature of life. There is no finish line. Sometimes, we just need to quit. Sometimes we need to learn when to give up and stop, this can be a win. Our daily lives are not all about winning. "Success is an event. Success is the path of unfinished business, always incomplete, never the end. Mastery is a constant pursuit."[1]

It is easier to pursue than to stop or quit. If one doubts this, look at the number of sports legends who held on for one, two, or three seasons too long. Even Michael Jordan, the subject of an interesting documentary, *The Last Dance* only talks of the glory years. It does not mention his last three pedestrian years playing for the Washington Wizards. Knowing when to quit is important. The reality of injury, sickness, or aging can force us to stop, thus opening the door to different directions or new horizons. Our journeys will inevitably face setbacks and challenges. Our journeys may weigh us down. There will unquestionably be triumphs and success, but in the end, we all find that life comes to an end. Sadly, everyone will "quit."

ENDNOTES: CHAPTER 28

1. Sarah Lewis, "Embrace the Near Win," filmed March 2014, TED video, 11:27, https://www.ted.com/talks/sarah_lewis_embrace_the_near_win/transcript?subtitle=en

CHAPTER 29

WINNING FOUNDATIONS

WISDOM POINTS OUT THAT THERE ARE certain components essential for developing an exceptional athlete. Important key qualities lay the foundation and create the possibility of being successful or winning. A foundation is not needed to lose. A friend said to me, "One does not have to practice or expend energy to lose." Before a person pursues "the win" one must have some prerequisites: God-given gifts, resiliency, and character. These are foundational infrastructures necessary to build an outstanding athlete. Here are eight additional prerequisites necessary for a person who seeks achievement as a top performer. And even possessing all eight qualities, the chances of becoming a professional athlete are minuscule.

1. **Interest and Love:** Without a strong passionate connection to the sport or activity, future success is unlikely.

2. **Genetics:** Body attributes must align with the desired activity. Sport-appropriate size and physical attributes, speed, quickness of body and mind, and coordination are vital. An interest without the accompanying physical attributes will end the pursuit. Also, health is a prerequisite for success. Even with the right genetic make-up, injuries or illness can certainly derail outcomes

and plans.

3. **Help and Coaching:** Instruction is necessary to guide the athlete in what they need to do and know to accomplish an endeavor. This person comes alongside and assists in the accomplishment of the desired goals.

4. **Opportunity:** A platform or venue is required for skills to blossom in any endeavor.

5. **Discipline:** Structure is necessary to accomplish anything worthwhile. A strong disciplined drive creating strength, stamina, and power is important to be a top athlete.

6. **Work ethic:** An athlete must dedicate oneself relentlessly to pursue the said activity. It requires passion, intense desire, and at elite levels, a singular focus is required. Some researchers believe excellence requires a minimum of 10,000 hours.

7. **Failure and emotions:** Challenges need to be handled correctly. There should be a willingness to get up, dust oneself off, and try again.

8. **Breaks:** Even if everything falls into place, breaks are usually required for outstanding success and opportunity. Everyone needs someone who will take a chance and direct toward success.

Who will help the athlete? Who will they look to for direction, help, and training? One cannot do it alone. In the above list, four of the eight ingredients toward accomplishing extraordinary feats involve someone else. Speaking with utmost humility, 50 percent of an athlete's future is out of his or her hands! *Who do we find in life that is willing to invest in our success?*

As an athlete grows, trains, and develops, they should strive to attain the best performance possible; excellence is always a worthy endeavor. Athletes can find their best performance by embodying *HC3*: Hustle, Caring, Coachable, Commitment. These are minimal building blocks in four easy-to-remember words; words simple enough to memorize and use as a daily evaluative tool.

Those who strive to be their best will need to examine themselves to see if they have these raw materials necessary to take part in competitive athletics. One can nurture the way they build requisite internal and external qualities through preparation and thought. Spending time examining the heart and planning the effort will be worthwhile. "Do not think of yourself more highly than you ought, but rather think of yourself with sober judgment, in accordance with the measure of faith God has given you" (ROMANS 12:3b). And "we have different gifts" (ROMANS 12:6a). Therefore, it is crucial to honestly examine ourselves and assess our talents and resources in the presence of God. It is vital to refrain from inflating our abilities while also recognizing and valuing our own talents and gifts. An accurate self-examination is of great value, a mark of maturity, and part of a firm foundation. It is advisable to:

1. Set proper priorities at the start.

2. Work diligently in preparation.

3. Rest in the outcome, "Wait upon the LORD. Wait for the LORD; be strong and take heart and wait for the LORD" (PSALM 27:14).

4. Recognize and embrace the importance of balance.

5. Never forget, winning is by the hand of God.

Michael Jordan says, "Winning has a price."[1] He speaks the truth. Amidst a philosophical conversation about values and winning, one must not overlook that winners pay a price. Those who achieve what is traditionally considered success and winning consciously decide to embrace discipline. Discipline is not a four-letter word. It's the watershed between intense focused work and positive results and lackadaisical haphazard effort and negative results. Discipline, or being undisciplined, has the potential to be a very slippery slope on either side. Discipline is a critical component and not something to underestimate. On the one hand, a person can be so disciplined that success is pursued at all costs, leaving a wake of carnage and wreckage. But the flip side of the coin, the haphazardly constructed "pell-mell", anything goes, poor quality effort that results in failure is equally invalid. Often outstanding results and outcomes are in direct proportion to hard work, discipline, and organization. When hard work, discipline, and organization are implemented and failure still results, internal growth, even eternal growth may blossom. This mindset does not look simply at the outcomes, but qualities of true worth, diamond-like values of eternal quality.

If teams and athletes, regardless of the level of competition, do not pursue the above qualities and are undisciplined, they become devastated. They're devastated because they didn't win; they're not "the best;" they failed. By not paying the price of discipline, they will be unprepared. This lack of preparation results in loss, and in the loss, handwringing occurs that eventually produces brokenness. This happens because a quality of effort, embracing sacrifice, and a willingness to examine themselves was missing. But even if the athlete did not pay the "price" and their efforts lead to brokenness or failure, God can still provide superabundant eternal rewards. Even when we stumble, He can rewrite the script and build good out of our mess.

Some teams and players use comparison with others to self-critique seeking to skirt discipline, hard work, and accountability. They base their performance and efforts against those around them. Teams who manage their success only by whether they won the championship follow "the road most traveled." Success can cause us to follow "roads" blindly. We aimlessly follow the crowd; we do this without pursuing higher ideals. These athletes are not seeking a higher goal, effort, or purpose, and they aren't interested in personal excellence or in being champions.

Champions build goals and ideals from within, not relying on external comparisons. The trophy does not validate who they are. It matters to them whether they have pleased and honored God. God builds qualities in the individuals who fail and get back up and try again. Humans trusting God, who persevere in spite of hurt, defeat, and pain embody the substance of what champions are made of. True champions are rare. These types of individuals encourage the rest of us to be better people who live to a higher standard. These are our leaders.

ENDNOTES: CHAPTER 29

1. Hehir, Jason, director. Jason Hehir, Michael Tollin and Peter Gruber, producers. *The Last Dance*, a ten-part documentary. ESPN Films & Netflix, 2020.

CHAPTER 30

SUPERPOWER HUMILITY

ODAY AS I WRITE, THE DENVER NUGGETS ARE riding through downtown Denver on firetrucks celebrating their NBA Championship. I know this because my son is sending me "Marco Polos" of this event. It is exciting and fun to see celebrities up close and vicariously enjoy success through their accomplishments.

Children aspire to become professional athletes for good reasons. We make our athletes out to be bigger than life. (Note people always have. We are just getting better at inflating them.) Why has society skewed values? It's not surprising we would drink the "Kool-Aid" that encourages a mindset focused solely on winning. Do parents and their children go crazy? What role does pride play? Pride finds its incubation in the winning!

We see pride when a football player who has a breakaway catch or run drops the football before crossing the goal line. An act of extreme arrogance, he lets the ball go to show I just embarrassed "you." The arrogant act grossly displayed his own aggrandizement, but resulted in a failure to accomplish the touchdown that he is celebrating. Similarly, track stars have been defeated because they begin a premature, prideful celebration believing they have won, only to lose because they celebrated their win *before* crossing the finish line.

This pride was on display when a baseball team lost a state championship game because the catcher bobbled the ball on a third strike. Instead of throwing to first base to insure the out, he celebrated. He seemed to imply they would bend the rules for him. I just want to get on with the celebration; the other team ran the bases for the ultimate win.

In each NBA game, spectators witness arrogance hundreds of times when the athletes challenge the officials' calls with great demonstrative arrogance. The athlete one ups the officials with a headshake, face growl, or some other gesture. Athletes in Major League Baseball display arrogance by flipping their bats. And in the NFL, it is shown in end zone celebrations. Pride run amuck!

Pride can misshape our perspective and lead to downfalls. A genuine hero boasts in God. Heroes humble themselves before God, because God provides the talent and God raises up one team or army to victory and allows the defeat of the other.

> "No king is saved by the size of his army; no warrior escapes by his great strength. The horse is a vain hope for deliverance; despite all its great strength it cannot save. But the eyes of the Lord are on those who fear him, on those whose hope is in his unfailing love, to deliver them from death and keep them alive in famine. We wait in hope for the Lord; he is our help and our shield. In him our hearts rejoice" (PSALM 33:16–21a).

> "It was not by their sword that they won the land, nor did their arm bring them victory; it was your right hand, your arm, and the light of your face, for you loved them" (PSALM 44:3).

> "No one from the east or the west or from the desert can exalt a man. But it is God who judges: He brings one down, he exalts another" (PSALM 75:6–7).

"The horse is made ready for the day of battle, but victory rests with the Lord" (PROVERBS 21:31).

Paul, an apostle, defending his apostolic apostleship, speaks about credentials and boasting and why his boasting is only about the Lord. He truly had impressive credentials and insights and good reason to boast, yet he says,

> "I must go on boasting. Although there is nothing to be gained, I will go on to visions and revelations from the LORD. I know a man in Christ who 14 years ago was caught up to the third heaven. Whether it was in the body or out of the body I do not know—God knows. And I know that this man—whether in the body or apart from the body I do not know, but God knows—was caught up to paradise. He heard inexpressible things, that man is not permitted to tell. I will boast about a man like that, but I will not boast about myself, except about my weaknesses. Even if I should choose to boast, I would not be a fool, because I would be speaking the truth. But I refrain, so no one will think more of me than is warranted by what I do or say.

> "To keep me from becoming conceited because of these surpassingly great revelations, there was given me a thorn in my flesh, a messenger of Satan, to torment me. Three times I pleaded with the Lord to take it away from me. But he said to me, 'My grace is sufficient for you, for my power is made perfect in weakness.' Therefore I will boast all the more gladly about my weaknesses, so that Christ's power may rest on me. That is why, for Christ's sake, I delight in weaknesses, in insults, in hardships, in persecutions, in difficulties. For when I am weak, then I am strong" (2 CORINTHIANS 12:1–10).

Most of us do not find true strength, true power, and true victory where it is typically found. Strength, power, and victory are found in God. This knowledge is where we find truth. The real engine which empowers us is humility. Knowing we depend on God for life and sport outcomes should bring us to our knees and produce dependence and humility.

Humility is not popular today. Alistar Begg states, "Humility pleases God, but humility is not in fashion. It would be sad if we had simply forgotten about it, allowed it to fade from view with the passing of time. But the evidence suggests that it is not that we have merely allowed it to slip; we have voted it out of the public domain. We appear to have concluded that just as smoking is hazardous and should be restricted, so too should humility."

Referencing education, Begg goes on to say, "I suggested that our culture's preoccupation with brains, bodies, and bucks needed to be reexamined in light of the product emerging from our homes and schools. I was always interested to see their program [teacher workshops] for the day and to note the areas of emphasis in child development and teaching strategy. On each occasion, I searched in vain for any hint that humility might be considered as a necessary prerequisite for effective education. Rather, the drift seemed to be to encourage children to write papers on such subjects as 'Why I am important' or 'Why I love myself.' Far from encouraging the children to see humility as a positive attribute to be cultivated, too often it was depicted as a liability to be avoided. In contrast, the scripture says, 'These are the ones I look on with favor: those who are humble and contrite and spirit, and who tremble at my word' (ISAIAH 66:2) . . . This absence of humility is so pervasive we are liable to miss it unless someone points it out."[1]

> "Instead of despising humility, as the Greco-Roman culture did and as our present culture still does, God exalts it and promises to bless those who pursue it. Does this not cause us to realize that the pursuit of humility is not an incidental thing—something we seldom think about—but rather a character trait that we should

give diligent attention to? The very fact that we are so casual about humility should in itself cause us to humble ourselves in the dust before such a glorious and gracious God."[2]

A twenty-four-page sports faith-based document written to pursue excellence, mentioned twenty-four different virtues of character and team values one should pursue. However, glaringly they left out humility. The authors left out humility, even though humility is indispensable as a factor for true success.

God opposes the proud, "All of you, clothe yourselves with humility toward one another, because, 'God opposes the proud but gives grace to the humble.' Humble yourselves, therefore, under God's mighty hand, that he may lift you up in due time" (1 PETER 5:5b).

So many times, in sports, athletes shout their greatness only to experience humility in due time. They declare their greatness even though God HATES it and opposes those who are arrogant and proud. A pathway that is inflated with arrogance is doomed to fail. *The Bible* declares this truth repeatedly.

"He mocks proud mockers but gives grace to the humble" (PROVERBS 3:34).

"To fear the LORD is to hate evil; I hate pride and arrogance, evil behavior and perverse speech" (PROVERBS 8:13).

"When pride comes, then comes disgrace, but with humility comes wisdom" (PROVERBS 11:2).

"The fear of the LORD teaches a man wisdom, and humility comes before honor" (PROVERBS 15:33).

"The LORD detests all the proud of heart. Be sure of this: They will not go unpunished" (PROVERBS 16:5).

"Pride goes before destruction, a haughty spirit before a fall" (PROVERBS 16:18).

"Before his downfall a man's heart is proud, but humility comes before honor" (PROVERBS 18:12).

"Haughty eyes and a proud heart, the lamp of the wicked, are sin!" (PROVERBS 21:4).

"Let another praise you, and not your own mouth; someone else, and not your own lips" (PROVERBS 27:2).

These words guarantee pride will produce failure regardless of the sport and the athlete. Pride will produce a fall.

Challenging the faces of pride may be met with contempt. Even within the church, outcomes are often the evidence of truth or right. We relegate truth to situational ethics when measuring success by outcomes. The so-called success or desired outcome may have nothing to do with real value, character, or God.

Humility will produce a counterculture mindset. Winning, success, money, all fall short when examining results through a lens of humility. It is humbling to boldly place values ahead of winning in today's culture.

A college golf coach, Bill Brogden, decided he was willing to forfeit the Western Athletic Conference Golf Championship rather than miss his team's flight. It was the last flight out of town, and since during recruitment he had promised his team to do what was right and best for his student athletes, they left. A playoff to determine a winner would cause the team to miss the plane and they would not get back in time for study, classes, and finals. This decision was so counterculture that professors at the university were shocked when they learned of this decision. The Tulsa University president said, "I have never been more proud of a coach or a team," adding that the decision "shines brighter than any trophy."[3] Results did not rule the day, but a counter-cultural mentality that put values ahead of sport outcomes. This story is the opposite of pride. Coach Brogden's decision demonstrated values that are higher—on a different plane.

It might even appear foolish.

Paul declares the foolishness of God is stronger than man's strength. "For the foolishness of God is wiser than man's wisdom, and the weakness of God is stronger than man's strength" (1 CORINTHIANS 1:25). The way God perceives life is different, just like Coach Bill Brogden.

In my personal journal, I recorded my struggles. I depended on God and sought to humble myself before Him. My entry recorded in 2003, "Where do we find success? Is it in our efforts? Is it in our talents? Is it in the breaks we receive? No, it is when we recognize our weaknesses and failings, and find we are helpless, that we begin down the path toward true success and greatness. We are mistaken when we think we can somehow pull it off. It is only God who gives us everything; it is only God who pulls it off; it is only God who makes us great. Failure does not stop God's hand in our lives. Mistakes do not thwart the majesty and power of almighty God. In fact, just the opposite. When we are weak, God steps in and makes us strong. In weaknesses is power, not in a fake human mock heroism. When we recognize how desperately we need him, only then can we truly enjoy and experience his blessings, growth, and opportunities. The Bible is full of kings who were outnumbered, battles that could not be won, and situations that looked like certain failure, and yet that is when God appears.

> "My son admitted he had learned a lesson the hard way. He told me it was too late. He had squandered opportunities, not pursued his dreams, and failed to do what he knew in his heart he should have been doing. He knew he should have been training for excellence in basketball, but instead, he had been undisciplined, lazy, soft, and missed opportunities. This was doubly hard,

because as his dad, I watched from "the front-row seat of life" sitting helplessly observing him struggle, watching him make mistakes and fail, and seeing his anguish and ache.

"On this day, we knew God would step in, like the hero in a wild fictional saga. Satan stands ready to slay the hopes, dreams, and joy of a young man, and God steps in. The darkness is heavy and God steps in. Just like the cross, Satan believes he has won, only to see God break through and raise hope from failure, joy from sorrow, strength from weakness, like the power that raised Jesus from the dead. We have been endued with this same power for God's glory! In the sorrow and tears, the sky parts, lightning strikes, and in my son's confession of failure and remorse ushered in the power of God. In humility, we are reminded it is not our battle; the battle belongs to the LORD (2 CHRONICLES 20:15).

"We do not know how this story will turn out, but my son went to work and did everything he could do during his time remaining in high school. We wait in great expectation by faith to see what God will do."

ENDNOTES: CHAPTER 30

1. Alistair Begg, *Made for His Pleasure*, Moody Press, 1996, 145–147.

2. Jerry Bridges, *The Blessings of Humility*, NavPress, 2016, 8.

3. Rick Reilly, "A Stroke of Inspiration," *Sports Illustrated*, May 23, 2005, 72.

CHAPTER 31

OVERTIME
AND THE WIN

ON'T SAY IT'S ONLY A GAME! A GAME IS NEVER only a game! In life, outcomes carry meaning. In sports, results provide value and position. Games cease to become activities of play when meaning is attached. When we play for money, it immediately changes the play to work. But if we play for other reasons like success, self-worth, notoriety, power, significance, or the roar of the crowd, inherently, the competition has meaning. These may be reasons of lower worth, but if we are honest, we strive for these accolades.

Deep within our hearts, we understand that everything holds significance to God, even games! I have read, by well-meaning scholars, that if one puts their best efforts into an activity, and if they play with passion and intelligence, then the competitor is a winner no matter what the outcome. It does not matter who wins. "God is not concerned with the final score."

The founder of the modern Olympics, Frenchman Baron de Coubertin in 1908, has been famously quoted as saying, "The most important thing in the Olympic Games is not to win but to take part . . . The essential thing is not to have conquered but to have fought well." This is deeply true and yet one does not go to the Olympic games, train for years, pour out one's life only to "take part" and to have "fought well" We have two truths in tension!

Respectfully, it matters who wins. As we continue to work through the issues of winning and losing, success and failure, we have results that bring us satisfaction, even more than winning, but they grow out of the effort and desire to win. To have "competed well" with every sinew and fiber of your being, striving for victory, truly exposes those better things! So yes, it matters who wins, to the participants and to God. God cares about each of us on the fields and courts where people lose and win. It is through passionately pursuing victory, when we push ourselves beyond the pain of defeat, at that juncture, there is a leading of discovery to deeper values.

As we examine outcomes, we ponder the definition and aspects of winning. The quest to win can maximize one's talent. Has the athlete achieved the best that they are physically, mentally, and emotionally able to achieve? Of course, this is fluid and a moving target. Like much of life, the answers are not always clear-cut and easily defined. However, reaching for the highest achievement serves as a good foundation and significantly raises the standard for athletic performance. This goal places the athlete above a win or a loss and makes the outcome secondary to the excellence they can accomplish. This mindset creates strong intrinsic motivation and removes the idea; an athlete compares themselves to those around them. Intrinsic challenge is a tough-minded stance and worthy of someone foisting as a goal. However, it is a suboptimal position.

For example, a contest could include teams and athletes matched so perfectly that the outcome of the contest ends in a tie. This means under normal conditions, within the rules, the opponents were dead even. This is where things get interesting. Because ties result in equality of result, we have no winner or loser. This creates a problem in sports because sports need an experiential winner. Sport cannot tolerate equality, and for league purposes or tournament play, there must be a winner, regardless of the magnificence of performance. Two teams are not allowed to advance. So, the tie forces an extension of the game. Ultimately, one individual or team is declared the winner, even if they did not win during regulation play. Instead of both teams being applauded for an incredible exhibition and accolades shared, the game is extended, a winner declared, and ALL the accolades are bestowed upon the champion of the mini game. The loser drops off the radar and out of the limelight. They have now failed, even though they didn't really lose, technically. The tie is the best example of the dichotomy between winning and losing one is likely to find. The tie begs more than any other outcome that dynamics are involved in internalizing and digesting the results of contests. Another perspective exists.

The way God perceives life is different. His view is always the best view. And because God sees life differently than we do, it is appropriate to spell out a "new" definition for winning as we move toward the conclusion of this study. We cannot know what God thinks regarding events on the horizontal surface of planet Earth. But we can define real success and winning as:

1. How might God see outcomes from His perspective in His heavenly dwelling?

2. Am I being sharpened as I engage in an event, contest, or job?

3. Is the sharpening making me more conformed to the image of Jesus Christ?

4. Does one recognize that our work toward goals entails "a journey mentality," rather than a sprint? Do I consider those around me during my journey?

5. Has the activity glorified God? This is THE only real question; not did we win or lose? And not even how we played the game, or if we took part and fought well, but did we glorify God?

"According to all branches of Christian theology, the ultimate purpose of life is to glorify God."[1] Tim Keller says in a discussion of men in dire straits, "Their greatest joy was to honor God, not to use God to get what they want in life."[2]

God's honor removes fear and replaces it with courage, as our bar is set higher than just winning and losing. Failure does not destroy us. This fosters mental toughness since failure is never the end because all outcomes have eternal value. Outcomes within a contest have meaning. And the meaning can take on different shades, like the attitude of an athlete in the contest, or the building up of a teammate, or the respecting of an opponent, or in the listening to the coach.

Years ago, a women's softball player hit a home run, but while racing to and rounding first base before she realized she had hit a home run, she damaged her knee and collapsed in a heap, unable to move. To the amazement of all, two opposing team players carried her around the bases, which was in line with the rules of softball, so she could record her home run. This belies a different and one could say, "higher standard."

In the movie *Jesus Revolution*, a very poignant scene occurs when the pastor is lamenting his mistakes and failures. He has made terrible decisions, and he wants to give up and leave the ministry. His wife rebukes him, saying, "Don't be so arrogant to think that God can't use your failures."[3] God looks at our outcomes and our lives differently than we do.

Often, people with handicaps are seen as naive, impaired, innocent, weaker, or compromised by those who believe themselves to be able-bodied. But what if life is backward and their shortcomings and impairments are our example? What if they are the ones who are most normal? What if their handicaps give them "a take on life" that makes them the real example and leader? The oath for the Special Olympics is "Let me win. But if I cannot win, let me be brave in the attempt." Obviously, they are reaching for a higher standard. We too need to have a higher standard!

ENDNOTES: CHAPTER 31

1. Timothy Keller, *Walking With God Through Pain and Suffering*, Dutton, 2013, 167.

2. Timothy Keller, *Walking With God Through Pain and Suffering*, Dutton, 2013, 231.

3. John Erwin and Brent McCorkle, directors. *Jesus Revolution*. Kingdom Story Company and Lionsgate, 2023.

Part Five

Chapters
32–34

Stories of Triumph
&
Final Thoughts

CHAPTER 32

A HIGHER STANDARD— WINNING DOES NOT TELL THE WHOLE STORY

S A COACH FOR OVER TWENTY-FIVE YEARS, I have walked into countless locker rooms displaying the Vince Lombardi slogan "Winning isn't everything; It's the only thing." This locker room motivational mantra has always felt so shallow. It is such hyperbole. Everyone knows that not everyone can win, yet we deny, ignore, and believe the other opponent will always lose. We live in the nonreality that we will always be the winner, even though we know every contest must have a winner and a loser. It is a fixed law, like gravity. No one wins all the time.

When we grope for a higher standard or a different way to frame losing and winning, we realize we reveal and expose the beliefs deep within us. Nothing uncovers the motives of our hearts, like failed goals and dreams. The things we value get exposed. Often, sport pushes what we value to the surface, and we must deal with it. It is important to examine the thrill of winning, but we also should deal with the struggle in losing.

The following are four true stories which shed light on what it means to play to a higher standard, diamonds born out of a different dimension under tremendous pressure.

UNIVERSITY HEROICS IN MARCH

The final score does not tell the entire story. This story began on April 5, 2022, the National Collegiate Athletic Association championship game featured the University of North Carolina, Tarheels, and the University of Kansas, Jayhawks. Kansas was a number one seed and had defeated several opponents easily. North Carolina had to battle every step of the way and they were the underdog. Their season had started so poorly there was discussion about whether they would keep the coach for the next season. The best player for North Carolina had severely injured his ankle against Duke in the previous game. However, North Carolina won a hard-fought game overpowering Duke in the last minute.

The championship game started with Kansas jumping to an early 7-0 lead. North Carolina battled. Kansas fans relaxed, as it looked like they would cruise to an easy victory. Apparently, Kansas's basketball team relaxed too, shooting poorly. They missed sixteen of twenty-one close shots and went into the half down fifteen points, 44–29 to North Carolina. The halftime score was unbelievable partly because Armando Bacot, who had injured his ankle in the previous game, played on one leg, and Brady Manek had received a serious inadvertent blow to the head while defending Kansas's powerful star center.

Manek may have suffered a concussion, but stayed in the game, however one could tell he was seriously hurt. With two injured players, North Carolina built a lead in the NCAA tournament final that no team had ever overcome. The second half started disastrously for North Carolina, Kansas scored in rapid fire fashion, and before the ten-minute mark, Kansas had tied the game. This was a shocking lead lost by North Carolina, coupled with an extraordinary comeback by Kansas.

As the second half unfolded, North Carolina's guard Caleb Love turned his ankle on a routine non-contact change of direction. Yet somehow, astonishingly with a short bench, North Carolina fought off the comeback by Kansas and stayed even, as the game moved toward its conclusion. Oddly, during the last three minutes, a North Carolina substitute, Jackson Watkins, stopped, bent over, and vomited onto the court and had to be removed from the game. Bacot, driving for the go-ahead basket, re-injured his ankle and had to hop on one leg down the court with five seconds left. Manek collected an offensive rebound and made an errant pass that went out of bounds, giving Kansas the apparent win. But on the ensuing possession as Kansas broke the press, a player stepped out of bounds, giving North Carolina the ball with 4.3 seconds and plenty of time to score a three to tie the game. As the last play unfolded, Brady Manek slipped and stumbled to the corner, crawling like an elephant, and even when Love shot the potential game tying shot, Manek's head was still down. His disorientation was evident in those closing seconds.

Did the effects of a blow to the head earlier disorientate him in those closing seconds? Should he have been playing? We may never know, but with the University of North Carolina's best player, playing on a gimpy ankle, their second-best player playing with a hard injury to the head, their key guard twisting his ankle during the closing minutes of the second half, and a super sub bending over and throwing up on the court, and they barely missed a three-point shot to tie the game. Who won, Kansas or North Carolina? Kansas by points for sure. But with a roster of blue blood players with impeccable credentials, Kansas won on a missed three pointer at the buzzer, this against a team with three key injured players and a sick sub. Who is the winner? North Carolina over-performed, out worked, out hustled, and battled to the final tick with multiple crazy injuries. A resounding victory in the annals of what it means to find success despite losing. North Carolina displayed bravery and determination in their defeat, fighting with grit against overwhelming obstacles that couldn't be overcome, and ultimately laying the foundation for heroes in another story and a higher standard.

LIFE WORDS

Prior to Brett Farve and Aaron Rodgers, Bart Starr, an exceptional quarterback, led the Green Bay Packers. In 1965, a story unfolds that portrays a brief piece of folklore about this exceptional quarterback. Legend has it, when his son was young, Bart would give him a dime for every perfect school assignment. During the season, Starr had a disastrous day and played horribly. Bart returned home exhausted and discouraged and when he finally slumped into bed, he found something attached to his pillow. It was a note. "Dear Dad, I thought you played a great game. Love, Bart." Taped to the note were two dimes.[1] Gary Warner encourages with these words, "The Christian competitor follows a Lord who takes the sting out of defeat and keeps us humble in victory by judging according to a higher win/lose standard."[2]

A TOUGH CALL

Years ago, I received an inspiring email about two basketball teams in New York who played valiantly. New Rochelle and Yonkers High played an incredibly intense game with the roar of the crowd making referee whistles hard if not impossible to hear throughout the contest. At the end of the game, the winning shot was tipped in as time expired. The officials were not sure if the tip counted, but the home crowd was cheering wildly, believing New Rochelle had won. The referees asked the clock operator if the ball was tipped in before time expired, and the clock operator said it was not. This gave the visiting team, Yonkers, the win. The officials had the unenviable task of relaying that information to the coach of the home team. He was shaken and understandably dejected. But in the next moment, he introduced the scoreboard personnel to the officials and told the official clock operator he was proud of him. The clock operator, who had waved off the winning basket was his son. The father's love and pride in his son was demonstrated as they walked off the court together, with the coach giving his son a hug, profoundly demonstrating values greater than winning and losing.[3]

MY FRIEND

(*This is in the first person, in the writer's words. It describes an amazing comeback with bloody feet. Stick with the long story; the end is amazing.*)

In high school, I primarily identified myself as "the runner" at my school. I was good, but not great: 2:04 half-mile, 4:32 in the mile, and a 10:15 school record in the two-mile. Fast enough to place in most meets and win a few races. I had dreamed of running at a "big-time" school like Ohio State in college, but I was well short of their standards. I loved the sports of track and cross-country and knew my only real option to keep competing for four more years was the small school, NAIA, or NCAA DIII route.

I chose Taylor University because they had an outstanding coach and running program. I was OK with the fact that it followed Evangelical Christian standards. I bonded right away with my new teammates and enjoyed going to school there. The biggest area of growth, though, was in my faith in Christ as being the guiding light in my life.

Running-wise I did alright as a freshman, improving marginally in all my events. The big jump came my sophomore year. The world of the USA, track was transitioning from English to metric measurements, so some of our meets were in yards or miles and others measured in meters. I dropped under fifteen minutes with a 14:58 for three miles and ran 15:40 for 5000 meters (the three-mile time is better). I placed in meets including conference and state and was very proud of my season. I had great teammates who were graduating, and I felt certain I'd move into one of the leading positions on a very good team.

That summer I was obsessed with running. My training was the best it had ever been. I was killing it in road races, including a fifty-seven-minute, ten-mile race that I won. Then suddenly it was over. While competing in a 7.5-mile race in Sidney, Ohio, I had bad pain in the instep of my right foot. I pushed through and finished the race, but could hardly walk the next day. I took a few days off and tried to run again but couldn't. I went to a doctor and got the 1970s standard family physician advise: "Just take a few weeks off."

That began a long stretch of months, alternating between rest, treatments, and running with poor racing sprinkled in. I missed several cross-country and track meets my junior year because of the injury and performed poorly when I competed. I do not remember a single race from my junior year of college. In the fall of my senior year, I ran only one cross-country race and completely quit going to practice. Because my identity was still so wrapped up with running, I had doubts and depression about who I was and where I belonged. I avoided eating meals with my teammates because they would often talk about the team or upcoming meets at lunch. When they all walked to dinner together after practice, I just didn't feel like I deserved to be with them. None of them ever said anything to that effect or did anything at all to show I wasn't welcome, but I created a barrier in my mind. That mindset separated me from those who had been my closest friends. My inner thoughts told me I was done with running and done with them.

Since I had not worked out in a few months, my foot did not bother me anymore when just walking around, and one day in February, I went for a run for only a couple miles, but felt no pain. I ran again the next day, and then the next, and still no pain. I had no plan to be on the track team that spring, because it had been a year and a half since I had diligently trained, and months since I had run at all. I knew it was too late to reach peak physical condition, but the longing to reunite with my friends and the sport I loved compelled me to seek guidance through prayer.

I talked to my coach, and he told me just what I needed to hear and what had been true all along. My value as a Christian and a friend had nothing to do with how fast I could run. My heart was deeply involved. If I loved running, then I should be out there doing it. If I enjoyed the friendship of my teammates, then I should be out there with them. I prayed the Lord would help me swallow my pride and just help me enjoy the experience.

The season began, and I trained without pain. My mileage increased, and I had a few good workouts, but the races were below average. I failed to break eighteen minutes in my first 5000-meter race, then ran a three mile around 17:00 and a 5000 in 17:30. I didn't make the travel squad for spring break, and I didn't compete in a couple meets because I wasn't one of our top three runners in the 1500 meter (or mile) and 5000 meter (or three mile). Despite all this, I loved being part of the team and had a great time cheering on my talented teammates.

Our last meet was the conference championship held at Hanover College. I did not expect to compete, since I couldn't crack the lineup. But a week before the meet, Coach told me the conference had added a six-mile run event for the first time. If I wanted to compete, I could.

I worried that racing for six miles (twenty-four laps around the track) in my spiked shoes with no support which might worsen my foot injury, since it had been hurting a little again. So, I went out a few days before the race and got a new pair of racing flats. I jogged in them only once before race day.

The six miles were contested on Friday afternoon to begin the two-day championship meet. I went into the race wanting to do my best, but given the slow races I had run at half the distance that spring; I settled into what I thought was a realistic pace. I ran with the slower runners while the lead pack quickly pulled away. Two of my teammates were among that lead pack, but a mile into the six-mile race, our best runner, John Wilson, got the heel of his shoe stepped on by another runner. It pulled down off his heel and he tried to just keep it on by gripping his toes. When he realized he couldn't do that for another five miles, he pulled out to lane three and hopped along while pulling the shoe heel back on his foot, but couldn't do it. Finally, Coach yelled at him to just stop and get it on. John sat down on the track, but he had double knotted his shoes before the race and still couldn't pull it on, leaving him no option except to pick the shoelace knot apart so he could put it on and retie it.

While John was struggling with his shoe, my pack of slow runners caught up and passed him. I yelled encouragement as I ran past him, but I knew I couldn't help him. We had hoped to start the meet on a high note with both John and our other runner, Kurt Cornfield, earning points in the six-mile race, so it was disheartening to witness John being left behind.

John, now in last place, finally got his shoe on and set out after the other runners. Rather than panic and get all the distance back rapidly, he set off at a brisk but strategic pace as he began picking off runners. As he passed me, I said, "Go get them, John Boy" (his nickname) to which he replied, "You're coming with me, Crispy" (my team nickname).

That exchange was unremarkable, but something inside of me clicked. I locked my eyes on John's back and picked up my pace to match his. I blocked everything out except staying on John's heels, lap after lap after lap. I didn't listen to my splits to calculate my pace. I didn't count places to see how many runners we were passing. I didn't think about the months of injury, the lack of training, or whether I "deserved" to be running at that pace. I just focused on the only thing that mattered in that moment: staying with John for another lap.

After five miles, twenty laps, there we were in the lead pack of six runners. Kurt, John, and I were running fourth, fifth, and sixth with less than a mile to go. We were lapping the runners I had been with since the opening mile of the race. Kurt and John were running side-by-side just ahead of me and plotting their strategy. Kurt held up three fingers to John and turned to me, also saying we're going with three laps to go. Sure enough, with three laps to go, Kurt bolted into the lead, with John right behind him. Some degree of reality finally hit me as I realized I needed to stay right where I was and hang on to score. I also became vaguely aware that there was something squishy in my left shoe. The last couple of laps were painful, but as John and Kurt raced ahead to finish first and second, I finished a strong sixth place out of twenty-six runners. I scored a point for the team and earned a medal for myself. I lapped nearly half the participants in the race.

My last time was 32:25 for the six miles (equivalent to about a 33:40 for 10K). I could not break seventeen minutes for three miles in any race that season, but I had just averaged about 16:12 for back-to-back three-mile runs. It had been almost two years since I had a memorable race or scored in a meet, and here in my last college competition, the Lord gave me a race I still remember forty-five years later. [His coach remembered it too.] As I limped off the track following those twenty-four laps wearing the new shoes, I had worn the ball of my left foot right down to the meat. The skin from the bottom of the front half of my foot was peeled off and bunched under my arch, leaving a bloody mess soaking through my shoe.

I continued to train and compete for another twenty years (after finally getting orthotics). I have been a track and cross-country coach for over twenty years on the high school and small-college level. I start or officiate many track meets every year from elementary to Division I NCAA championship competitions. The sports of track and cross-country have been a source of entertainment and income for me ever since college. I can't believe I almost walked away from the sport that has been such a huge part of my life due to an injury. I discovered when I listened to the Lord (and my coach) and realized that sports were just something I do, they are not who I am, that I could be truly fulfilled." (As told by Dr. Randy Crist, Professor at the University of Kentucky, and Cross-Country Coach at Asbury University.)

As this book winds to its conclusion, it should be noted that these stories are just a few samples of competitors embracing a higher standard. There are many athletes who compete at a higher standard; these athletes have values and compete for reasons which demonstrate they are real heroes "men with chests."

ENDNOTES: CHAPTER 32

1. Jack Canfield, Mark Victor Hansen, Mark and Chrissy Donnelly, and Jim Tunney, *Chicken Soup for the Sports Fan's Soul: Stories of Insight, Inspiration and Laughter in the World of Sport*, Health Communications, 2000, 238.

2. Gary Warner, *Competition*, David C. Cook Publishing, 1979, 94–95.

3. Al Covino, "Winners and Winners." Rob Nelson, submitter. Jack Canfield, Mark Victor Hanson, Hanoch McCarty, and Meladee McCarty, authors. *A 4th Course of Chicken Soup for the Soul: 101 More Stories to Open the Heart and Rekindle the Spirit*, Health Communications, Inc., 1997, 133–134.

CHAPTER 33

IS IT A WORTHY CAUSE?

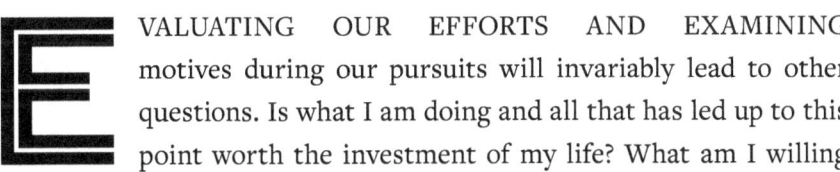VALUATING OUR EFFORTS AND EXAMINING motives during our pursuits will invariably lead to other questions. Is what I am doing and all that has led up to this point worth the investment of my life? What am I willing to die for? Sports analysts *never* ask these questions. Regardless of the activity, whether we are a doctor, lawyer, farmer, computer whiz, hamburger king, teacher, banker, or maintenance person, we invest our life. Is the calling worthy? Is it worth the daily minutes I pay?

We all spend our lives doing something. Did we invest well? Could winning be a goal too low? Is becoming a Super Bowl champion reason enough to spend a life? If we hold up the Larry O'Brien trophy at the end of a long NBA season, are we validated? We trade our life's minutes for whatever it is we pursue. Is winning any championship worth the exchange, and is it seen as completely fulfilling? Does it produce satisfaction that fills the soul with joy? What is winning? What is losing? Is having fewer points losing? Tough thought-provoking questions.

Entering the arena with sweat falling off the brow, sweat pulsing from the pores, muscles burning to cease, mind laser-focused, striving with full-hearted passion, this is our greatest effort. Being in the arena, tasting the entirety of victory or defeat, feeling it with every fiber of our body, going after something with all our heart, seeking to honor God, this pursuit is victory. Ryan Leak, in his 2016 video, "Chasing Failure," asks for and receives an opportunity to try out for the Phoenix Suns. Leak says, "Dreaming is free, living it out will have a price tag on it. And I think you owe it to yourself to find out how much it would cost," and if you pay the price and fail . . . "What do you do with failure? . . . You look back and realize that you tried, and no one can take that away from you."[1] Leak states there is incredible satisfaction in offering one's best. He says it is an incredible feeling of accomplishment.

Brené Brown says, "Having the courage to go into the arena and do battle is victory, [defining] winning as doing the really brave thing."[2] Brown, like me, loves the wisdom and power in Theodore Roosevelt's words mentioned earlier. He reminds us, "It is not the critic who counts; . . . [but the one] who spends himself in a worthy cause; who at the best knows in the end the triumph of high achievement, and who at the worst, if he fails, at least fails while daring greatly, so that his place shall never be with those cold and timid souls who neither know victory nor defeat."

So, the question we should ask is, "Is it a worthy enterprise, a worthy cause? Is it worth spending and being spent on such a task? Am I all in? What is the ultimate performance? What is the signature of greatness? What is the capstone?

Is the almighty win the signature of greatness? Does the outcome create worthiness? Who we are in the crucible and in pursuit of goals forces us to find out what's important. "What if we gain the whole world and forfeit our soul?" (MATTHEW 16:26). This question can stagger us. How are our strivings viewed by God? Walking with God does matter. Godliness is bringing the essence of who God is into our daily walk, into the noblest of tasks, and into the most difficult tasks. One cannot say it is only a game. Games absolutely matter. What parts of life do not? But when we say, "It is only a game," maybe a better phrase would be, "Do I put sports into perspective? Does sports have too much emphasis? Have we elevated sports to the status of God?" But it should not be said, "It is only a game," because everything is more than a game!

The intensity in the game and being all in, and handing this effort to God, with the intention of glorifying Him. This is the highest bar. God's glory requires the greater skill, effort, intensity, and mental preparation as we strain to honor God in each moment. This bar demands more of us, not less.

I was asked whether superstar athletes would have been as great if they had been a deep follower of Jesus? The answer is yes! An athlete could have been better. She could have pushed herself to develop her talents to the maximum capacity as designed and created by God. She may have uncovered abilities and talents in her life which would have dwarfed what she accomplished on her own strength. God's power within her could have produced blessings unknown to anyone. It is certainly possible in having a full and mature relationship with God she might have been far more accomplished than she or anyone else may have dared dream. God gives strength in the effort and balance in pursuing our utmost for God's honor.

How is a worthy effort defined? What is the greatest achievement? *Five* words: Glorify God with our best! He becomes the bar to measure our efforts, our life. A friend, Larry Maddox, riddled with an incurable painful cancer, bravely commented a couple of years before his death, "Winning is loving and obeying the Lord."

ENDNOTES: CHAPTER 33

1. Ryan Leak, speaker. *Chasing Failure*. YouTube Ryan Leak, a Ryan Leak film, November 24, 2015.

2. Sandra Restrepo, director. *Brené Brown, The Call to Courage* (documentary), Netflix, 2019.

CHAPTER 34

CONCLUSION:
IT'S PERSONAL

THIS LAST CHAPTER FRAMES MANY DEEPLY personal thoughts. I will conclude with candor and transparency. It's deeply personal, and yet it is my error to compare sufferings. My prayer of confession is, "Lord, I sometimes compare pain and sorrow. A one-upmanship for grief, so to speak. I confess that sin to you."

I felt devastated by the loss or failure of another job this winter. I wondered if you (God) knew what you were doing. You opened doors for coaching, yet, seeing me make the same mistakes and watching me fail over and over, I questioned you and my very existence. Why did I love sports? Why was I deeply interested in sports? Why did I spend so much of my life digging into this arena? This way you created me has been bittersweet. In the squirming, in the struggle, I found truths I could not have realized if I had not gone through these tragedies. I found you allow darkness and then blind us with the beauty of your light and truth. People so often miss the things we really need when we get what we want. I found that suffering is the avenue to deep understanding.

The glory in intimately knowing God through hurt is a gift for those select few who have experienced deep suffering and sadness, a breaking of one's inner being. Broken. In this brokenness, sometimes people may believe God to be aloof, only to be surprised that God is closer than imaginable. His resplendent glory fills the room and like Job, we repent in sackcloth and ashes; we asked about things we truly did not understand and things too great for our minds to even comprehend. "One bold message in the book of Job is that you can say anything to God. Throw at him your grief, your anger, your doubt, your bitterness, your betrayal, your disappointment—he can absorb them all."[1] God's character and grace bursts into life and sears our heart with unspeakable love, superabundant love, love beyond understanding.

During our lives, we may pursue an objective, whether in sports, work, ministry, marriage, a family, or a career. There may be infinite influences that direct these choices. Factors affect us that would be difficult to catalogue or enumerate. God calls us, points us in a direction, and we respond by following Him to the best of our ability. Our best may bring success, rewards, accolades, notoriety, fame, and fortune. Solomon speaks, "that if a man is diligent in his work he will stand before kings" (PROVERBS 22:29). We can see this wildly in the life of Joseph, who excelled so much in his work that he managed an entire family business, ran a prison, and eventually governed the most powerful kingdom on earth (GENESIS chapters 37–50).

However, our best efforts may cause ashes. We may be called by God to a task and reap heartache, loss, failure, and despair. The calling and the results, though linked, do not guarantee horizontal success as defined by humanity. The faithful use of gifts, talents, and the administration of our "calling" may cause a positive outcome or a negative outcome. We may not even be that good, by human standards, in performing our calling. But the resulting outcome or endgame is not as important, regardless of consequences, if we are driven to a deeper relationship with God, producing maturity, godliness, and love. The execution of our gifts and talents for some may result in wild success and opportunities like Joseph, or it may cause gloomy circumstances and failure, by the world's definition, like Job. The endgame is not the product. The endgame is a depth of quality relationship with our creator. Relationship with God is the greatest calling and gift known to man. Results do not substantiate, validate, or prove whether we are doing what God created us to do. The results are products of our opportunities, skill, efforts, work, and most importantly, the very hand of God. Regardless of success or poor performance or failure, results are not the last word. In fact, failure may optimize our need and dependence upon God and may result in tremendous growth in maturity, intimacy, spiritual zeal, or love, but nobody on planet Earth may recognize, know, or appreciate it. The failure may reap tremendous spiritual benefits while crushing the participant in the activity.

This quote by Phillip Yancey bears repeating. "Saints become saints by somehow hanging on to the stubborn conviction that things are not as they appear, and that the unseen world is as solid and trustworthy as the visible world around them. God deserves trust."[2] A study into the existence of God will reveal that He is personal. And we know he cares about us and watches over us like the birds of the air and the flowers of the field. We usually pray for things we want or need, sometimes with pure motives and sometimes with not so pure motives. Our prayers are a mixed bag of communications to a personal creator. We pray for a job; we pray for strength; we pray for those who do not know God; and we pray for mothers carrying children. If everything does not turn out okay, or our prayers appear unanswered, how do we respond? What is the reason behind these prayers not being answered as we had hoped? WHY?

Suffering presents a matrix of difficulties to mankind. Suffering leaves us tossing and turning on our beds and troubles us beyond expression or words.

Suffering hurts intensely!

God loves us.

He wants us to love Him. He wants us to trust Him. He wants us to communicate with Him. He wants us to grow in Him.

A devastating loss, mistake, or tragedy becomes a well-established fact in the tapestry of our lives which profoundly impacts us. It has ceased to be an outcome or an idea, it is reality. We may writhe in sorrow, pain, regret, shame, and sadness. We may hate ourselves for our weakness, folly, lack of skill, or lack of foresight. But yesterday is an unchangeable, historical event with lasting consequences. Failure of a marriage, failure of career goals, the failure of friendship, the failure of living (body aging), failure to win.

What do we do?

Fix our eyes on Jesus.

God's economy differs completely from how we view life. In God's economy, being last is being first, the prisoners, the orphans, and the widows are the ones who really have something to teach us. Paul, the apostle, sang joyously in a prison cell because he fully understood God's economy is backward; it's upside down; it's otherworldly; we can't, and we don't think like this. I could not have understood this, even a little, if we had won the playoffs and emerged as champions, if I had played in the NBA, if my career had been what I was seeking, if I had won and things had worked out as I had dreamed. The understanding shared in this book can only come from the inside-out, the backward, the upside down. The only way it can be seen in the upside down and backward is by being in the unwanted place at the bottom of the heap looking up seeking to make sense of what's happened.

Had my sister been healthy, if I had two sisters where everything went pretty well for them, I would not understand. To the upside down, inside out, backward outcomes, Jesus says, "the first shall be last and the last shall be first." He looks at people and the ones that are broken, the ones left outside, the ones that he speaks about as if they're heroic, and we don't get it! I don't get it. It's completely backward, convoluted, upside down— our world values' winning, our world values' success, our world values' financial accomplishment. We read books chronicling achievement and success, and we study how to motivate people to reach the top and how to never give up. We repeat phrases like "never give up," "work hard enough and you will succeed," "if you believe it, you can achieve it." However, in God's economy, achievement is powered by humility. God "opposes the proud but gives grace to the humble." Pride goes before a fall; pride was by some commentators and some theologians Satan's primary crime. In this book, we examine humility in depth. Humility is upside down from the "intimidate one's way to success" mantra. People often ridicule humble individuals, despite humility being the engine for all of life's success. Humility's depths produce God's blessings. Humility is the real motivational power. We often look for power in all the wrong places, but the real power is hidden.

In the Bible, Luke 16 describes humility through a story about a rich man and Lazarus. Lazarus longs for the crumbs that fell from the rich man's table. He had been a beggar having his sores licked by dogs. The rich man had everything, and yet after he died, the rich man had nothing. In fact, the rich man was in anguish and pleaded with Abraham for a drink, but he couldn't find comfort because of the chasm between them. A chasm between the place of God, where Lazarus resided, and the place of the rich man is a powerful story of humility. The weak and the broken being exalted, the last being first, the "upside down-inside out" economy of a different perspective.

My son experienced the upside-down nature of life. He was one of the most outstanding basketball players in New Mexico and played college basketball. In the very challenging Rocky Mountain Athletic Conference, he was nominated as one of the most outstanding freshmen. However, during his tenure in college, he experienced four years of being beaten down and treated as though he was not talented, as though he was not gifted, and as though he was not skilled. The truth was just the opposite, but his coach couldn't see these truths because God was building, at the early age of twenty-one, the understanding that it took me a lifetime to learn. An unbelievable gift given by God; the lesson: suffering produces diamonds of joy in our heart.

God's formula for this world, what He values, is not produced at the pinnacle, championship, MVP, but rather in the broken, the suffering, and the being crushed. Chunks of scriptures highlight individuals who were crushed, and we tend to overlook the lesson. In that crushing, God pours out all that is good.

David is crushed by his own failure and in that crushing he becomes a man after God's own heart.

Noah thinks people will want to get on the ship and escape certain death. They did not. He was crushed, maybe that's why he got drunk. He couldn't take it. Noah became the father of all nations.

Abraham was crushed. He was sure there were at least ten people in Sodom who were righteous. Abraham fathered the nation of Israel.

Joseph was crushed. He obeyed his father, and his brothers sold him as a slave. He did his best for his owner, but they put him in prison. In prison, his friends forgot him, and he spent years there. Joseph was crushed repeatedly, but he ruled the greatest civilization on earth. He saved his ancestral people.

Jesus, who was God, was the consummate beaten one. He spoke words of heaven—words of love and peace, joy and contentment, other worldly ideas, yet people hated him. His attackers lied about him, tortured him, and hung him on a cross to die. All of this is obvious and yet invisible.

This economy of God fills the Bible, and it's at the heart of love. God's values differ from earthly thinking. Life's benefits can slip through our fingers, and we can lose the very things we think are heroic. Notoriety, fame, success, money, all are elusive.

It's amazing how deceptive money can be. Money generates the illusion of value, importance, wisdom, wealth, influence, and prestige. Yet, it's just a vapor and a delusion, just like winning. If winning or getting money is our only objective, it doesn't matter how it happens. It doesn't matter if we cheat. It doesn't matter if we bend the rules. It doesn't matter if we keep someone eligible that is not eligible. It doesn't matter if we recruit illegally. It doesn't matter if we practice or play the games when we should be in church as long as we win! Situational ethics, the ends justify the means.

We may miss God's upside down-inside out economy. I miss it knowing pain brings joy, and I still don't want to drink that cup. I still don't want to taste profound sorrow or deep sadness. A place where one's heart is crushed with a sledgehammer, and we question God and ask all the God questions. How could He? Why would He? Where is He? Challenging his character over and over and yet that's even part of the crushing and the growing. Without the intense agony and pain, the mind wouldn't go anywhere else. The mind and spirit wouldn't explore any other alternative. The mind would just "mindlessly" enjoy floating downstream, soaking in the day's culture.

Whether it's in the Roman period, the Renaissance, or whether it's in the modern era, we float down the stream wherever it carries us. The stream of cultural values carries us rapidly over dangerous rocks and rapids, and nobody wonders. Humanity defines winning and success the same way: the pinnacle of all effort, we must win. Winning is all that matters.

God examines the heart and looks at life with different eyes, a different perspective.

God's thoughts are not our thoughts. God's ways are not our ways. Occasionally, men get this idea, and they say amazing things in our contemporary culture. Francis Chan understands it. He sells his large home to buy a small home, to spend the extra money on others. He lives more frugally, so he can do things God calls him to do.

The late Larry Crabb got it right in his books, *Inside Out* and *Shattered Dreams*. He tells us suffering is a gift bestowed by God. We couldn't think this up. We couldn't understand it. To understand this would take a crushing and brokenness few of us want to experience. Who wants to roll pain around in the palm of their hand and attempt to make sense of it? Who wants to experience pain, let alone understand what it's teaching? I don't. I don't need a handful of exquisite diamonds formed in the throes of pain and suffering.

I would have missed the extraordinary lessons of suffering, knowledge more beautiful than any sight the eye has beheld, more beautiful than diamonds, greater beauty than anything in all of God's creation. I would have completely missed it and would have joyfully missed it.

The reality is we are looking into another dimension. When we seek to live out of the other dimension, an act of kindness is a portal into the world of truth and love, otherworldly gifts. We rarely want to live out of the other dimension, whether we believe in God or not. We rarely want to live for others. Born out of love and theology, out of His word, flows worship. It's beautiful and breathtaking. It's really knowing God and we have no words.

Eternal values are easy to overlook. The pleasures of this world can often blind us to what is of real value and worth. Prosperity often affords us too many luxuries. It's simple to overlook our dependence on the Almighty. A study of the life of Solomon, king of Israel during the nation's greatest prosperity, suggests Solomon depended less and less on God as possessions and wealth increased.

After a long time, God judged Israel, and a period of silence followed. Undoubtedly, this time of silence was vacuous and painful. It occurred during the time between the Old and the New Testament. Four centuries of silence where God was deafeningly quiet. The Jewish people must have wondered if God existed, if He cared, and if all they had been taught about Him was real? It seemed like God was not listening to their cries or prayers. "Still, despite everything, they waited for a Messiah—they had no other hope. 'What else can I do?' God had asked. There was something else. What could not be won through power, he would win through suffering."[3]

He would win through suffering. He wins by humbling himself, pouring out himself for us. Real winning, whether in sport or in life, is upside-down and inside-out thinking. Sports and suffering go hand in hand, and we separate them. These truths explained over these last several pages may at first blush look like they have nothing to do with sports. Yet, wherever we find disappointment, sorrow, pain, and frustration, we can see God. Sport forces us to an end of ourselves in a myriad of ways. Sport speeds up and crystallizes life's challenges in rapid fire, time and space. In sport, as in a few other venues, we are all in; participants and spectators are deeply invested. This process opens the portal where Jesus shows us the path to wholeness in life by his example, and he suffered. Do we have to suffer? Do we get to suffer? We find victory in the most unexpected places.

MY WIFE

As we grapple with sport through a different lens, I will share the brief speech and lessons I offered at my wife's retirement party.

Retirement holds a unique suffering. It represents a significant achievement, a triumph, yet it also evokes a mix of nostalgia and sorrow. These were my thoughts which I penned on my wife's last day of work. She is retiring after over fifty years in banking, forty-eight and a half at the same bank. Her signature over this body of work has been her best. Karen has pressed toward the goal of daily offering her best to her God, her family, her employer, and her friends. All efforts are measured against this standard. Whether it is a sport, a job, a career, or our God; we strain to offer the only thing worthy of all the time, energy, blood, sweat, and tears. This worthy achievement, simply put, is our best, an effort framed in the context of bringing God glory, "And whatever you do, whether in word or deed, do it all in the name of the Lord Jesus, giving thanks to God the father through him" (COLOSSIANS 3:17).

These sentiments are echoed in a very brief and simple book by John

Wooden. He, by many basketball aficionados' standards, was the greatest college basketball coach of all time. He concludes his book describing the importance of love and its crucial nature in the life of his family and friends. He mentions that we must live each day acknowledging the brevity of life and enjoying the precious quality of the gift of life. Wooden offers a prayer that our lives are filled with love. "And that along the way you never cease trying to be the best you can be—that you always strive for your personal best. That is success. And don't let anybody tell you otherwise."[4]

This effort which is a love offering to God produces the only outcome worth truly celebrating. Too often, we measure performance by success, money, fame, power, praise, significance, and winning. But when we reach the end of our career and receive the final applause, the measure of perfection lies in loving God and giving Him our best. This and loving others is the greatest motivation; this is the greatest of achievements.

I felt these thoughts were apropos for this day; words Karen would pen to you, her friends and loved ones, if this were her book.

MOVIE ENDING

The movie *Seven Days in Utopia* unearths an important additional perspective as it confronts a bedraggled golfing failure with the values of winning and losing. He is faced with a challenge from a retired has-been, who imparts the values of true winning and a proven mindset. The movie moves toward its conclusion and the young upstart golfer playing with these newfound values finds himself one successful putt away from winning a prestigious golf tournament against some of the best players in the world. As he sized up the game-winning putt, with great drama, the narrator of the movie declares boldly, "and stroked the putt of his life . . . I guess you're asking yourself whether or not he made the putt? Does it really matter? How can a game have such an effect on a man's soul?[5]

This movie argues that purpose and calling go far beyond the scoreboard.

Besides being a must-see movie, which challenges traditional thinking, this movie runs head on into the mantra heard on sports talk shows, which speaks juvenilely, as if everything boils down to winning and losing.

An ESPN analyst spoke this rhetoric with authority. Commenting on the NBA, he said, "In the NBA, there are winners and losers."

No, it's not that simple! Life is an infinite number of points. Each moment tests us. Thus, the definition of our values holds the key, and the meaning turns on that point. What's at stake? A life of brilliantly refracted light through suffering, offering hope, and revealing the brilliance of joy like sparkling diamonds.

ENDNOTES: CHAPTER 34

1. Phillip Yancey, *Disappointment with God*, Zondervan, 1988, 284.

2. Phillip Yancey, *Disappointment with God*, Zondervan, 1988, 244.

3. Phillip Yancey, *Disappointment with God*, Zondervan, 1988, 105.

4. John Wooden with Steve Jamison, *My Personal Best*, McGraw-Hill, 2004, 204–205.

5. Matthew Dean Russell, director. *Seven Days in Utopia*. Utopia Pictures & Television, 2011.

AUTHOR BIO

BRADLEY D. BAILEY is an accomplished coach, teacher, counselor, theologian, and now, an author.

He loves sports and enjoys coaching and competing. He is an athlete's athlete. He required of himself what he asked of his players. As a coach for over twenty-five years, it was his job to help players and coaches realistically face their mornings-after. It was Bradley's own journey and faith-between mountain tops and valleys-that shaped this book. The title says it all: *Winning is Never Enough: Suffering, Sports and Hope* (*How to Deal with the Friday Night Loss on Monday Morning*).

Bradley thrived in competitive contests playing baseball, basketball, track, and cross country in high school. He coached basketball, football, track, volleyball, and cross country. He was a head basketball coach for over 18 seasons and was named Coach of the Year in his first season in a small high school in Arizona. He pursued excellence for himself and his students. This pursuit in college allowed him to letter in basketball, complete 2,000 sit ups in an hour and ride on a thousand-mile bicycle trip along the Gulf Coast. During middle age he ran dozens of road races, bicycle races, and mini triathlons. At fifty he began participating in the Senior Olympics, winning a state champion gold medal in the high jump, 100 m. dash, 400 m. run, and the 100 yd. breaststroke.

He has traveled the world, too, and some of these travels included adventure. In Uganda, he was chased by a 12,000-pound, fourteen-foot-tall elephant. In the Middle East, he rode camels and marveled at the rock-cut architecture and rock formations at Petra in Jordan, a UNESCO World Heritage Site. In Mexico, he played basketball on a traveling All-Star team in Mexico City, Tuxtla Gutierrez, and Tapachula.

In short, Bradley is an interesting and educated man with much to say. He earned a Bachelor of Science in Health and Physical Education from Taylor University (Indiana), Master of Divinity with extensive study in Greek and Hebrew from Grace Theological Seminary (Indiana), and a Master of Arts in Counseling from Western New Mexico University. As a teacher he taught biology, anatomy and physiology, earth science, general science, chemistry, psychology, health, history, and P.E. He has served as Spiritual Director at an Emmaus retreat for men near Ruidoso, New Mexico. At the retreat, all witnessed God sparring a man from certain death, after he succumbed to a heart attack.

Bradley resides in New Mexico with his wife and enjoys spending time with his children and 31 grandchildren.

You can reach the author at bdbaileysports@gmail.com.

www.ingramcontent.com/pod-product-compliance
Lightning Source LLC
Chambersburg PA
CBHW061140120626

46546CB00005B/1865